W9-BDB-871

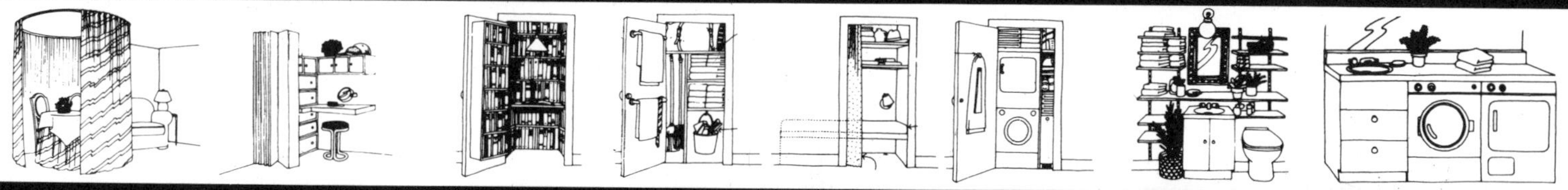

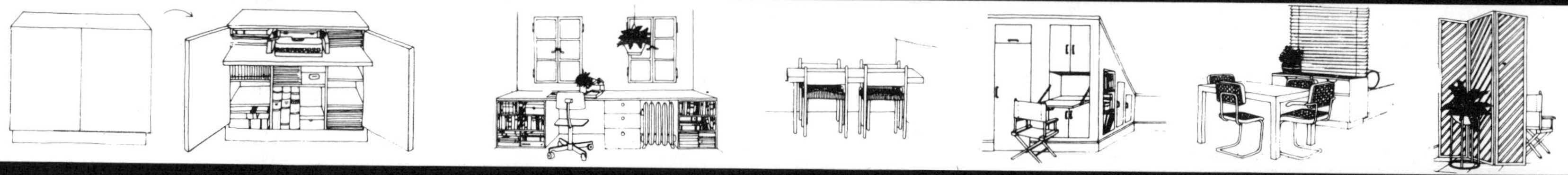

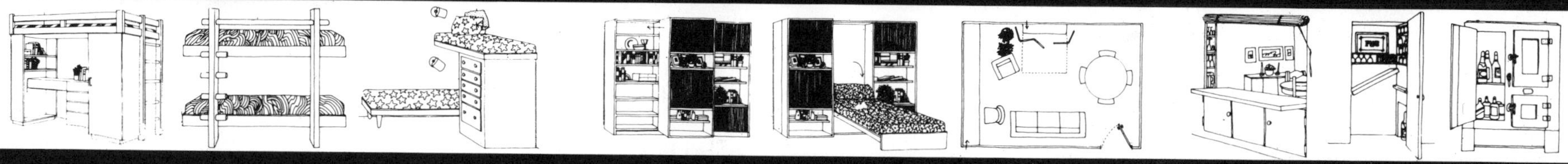

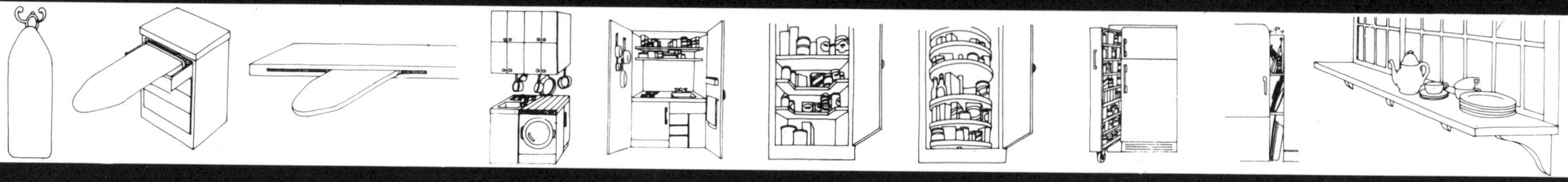

THE SPACEMAKER BOOK

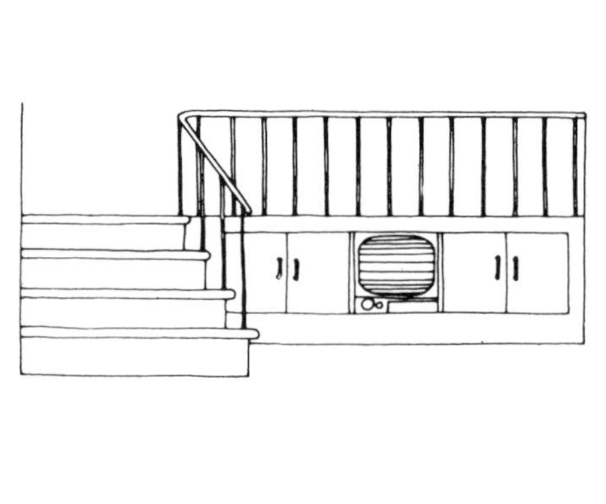
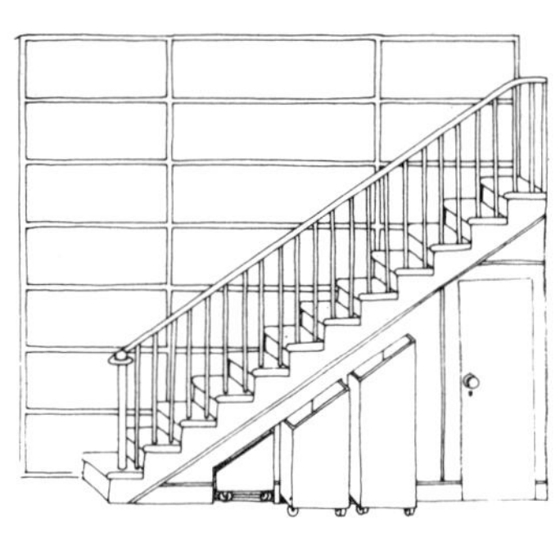
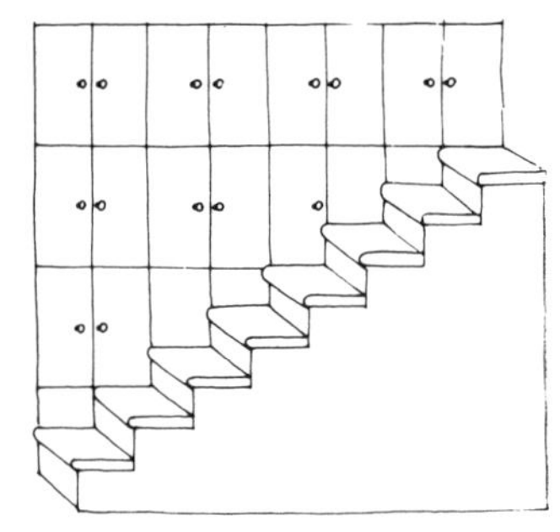
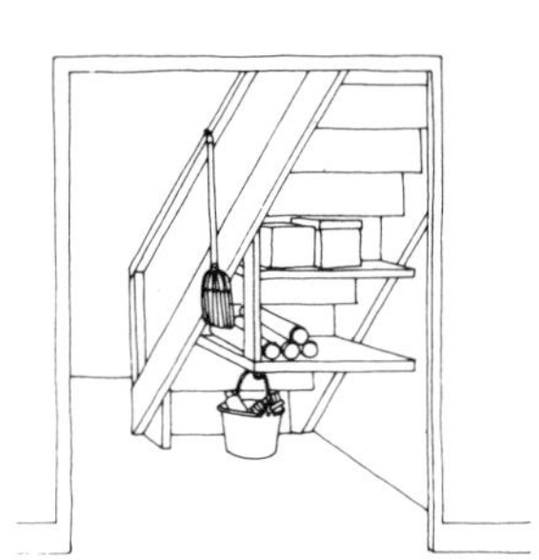
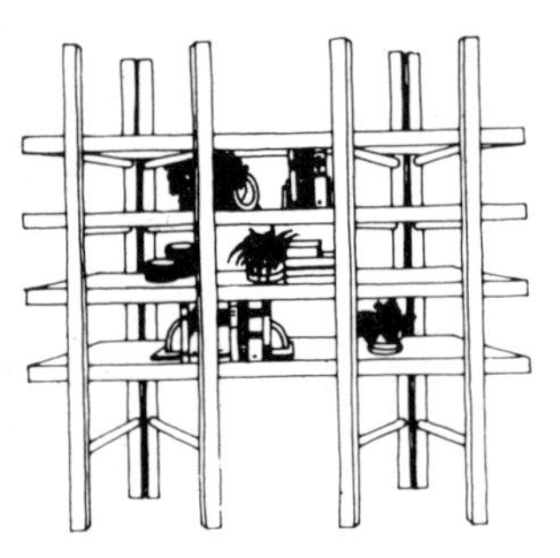

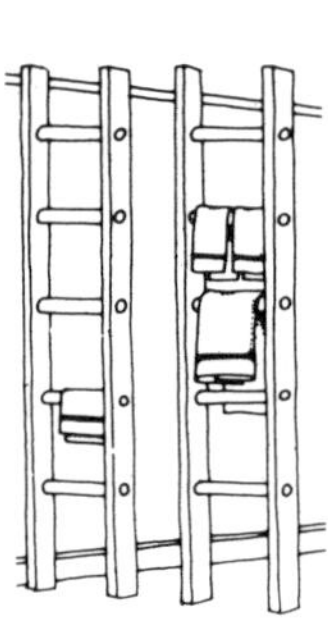
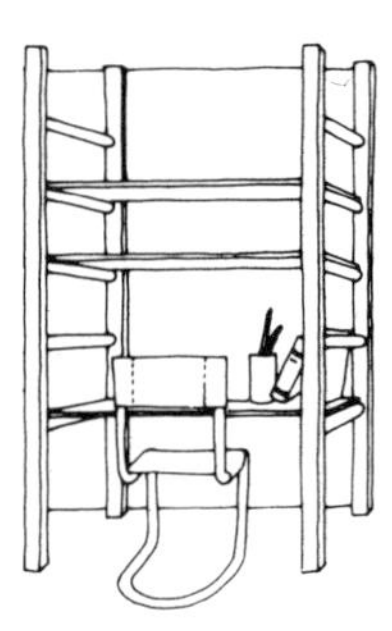

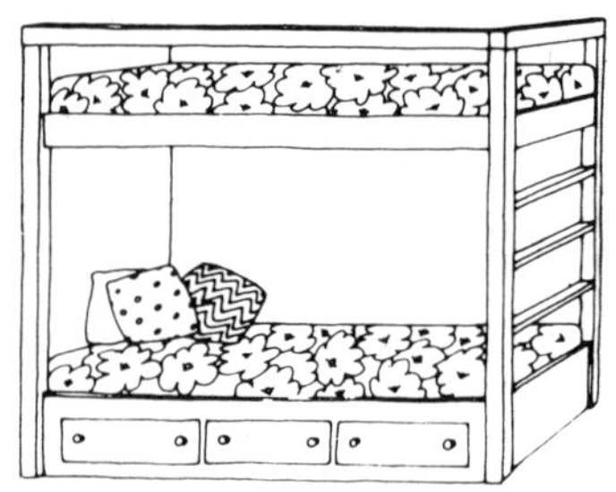
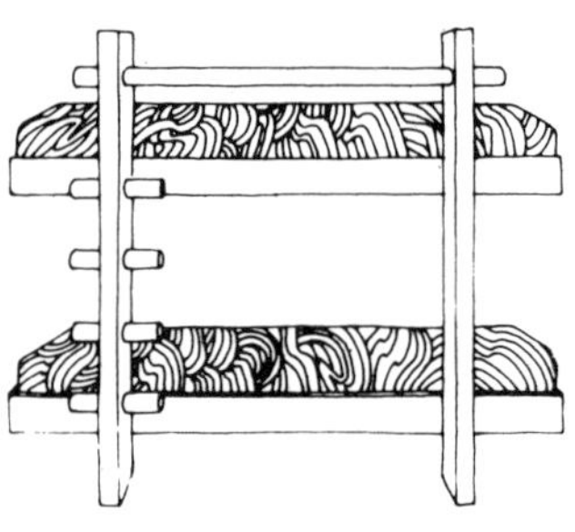

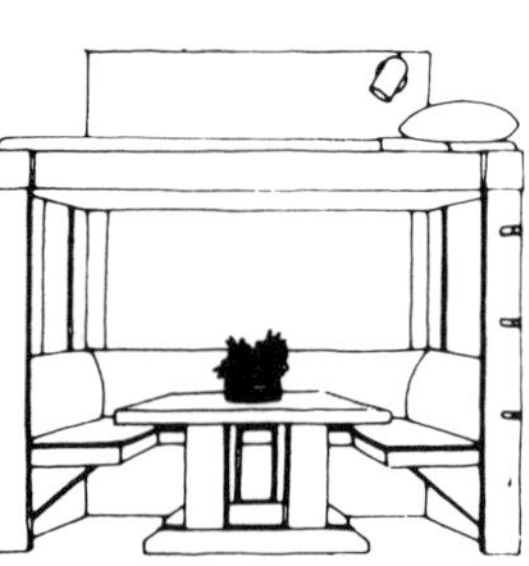

THE SPACEMAKER BOOK

ELLEN LIMAN

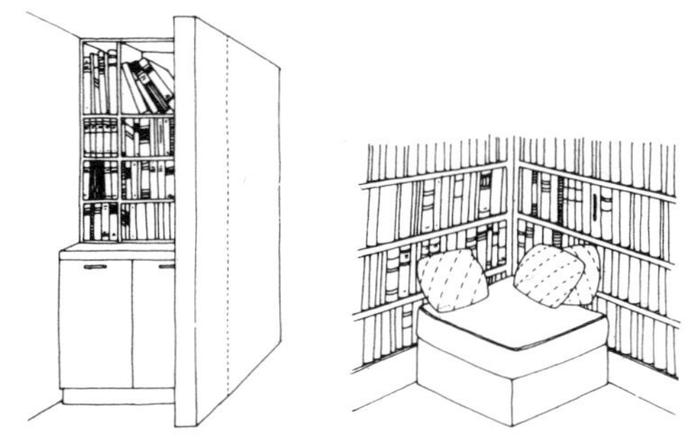

DRAWINGS BY NANCY STAHL

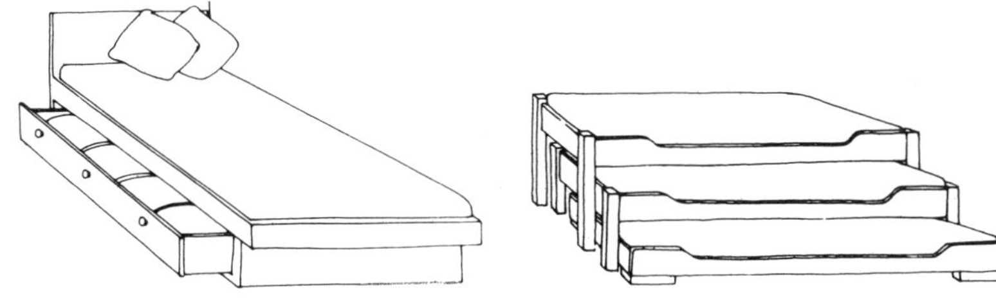

A STUDIO BOOK
THE VIKING PRESS
NEW YORK

Dedicated to Arthur, Lewis, Emily, and Douglas

First published in 1977 by The Viking Press
625 Madison Avenue, New York, N.Y. 10022

Published simultaneously in Canada by
The Macmillan Company of Canada Limited

Library of Congress Cataloging in Publication Data

Liman, Ellen.
The spacemaker book.

(A Studio book)

1. Interior decoration. 2. Personal space.
3. Room layout (Dwellings) I. Stahl, Nancy.
II. Title.
NK2113.L55 747'.8'8 77-714

ISBN 0-670-66012-4

Printed in the United States of America

Designed by Gael Towey Dillon

CONTENTS

INTRODUCTION: THE CONQUEST OF SPACE

Designing domestic space—isolating and organizing it, stretching and saving it—is a universal concern that has challenged man's ingenuity since he devised his earliest shelters. In the beginning, the conical shape of primitive huts was determined by the flexibility of the tree branches from which they were made; two-storied houses were a solution to cramped quarters as far back as the second millennium B.C.; and Babylon houses were divided into three separate spaces, one for men (the public area), one for women and children (the private area), and one for servants. Sleeping balconies were prevalent in ancient Egypt, built-in furniture dates back to the caveman, and our revolutionary ideas about open-plan living are a reversion to the earliest one-room mud hut.

Today the problems and solutions are similar. Building materials still determine the shape of space, double-decker living is a popular space stretcher, and areas of a home are allocated according to private and public needs. But the quality and quota of space available for a family are determined not so much by limitations of technology as by cost—and these costs will undoubtedly grow bigger even as rooms and closets grow smaller. Most people cannot afford all the space necessary to live comfortably, and even those with space to spare need to know how to plan it. I hope the pages and pictures that follow will help.

THE ELEGANT JAPANESE HOUSE
IMPERIAL GARDENS

Anecdotes about the Fibber McGee closet entertained a generation of radio listeners in the 30s and 40s, but similar crazy and chaotic situations are as much a reality now. In these days of small rooms and high construction costs, it is not only the closet but also the bedroom, dining room, living room, and kitchen (or lack of them) that pose problems for home and apartment dwellers alike. And all of us, even those lucky enough not to live in cramped quarters, must plan our space to provide the maximum in convenience, utility, and comfort.

In addition to organization, decorative effects are also an important part of the plan. Just as generous space is no guarantee of elegance, what is lacking in space can be made up for in charm, taste, and warmth. A small space does not mean "small decorating," but rather requires a bold creative approach. For example, an insignificant room can be transformed into something special with large-scale furniture (a beautiful big bookcase instead of a small boring one) and dynamic patterns (a bright wallpaper, or an assertive fabric).

In modern architecture the space in a building is not restricted by walls. Free from the traditional division of space into separate rooms, newer interiors can be planned starting from an open, free-flowing space with partitions or dividers sparingly added only where essential. Although most of us do not have the opportunity to design the limits of our rooms—having inherited the plan of an apartment or an architect—the openness of modern architecture undermines formerly rigid rules and allows us to think not strictly in terms of rooms but more loosely in terms of spaces. It is wasteful to use rooms or areas only according to their predetermined labels if these do not suit our needs, and it is certainly extravagant to use rooms or areas only part time.

This 13′ × 15′ one-room apartment is so well planned that there is space for three distinct areas: entertaining, sleeping, and eating and working. Ample storage is also provided in compartments and on shelves in the bed alcove (concealed behind the draped fabric) and in the trunk–coffee table. The use of a few large and important pieces instead of smaller insignificant items, and the simple backgrounds (vertical blinds, grass-cloth floor covering, and moiré wall covering), produce a sense of spaciousness and luxury.
In the summer, cheerful chintz and white duck replace the winter fabrics—brown taffeta and gray silk (*above right*).

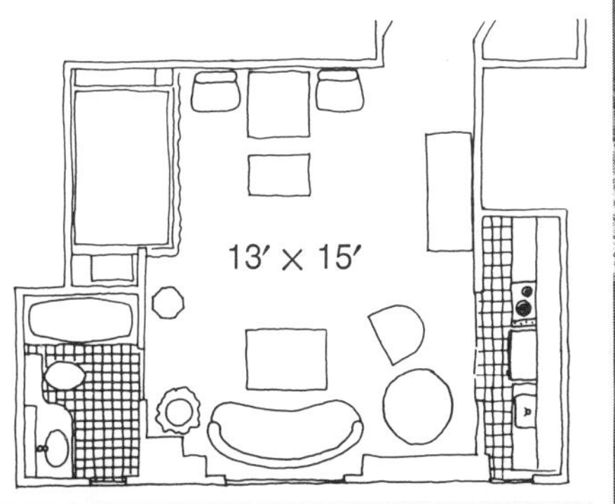
13′ × 15′

How to Measure a Room

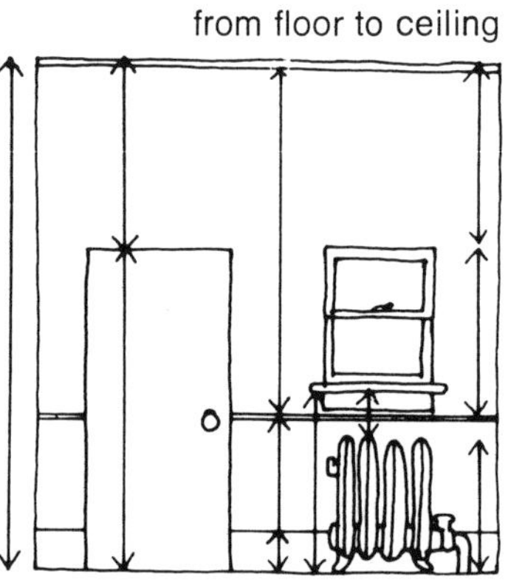

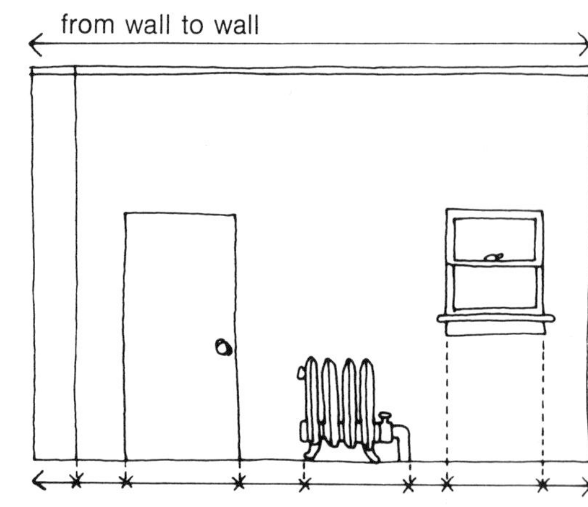

ROUND-THE-CLOCK USES FOR PART-TIME ROOMS

Here are some combinations that make full use of rooms that normally would be used for only a few hours of the day:

- The living room can double as an office, den, bedroom, nursery, library, or dining room.
- A bedroom might be part office or library.
- The off-duty dining room can become a playroom, studio, library, office, or bedroom.
- Foyers or large hallways are perfect for dining; or, with a hideaway bed added, as a guest "room"; or, with book storage and seating space, as a library or office.
- Even a bathroom can be a proper place for clothing storage, and with the right accessories —radio, television, magazine rack, or lounge chair—a quiet retreat for rest and relaxation.

A PLAN TO EXPAND SPACE

No matter how much, there is never enough. If it is not a problem of where to put the baby, it is a question of where to put the baby's carriage, diapers, or the baby's grandmother. Here are some ways to make the most of—and to make more of— the space you already have.

SIMPLE WAYS TO STRETCH SPACE

- *Get rid of everything extraneous.* Edit out the nonessentials and clear out that cluttered closet or corner.
- *Remove distracting decorative elements* and architectural details. In an older home this might be moldings, carvings, and fireplaces (use the inside of the chimney for storage).
- *Plan even the smallest detail with care.* For example, do not hang a hook for a bathrobe over a mirrored bathroom door or the view of the mirror will be blocked.
- *Try a monotone color scheme and simple furniture.* Use fewer free-standing, ill-fitting pieces of furniture and more furniture that merges with the space. (Note, however, that the fewer the pieces, the more noticeable they will be.) Instead of several storage units, install one, wall-to-wall and floor-to-ceiling, or two, floor-to-ceiling with a couch or other large piece of furniture in the alcove between them. This is a cleaner look.
- *Use multipurpose, folding, movable furniture,* but not so much of it that everything has to be set up to eat or entertain.
- *Analyze areas and reorganize.* Set priorities: most used, least used, and in between. Again, think of space, not of labels relating to function. For example, if the bedroom is too tiny, put a convertible bed in the living room and use the bedroom as a work area or, with a large armoire added, for storage; put the laundry room where it is most handy, not downstairs but upstairs in a closet next to the bedroom.

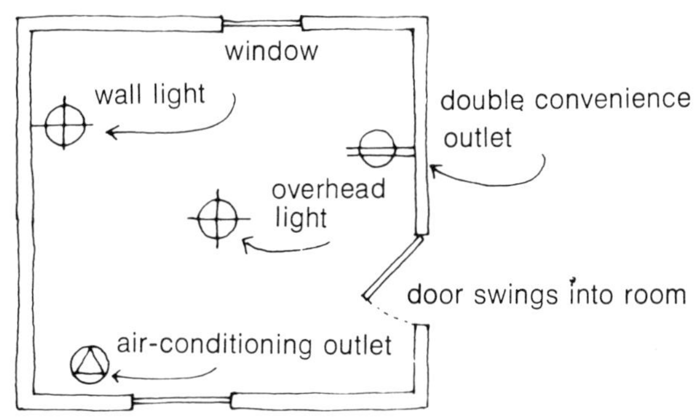

Similarly, convert a wide underused closet into a seating alcove (with plenty of storage space remaining above and below the seat) by removing the closet header, rod, and doors; or make a small office out of the back-hall mud room by adding a telephone, chair, shelf, and bulletin board.

• *Do things with doors.* Rehang a door to open in a different direction; change a swinging door to a space-saving one, to a sliding, pocket, folding, even a bar-style door; take off a door to add a feeling of movement through space, and close off a door altogether to gain more wall space.

• *Remove temporary partitions or room dividers.* These may block traffic and the visual flow of space. Let rugs, furniture, color—not walls—define an area.

• *Cut out unimportant items.* Instead of heavy draperies, use mini-slatted blinds, shades, or shutters or leave windows bare; instead of table lamps, use wall or ceiling-hung chandeliers, sconces, or track lights.

INEXPENSIVE STRUCTURAL SOLUTIONS

Without investing in extensive remodeling, there are easy ways to redesign an area simply to give the appearance of more space, or actually to increase it.

• Open up space by tearing out a wall between two rooms where a permanent partition is not necessary, for instance, between a living room and dining room. Close with folding screens, when desirable.

• Visually enlarge and brighten a dark room by adding a window: a skylight, a picture window in place of a mullioned window, a wall of windows. (Remember, however, that a larger window will let in not only more light and view, but also more heat and cold!)

• Add on a new outside deck or patio.

• Convert a porch into a dining area or a garage into a family room.

• Modernize the bathroom and kitchen.

FURNITURE ARRANGEMENTS AND FLOOR PLANS

Arranging furniture is like placing shapes in space to form a pleasant and practical relationship. Furniture should fit in a room so that people do not have to climb over chairs or move the bed to open windows or to gain access to dresser drawers; so that people sitting on one side of a living-room area do not have to shout to people on the other side, or use binoculars to watch television. Ceiling and wall lights must be placed so as not to be hazardous to the head; adequate sockets must be nearby for these and other electrical accessories; and major pieces, such as the couch, dining table, bed, and desk, should be arranged to take advantage of a nice view and good light.

good traffic patterns

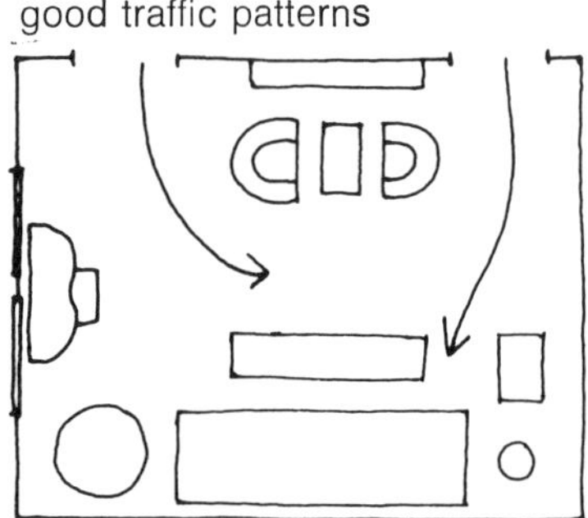

poor traffic patterns

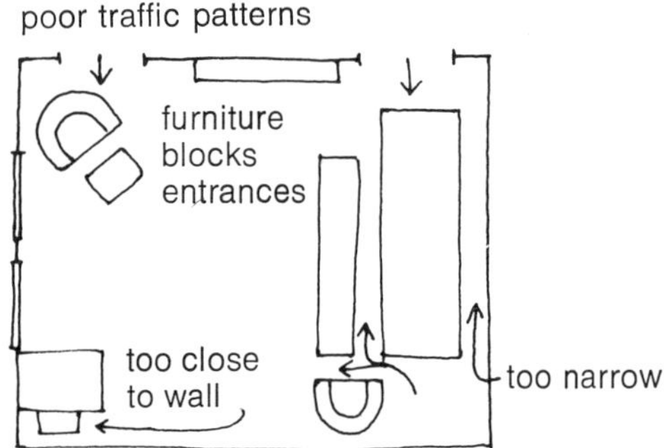

good balance and contrast of shapes

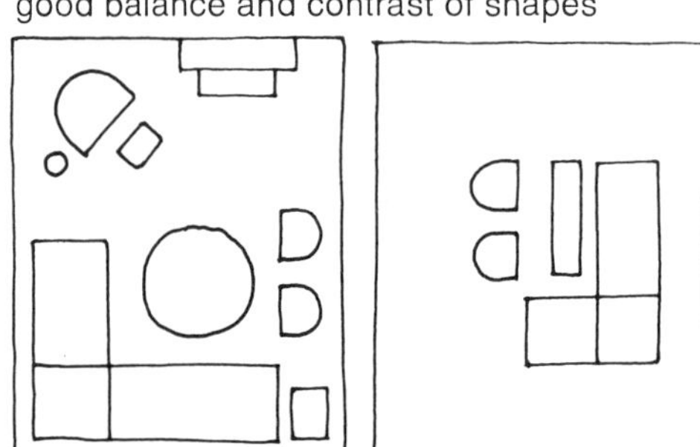

poor balance and contrast

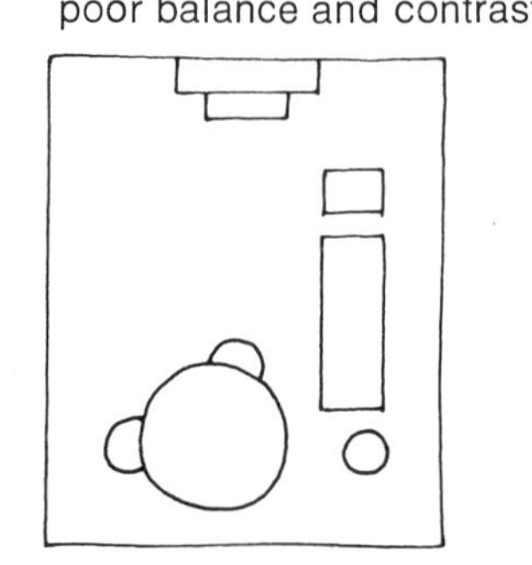

good color balance

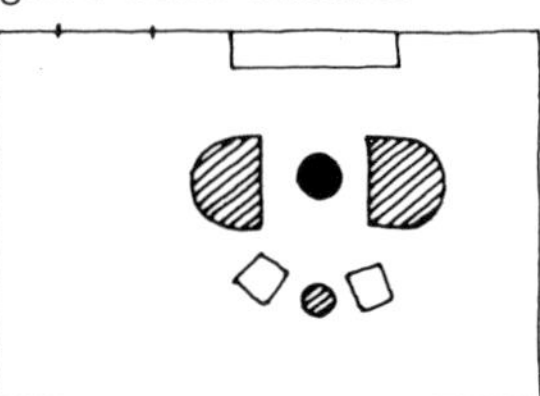

poor color balance

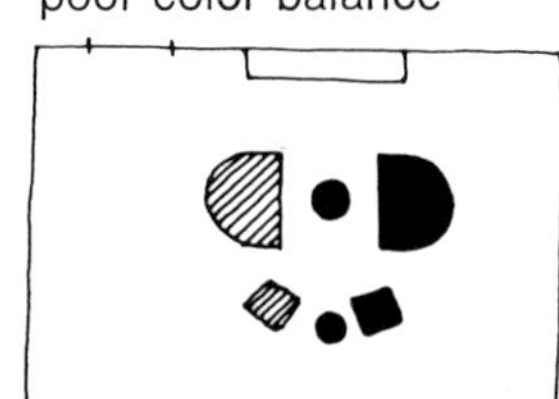

CIRCULATING THROUGH SPACE: TRAFFIC LANES

When arranging furniture, keep in mind that traffic should move easily in and out of a room as well as around furniture. Opened doors should not bang into furniture, and people should be able to sit down and get up without being squeezed.

- Allow about three feet minimum for traffic lanes.
- Allow about eighteen inches between two low pieces, such as coffee table and adjacent sofa or chairs.
- Allow about two to two and a half feet between two higher pieces, such as a breakfront and a desk.
- Allow two feet between dining chair and the wall behind it and three feet for passing behind a chair when serving.
- Allow approximately two to three feet around at least two sides of a bed so it is not cumbersome to make up.
- Allow access space in front of drawers and closets that open outward (about three feet).
- Allow room for furniture that expands, such as a sofa bed or flip-top table.

MAKING A FLOOR PLAN

After you have some idea of what goes where, sketch it out on paper. Even if there is already a floor plan, double-check measurements (architects' plans show both feet and inches; that is, 5′0″). Draw a plan of the room showing all fixed features that will affect or interfere with the arrangements, such as air conditioners, radiators, windows, door, pipes, and beams. To measure, use a folding wooden rule or a flexible steel tape or a yardstick. Go around the room, measuring and noting sizes and, for greatest accuracy, put it all down, to scale, on graph paper. (The standard scale is ¼ inch to 1 foot.) Calculate the distance at the base of the walls from corner to corner and from point to point; that is, the measurement from one corner to the outside edge of the first permanent structure that you come to, such as a window. Measure the size of the window and then proceed, in the same manner, around the perimeter of the room. Note sizes of door openings as well as the direction of the swing of swinging doors.

A floor plan will show horizontal measurements, but an elevation plan is important because it indicates vertical measurements. For example, although a window is indicated on a floor plan, the height of the window and how high up it begins and ends on the wall is not. Nonprojecting wall-heating or air-conditioning units will not show up at all.

To make an elevation plan, draw the distance from floor to ceiling and note the distance from point to point; that is, the measurement from the floor to the window apron and sill, from the sill to the top of the window casing, from that to the moldings, and on to the ceiling. Do the same for doors. The

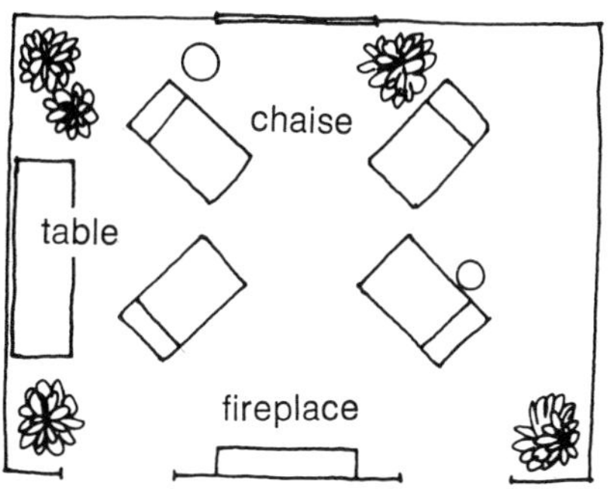

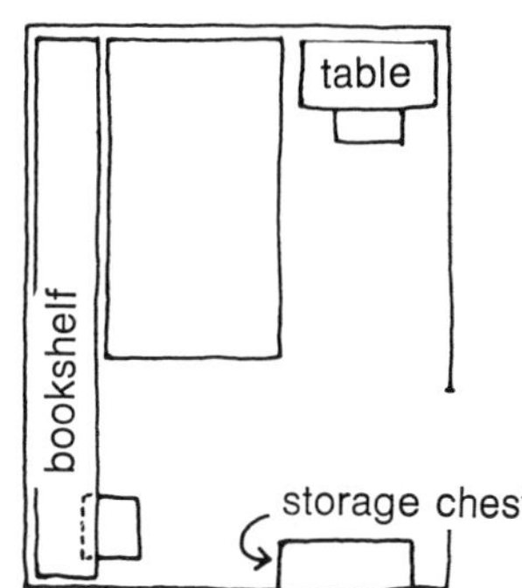

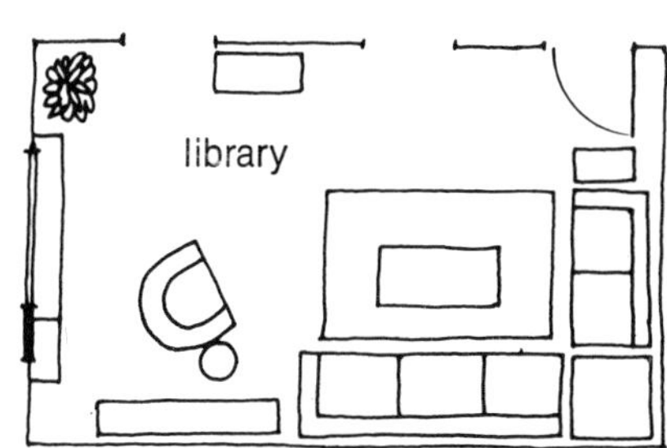

An "Island" Arrangement

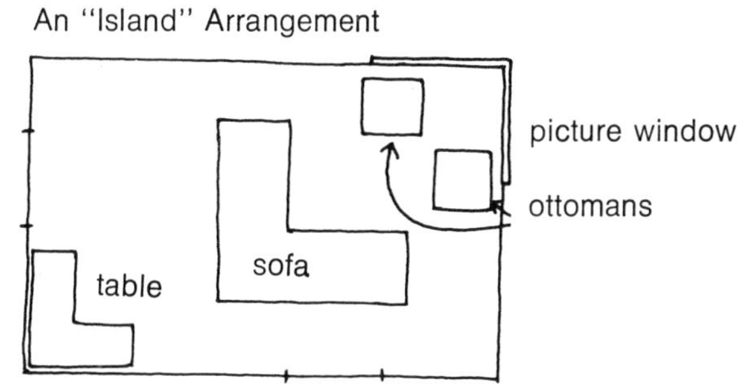

elevation should show the height and width of all doors and windows, all heating and cooling units and electrical outlets, as well as their location on the wall. If walls are uneven, particularly if exact measurements are needed for built-ins such as wall-to-wall bookshelves, measure the distance between areas in several places and then use the smallest measurement.

Incidentally, a floor plan will tell not only how much space there is and what will fit within it, but also the size of areas to be covered with wallpaper, paint, or a floor material. For example, in an average room, the floor and ceiling area is calculated in square feet by multiplying the width by the length of the room, one wall by multiplying the length by the height.

HOW A FLOOR PLAN MAXIMIZES SPACE

• Sketch in ideas for furniture placement or move around cutouts of the furniture on the plan to help determine the best use of the space. Sometimes it is surprising to find that a certain space is larger than it appears and that a piece of furniture that seemed too big will really fit into it. (A good way to determine if colors and materials will be evenly distributed around an area, without too much clustered in one place, is to color cutouts to approximate the color of the furniture—wood, chrome, wicker, and its upholstery.)

• Furniture in corners makes a room seem larger, solves traffic problems, and creates more floor space, so this is a good place to start planning a furniture arrangement. For example, a bed will look smaller and the room larger and there will be more floor space if the bed is put in a corner. (See Chapter 9.)

• To gain more floor space, place furniture around the sides of a room or cluster it in a tight island in the center; for example, couches in a U or L arrangement or back to back, or facing each other, with perhaps a storage place—a bookcase or cabinet—incorporated into the arrangement. Note that free-floating furniture (furniture that is not up against a wall) should have a "finished" back.

• Finally, and most important, be flexible and allow for change. Furniture should be moved around from time to time for variety or to suit changing needs and tastes. Often it is better to live in a new home for a while to determine these needs before a permanent plan is attempted.

Selecting furniture for limited space involves more than aesthetics. The smaller the space, the more care must be given to function and scale. Each piece of furniture must do double duty or more.

FURNITURE CHECKLIST

The process of selecting furniture for small spaces must begin with a realistic assessment of a family's needs. The following checklist may serve as a guide:

• *The living-room area.* For normal use, how many persons must be seated? To what extent should seating be expanded for special occasions? Is comfort in seating important? (It will be if hours are spent reading books or watching television in a chair, but not if the living room will be used primarily for entertaining and other socializing.) Should provision be made for an overnight guest? How much table room is necessary for drinks, ashtrays, coffee, backgammon or other games? What kind of music equipment and television must be accommodated in the room? What storage space is required for books, records, and so forth? Will there be a telephone? If so, where? What kind of lighting is essential?

• *The dining area.* For everyday use, how many must be seated? What is the largest number of guests that can be served? Is a serving surface necessary for buffets? Must dishes or other equipment be stored in the dining area?

• *The sleeping area.* Will the bedroom be used as a study, for television viewing, or for other purposes beside sleeping? If so, what kinds of work surfaces, seating, and lighting are needed? Should the bed be a convertible style? Must the room be able to accommodate a guest? How much clothes storage is required? What other storage, for linens, games, toys, and so on, is essential?

Once these needs are determined, it will be necessary to find out what will fit in an area. This requires a knowledge of measurements.

A dining area can be created in any empty space with commercially available furniture that comes with its own matching room dividers. These low curved pieces have clip-on shelves and are covered in the same wool rib cloth as the tub chairs and table base.

Furniture that fits compactly into corners—such as these modular seating units with triangular tables—occupies less space. The entire angular arrangement, including the carpet, echoes the herringbone pattern of the floor. Other furnishings, plants, pictures, and a piano (not shown) reinforce the division of the room into three conversation groups (the third one is behind the plant next to the window).

Multipurpose Furniture

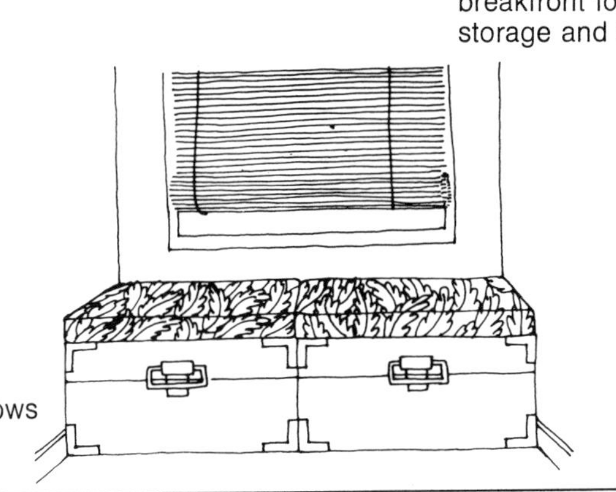
two storage chests with pillows as window seats

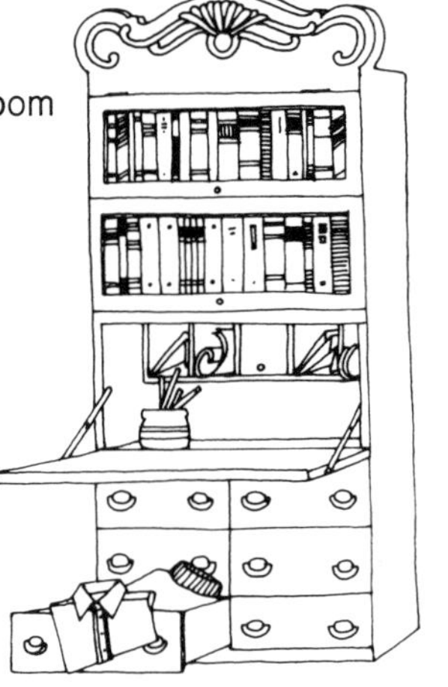
breakfront for bedroom storage and work

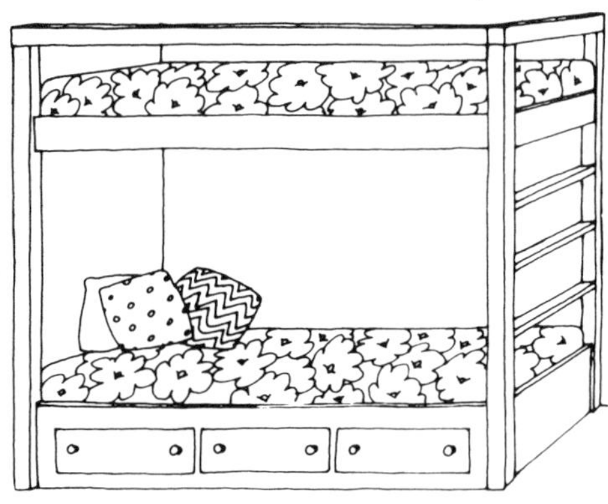

Foldable, Movable Furniture

tray on a luggage rack

wooden or aluminum director's chair

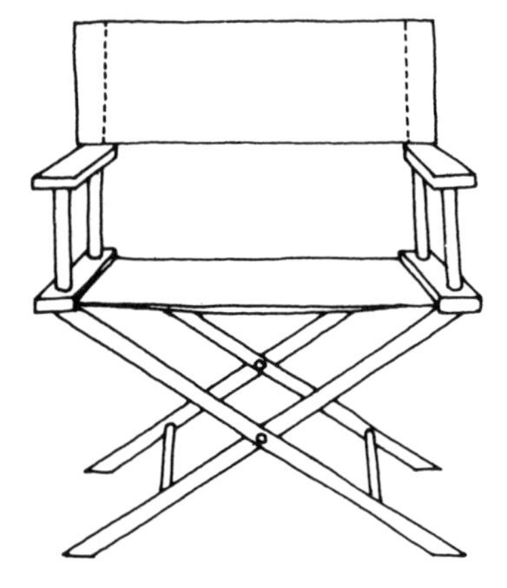

sling chair

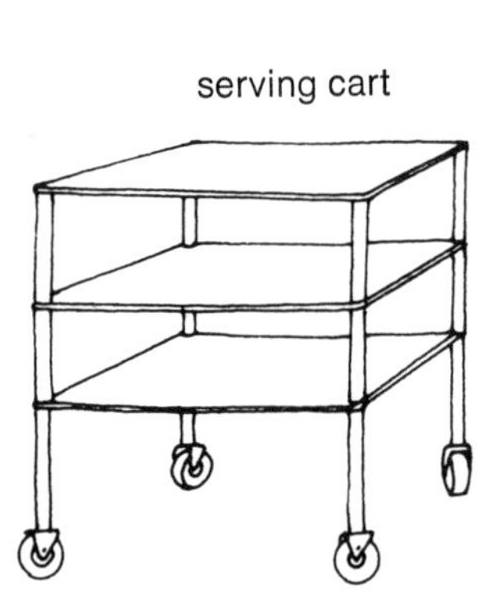
serving cart

Stackable Furniture

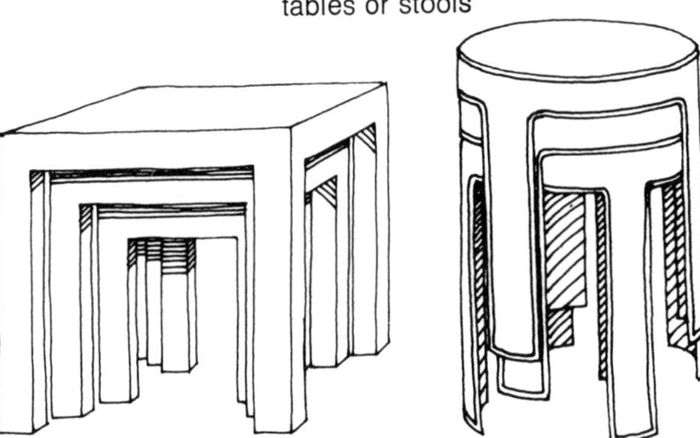
tables or stools

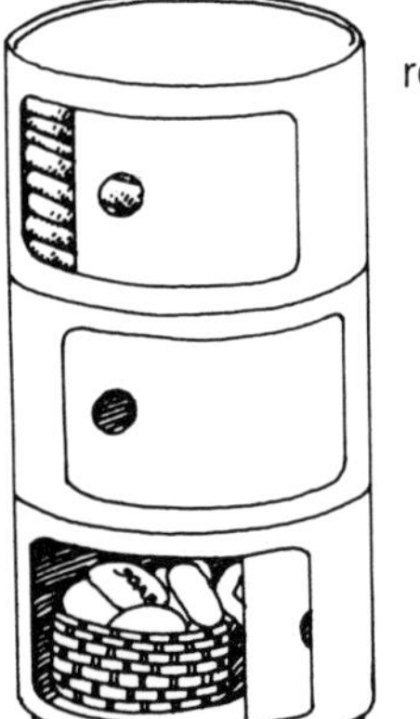
round plastic cabinets

MEASURING AND SIZES

Furniture must fit in the elevator and through the front door as well as in the room, so measure carefully and measure both what you now own and what you plan to purchase. Use a flexible metal or cloth tape (cloth is slightly less accurate, as it stretches). Both are better than a wooden rule, which cannot bend for measuring curved and upholstered furniture. Measure and note overall height of furniture, the width from side to side, and the depth, and any other details unique to the piece, such as the size of a sleep sofa when opened.

Furniture is manufactured in a somewhat standard range of sizes that are determined by the measurements of the human body. Therefore desks or dining surfaces are approximately 26″ to 30″ high, with a few inches less on the underside for leg clearance; the seat of an accompanying chair about 17″ to 18″ high, and of an occasional chair 2″ to 3″ lower. Although the height of furniture is important for comfort, the crucial measurement for those with limited space is width or length.

LIST OF TYPICAL SIZES OF FURNITURE

The following figures represent how much floor space the average piece of furniture in a category will take up, in inches and not their overall measurements:

Bed (single): 30″, 33″, 36″, 39″ × 75″
Full-size: 54″ × 75″
Queen-size: 60″ × 80″
King-size 78″ × 80″

Couch: 72″ to 84″ × 30″ to 40″
Love seat: 54″ × 30″
Chair for eating or sitting: 14″ to 24″ square
Tables (based on a chair 16″ wide):
Round: 48″ (for 6 to 8 persons)
36″ (for 4 to 6 persons)
24″ (for 2 persons)
(Calculate other sizes by multiplying the number to be seated by 6 or 7.)
Rectangle: 72″ × 36″ (for 6 to 8 persons)
24″ × 24″ (for 2 persons)
(Calculate other sizes by allowing 24″ around the table per person.)
Chaise longue or armchair and ottoman: 72″ × 24″
Arm / lounge chair: 30″ × 30″
End tables: 24″ × 24″; 18″ × 30″; 18″ × 18″; 12″ × 24″; 12″ × 12″
Coffee table: 20″ × 48″
Dresser: 18″ × 60″, 72″
Small chest: 18″ × 36″
Buffet: 18″ × 48″, 60″
Bookcase: 1′4″ × 2′ to 6′
Ping-Pong table: 108″ × 60″—allow 4 feet of runback for each end and 3 feet at sides.
Billiard table: 4′ to 5′ × 7′ to 10′—allow 5 feet for playing around table.
Card table: 30″ × 30″

How to Measure Furniture

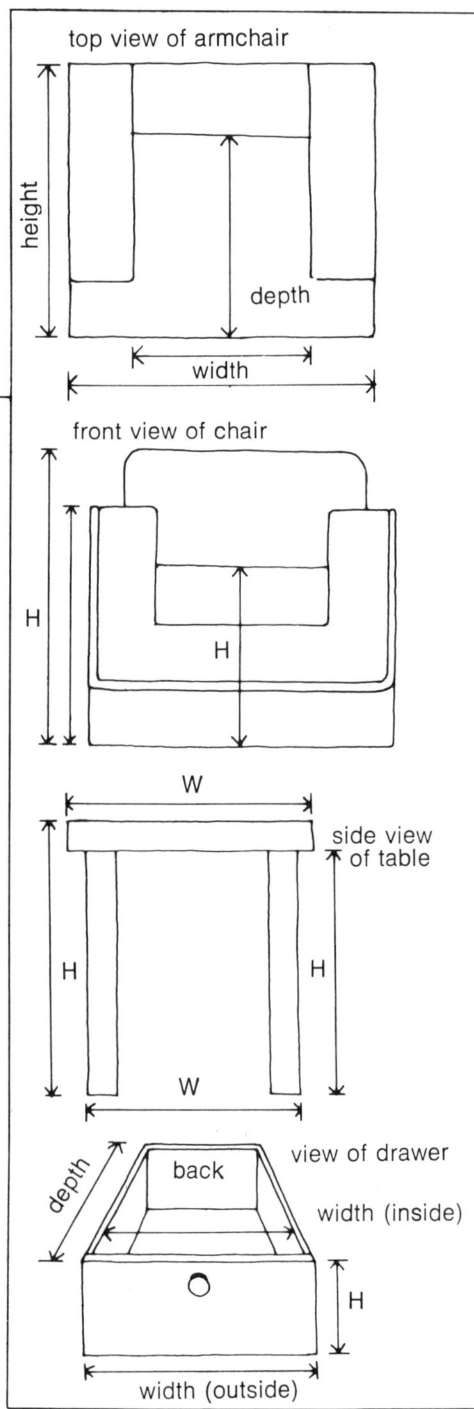

custom-cut top over assorted furniture

HOW TO SELECT FUNCTIONAL FURNITURE

There are ways to make the most of every inch of space and, at the same time, to avoid the cluttered look. Here are some of the tricks of the trade:

- *Eliminate the unnecessary.* Limit the number of different pieces of furniture: use two sofas instead of a lot of chairs; use stools and ottomans that store under tables, and chairs that stack or fold; put possessions in closets, not in cabinets; use built-ins (see following section on "Built-In Furniture").
- *Be alert for substitutes.* Instead of furniture, use an existing architectural feature. An exposed horizontal beam can serve as a shelf, a wide windowsill as a buffet, the fireplace mantel as a bar.
- *Be flexible.* Use a love seat instead of a couch, or if space does not permit, a constellation of floor pillows instead of a love seat; allow for expansion—more books, more company; select compatible colors and styles so that rooms can be rearranged with ease.
- *Use imagination.* Try an old piece of furniture in a new way, perhaps a dining-room cabinet as a storage unit in a child's room.
- *Explore multiple-purpose potential.* Use a desk as a dining table, a dining table with an elasticized plastic cover (shower-cap style) as a work table, use a bookcase as a headboard, a headboard as a room divider.
- *Consider design.* Tables and stools in a hexagonal shape fit together in a way that takes up a minimum of space; furniture in a triangular shape goes compactly into corners. Plastic and glass see-through furniture will seem to disappear and visually take up no space at all; furniture with a reflective finish such as chrome, steel, or mirror will add to the illusion of space. Modular furniture (matching units placed together in groups) is trim and gives any area a neat look; new models of sofas have built-in bookshelves or cabinets.
- *Think about mobility.* Buy furniture that can be removed, stacked, knocked down, folded, deflated, rolled up, or taken apart (plan on storage space for this); or furniture that has parts that move, pull out, or fold down like a slant-top desk, or a breakfront that opens up for serving food and drinks, or tables that raise and lower from dining to coffee-table height. Consider pieces that can be moved from place to place—a wall lamp that can be clamped onto any protruding surface, like a bookshelf, or slipped into brackets installed in several strategic places, or furniture on wheels or casters, such as a wagon for tea or television, or even a piano. (Casters are either wheel or ball type; the ball casters are stronger and better looking but usually cost more.)
- *And storability.* Select tables, desks, and chunky chests with many drawers and shelves down to the floor, if possible, instead of open-

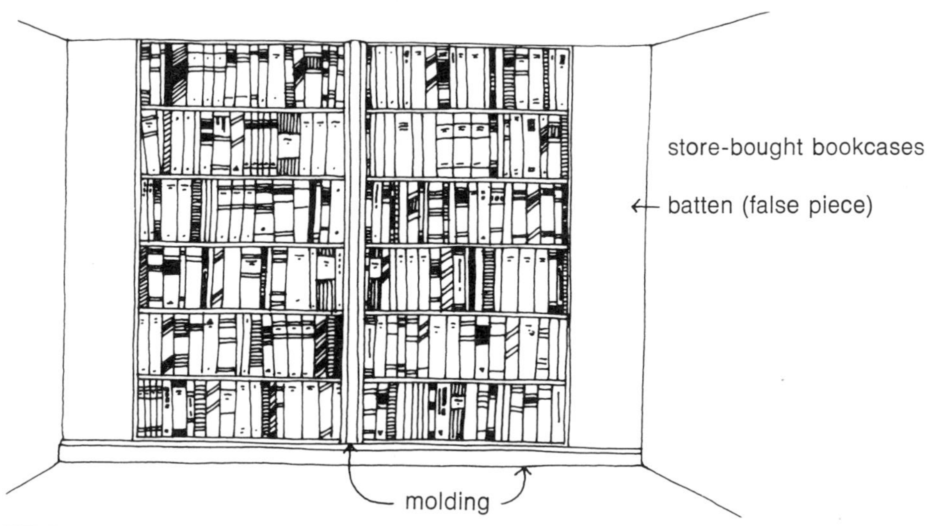

bottom furniture with long legs and one thin drawer. Choose a bed with drawers or with another bed, a trundle, beneath it. A trunk or cube not only can provide storage within but can double as a table, or, with pillows, as a seat.

• *Consider cost.* How much will an expensive built-in such as a Murphy bed be as compared with the cost of adding on a bedroom? Is the cost of having a cabinet made worth it as compared to the cost of buying a comparable piece of free-standing furniture? (The cost of built-ins varies as greatly as does the cost of a piece of furniture, and a simple built-in may be less or more expensive than its furniture counterpart.) Select furniture that can be easily installed by an amateur; otherwise include the cost of installation.

• *Add outstanding accessories to an under-furnished area.*

BUILT-IN FURNITURE

Built-in furniture can include bookshelves, closets, cabinets, and chests; seating, beds, banquettes, platform and bunk beds. Built-in furniture is popular, and for good reason: it looks trim, saves space, and, if constructed with a new or remodeled home, saves the cost of furniture.

Built-in furniture should be designed to go with and complement the area. For example, the style should be the same as the furniture and the finish the same as the wall. If the bottom of built-ins is recessed a few inches above the floor, it will seem to float and thus make the room appear to have more floor space. With built-in furniture every nook and cranny can be put to work. It is particularly suitable for such normally useless voids as alcoves where manufactured furniture cannot fill the space.

HOW TO MAKE FURNITURE LOOK BUILT-IN

The one drawback of built-ins is the expense. Carpenters are not cheap. There is an alternative, however. Ordinary furniture can sometimes be converted into built-ins at a fraction of the cost and without losing the custom-made look. Here are some possibilities:

• Saw off parts of standing pieces such as legs, also protruding moldings from the walls and ceilings, so that there is a perfect fit.

• Add a false front, a batten, or molding to fill in a gap in space; for example, between the top of a bookcase and the ceiling or between two pieces.

• Use a combination of ready-made and custom-cut parts. For example, to make a desk/shelf and bookcase unit that runs wall-to-wall under the windows, add a wooden top custom cut at the lumberyard to several assorted low bookcases, and a file cabinet of the same height.

• Paint furniture the same color as the wall, or cover it with the same wall covering.

• Group furniture together. For example, place three Parsons tables side by side on a wall; put three picnic benches in a windowed alcove (cut shorter, if necessary, to fit).

stacked chests—painted like wall

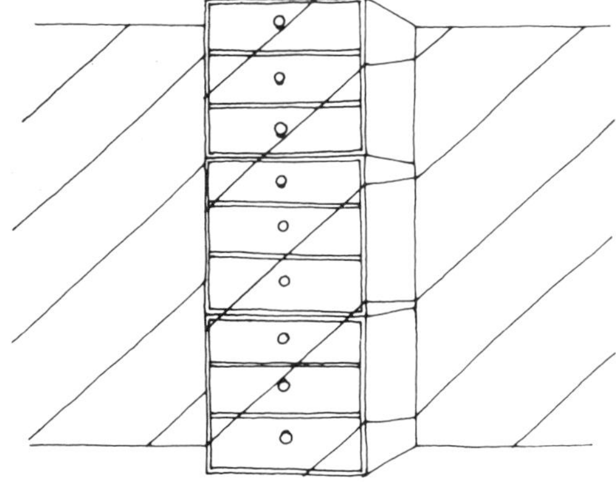

Clever use of paint, mirrors, and lighting can create a mirage of more space than there actually is. The techniques are not difficult to master.

SEVEN SIMPLE WAYS TO STRETCH SPACE VISUALLY

- *With a coordinated decorative treatment in adjoining areas.* One large room will give a feeling of space more than three times as great as the equivalent area in three small boxlike rooms. But if walls cannot come down, the effect of continuous flow from room to room can be partially achieved by using the same or similar floor and/or wall coverings. Compatible textures, colors, and patterns in other areas of the rooms will reinforce the effect.
- *With soft and subtle color schemes.* Light, neutral colors that are recessive and furniture, woodwork, floors, draperies, and wall coverings that are similar in color or pattern to one another are not only easy on the eye but create the appearance of uninterrupted space. On the other hand, an area full of different colors and patterns looks crowded and thus smaller because the eye must pause in many places. Example 1: An all white room, even including ash-

This foyer looks much larger than it really is, for several reasons: the decorating scheme—the floor covering and the black-and-white fabric—is continued from the adjoining dining room; closet doors are mirrored; and the furniture is unobtrusive—banquettes squeezed into corners, a near transparent steel-and-glass table and Lucite shelf, and wall-mounted lighting. With a table added, the formerly useless foyer can be set up for dining.

An overwhelming illusion of height is conveyed by the vertical columns in this house. The architect has added a minimum of free-standing furniture and has designed a carpet-covered conversation pit to further this effect.

reflected in the mirror, sconces and half-circle table "become" round

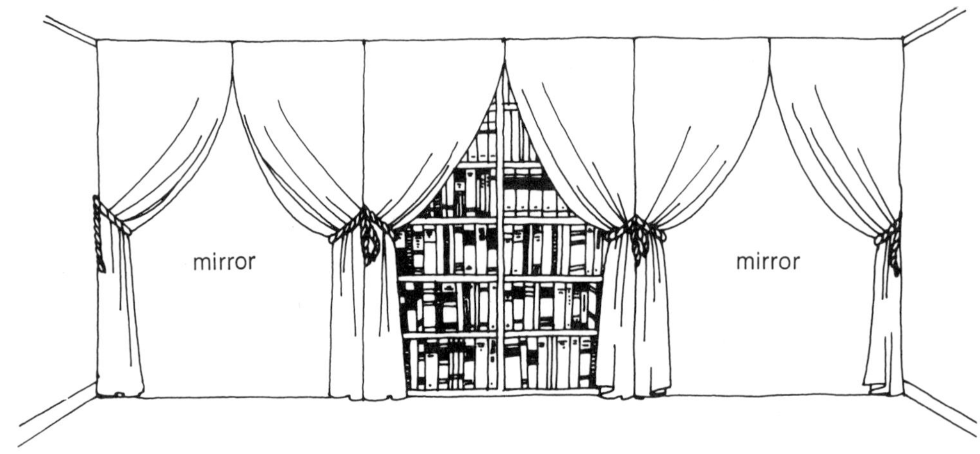

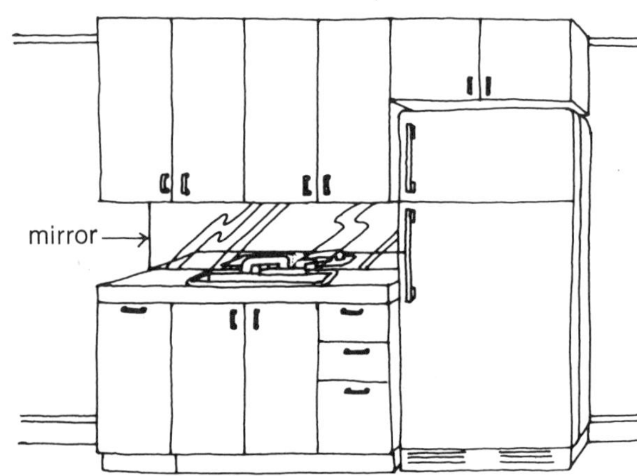

mirrored kitchen backsplash

trays and lamps. The interest is achieved with varied textures—white shag rug, white leather upholstery, bleached wood finishes. All architectural details have been painted out.

Example 2: A room completely covered—upholstery, curtains, bedspread, tablecloth—in one or two subtly patterned or textured fabrics. On walls the fabric is stapled, glued, or shirred on rods. (To preview how the pattern will look when shirred, bunch fabric together in your hand.) Different small-scale patterns that are in the same color range can be used in a similar way.

Example 3: A room completely carpeted, with a low pile commercial carpeting that travels over floors up onto built-in banquettes and onto walls, with an accent color or two in accessories such as pillows.

• *With a continuous flow of lines.* Seating, lamps, tabletops that are about the same height are less distracting than pieces of uneven heights, and contribute to a sense of uninterrupted space. This is most easily achieved with custom built-ins such as a fireplace stoop extending to become an end table, and then seating. The removal of extraneous architectural elements such as moldings will also help.

• *With simplified window treatments.* Draperies and curtains tend to close-in a room visually and actually take up more space for installation than shades, screens, shutters, panels of fabric, blinds (narrow horizontal or vertical), or curtains of beads or bamboo. If privacy or protection from light is not a problem, then leave windows —and glass doors—bare. Bring in the outdoors. Add hanging plants or put plants on sills. Decorate the room with nature's colors as though it were part of the view. If there is a deck outside, use an interior flooring that is similar.

• *With free-flowing floors.* Area rugs are good space dividers but do tend to make a space seem smaller; to make the floor appear to be larger, leave it uncovered (scraped, stained, waxed, or painted) or install carpet or floor covering wall-to-wall and, if possible, room-to-room. Or go one step further and paint the baseboard the same color as the floor covering, and several more steps beyond by extending the color up onto one or two walls.

• *With scale and placement of furniture.* A room will appear larger if lighter and smaller pieces of furniture greet the eye as one enters and if larger pieces are less conspicuous. Although small-scale furniture would be the most obvious choice for a small room, larger furniture in the background can sometimes lend importance and an element of surprise.

• *With wallcoverings.* Trompe l'oeil wallpaper, wallpaper with a trellis pattern, murals, and mirrors all "open up" a wall because the eye does not know where the wall ends.

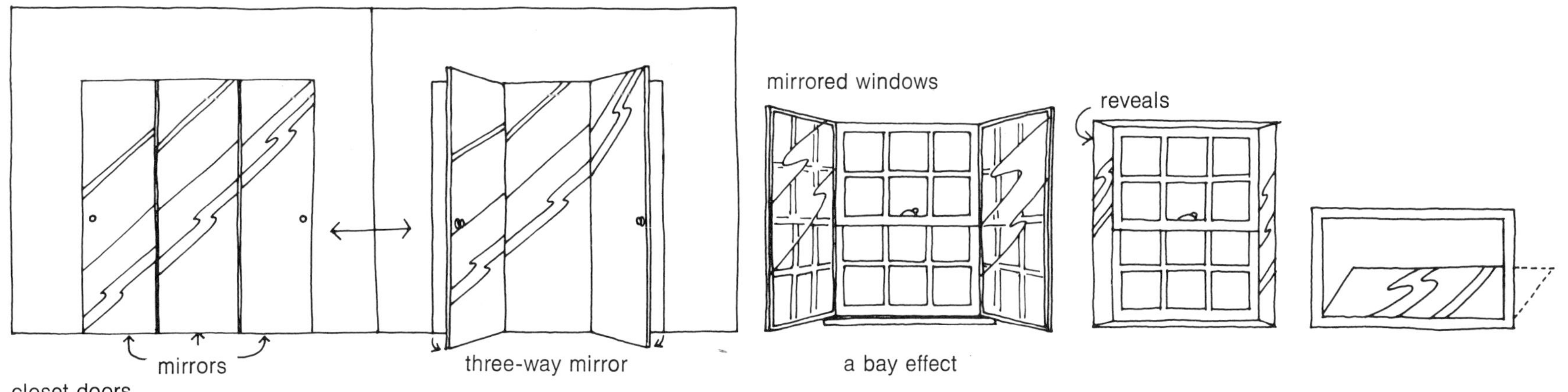

EXPANDING WALLS WITH MIRRORS

Short of tearing out walls, a mirror is the best device of all for re-creating space and changing the appearance of size, without remodeling.

Mirrors add perspective, depth, and height. Mirrors lighten and brighten—a trick known to the Egyptians, who put mirrors outside the pyramids to reflect light to the inside so they could see as they built.

The uses of mirrors are wondrous and almost unlimited:

- Put a mirror on a dark wall to catch the sunlight, to liven up the dead-end wall of a hall or a dull corner.
- Put a mirror on the long wall of a narrow room to make it look wider and on the short wall to make it look deeper.
- Put a large rectangular mirror hanging lengthwise on a narrow wall. It will seem to stretch the wall, and hanging vertically behind a table or bench, to push the ceiling up.
- Put a half-circle table against a mirror and it will look like a round table. Wall lights or sconces hung on the mirror will also double their size.
- Put a mirror on the ceiling, on the dining table, behind bookshelves, beneath kitchen cabinets for added dimension in an unexpected place.
- Put a mirror on a closet or room door. Mirror a set of sliding doors to make a mirror wall.
- Put mirror tiles on a screen or on ugly beams or partitions. Once mirrored they will visually dissolve.
- Put a mirror in alcoves. If, for example, both sides of a fireplace are mirrored, wall-to-fireplace and floor-to-ceiling, the fireplace wall will "disappear."
- Put mirrors near windows to bounce light into a room, either on an adjacent wall, on a nearby screen, or on window shutters or reveals. (When shutters are mirrored, the window looks like a larger bay window.)

TRICKS AND TIPS

Mirrors are marvelous space stretchers, but they can also be a mixed blessing. So proceed with a little caution.

- Consider first what a mirror will reflect—something pretty in the case of a mirror placed opposite or perpendicular to a window, or something unattractive, the mess in the kitchen. A mirror will increase the amount of furniture; although this may be desirable in a sparsely furnished room, it will make an already crowded room look even more cluttered.
- A large mirror is breakable and expensive to buy and to install. On the other hand, the space gained is cheaper than adding a new room.
- Place wall-to-wall mirror so that the extension

How to Change the Dimensions of a Room Visually

to widen

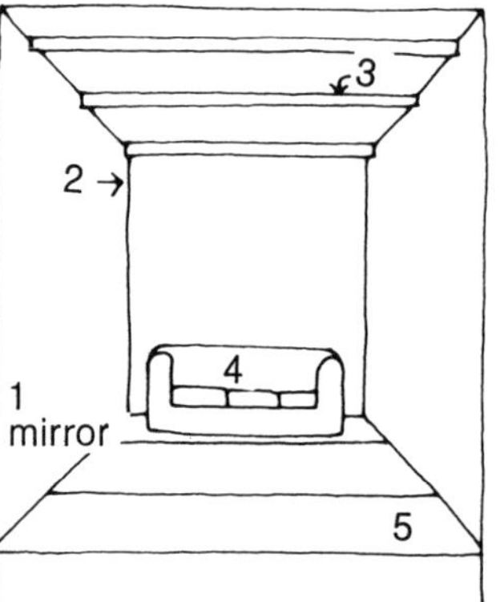

to lengthen

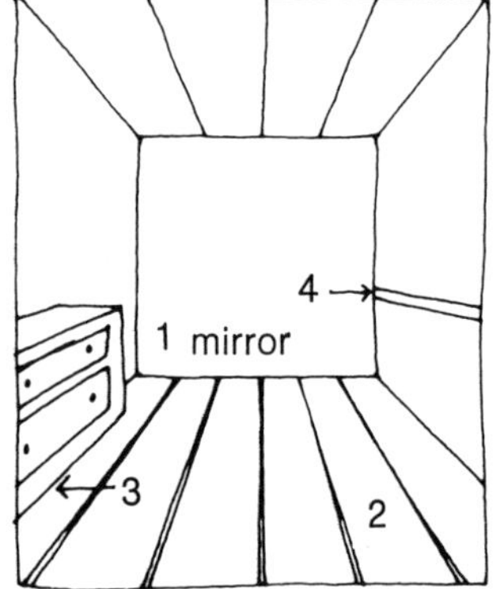

to raise a low ceiling

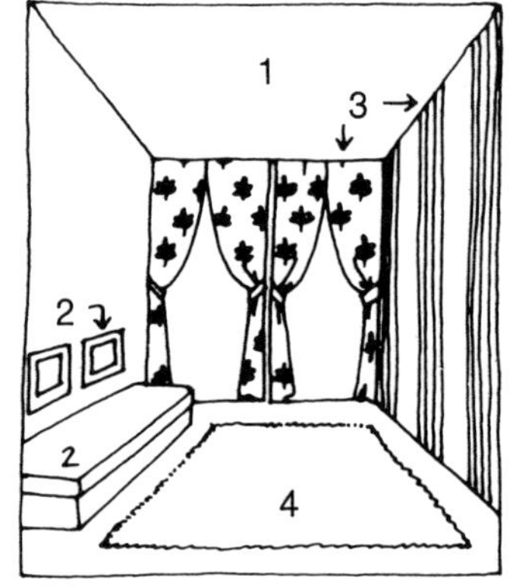

to lower a high ceiling

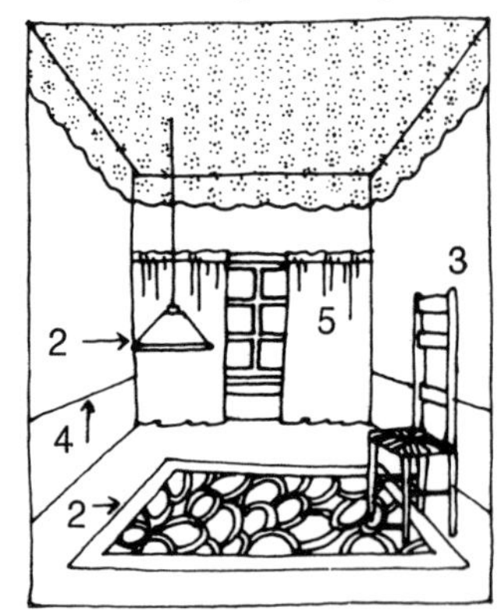

of space seems logical, so that there is a rational beginning and end, so that if the wall were not there, you could keep walking through the house (that is, not on a window wall). A floor-to-ceiling mirror is most effective if it starts at the floor, not above the baseboard, and ends at the ceiling, not below the ceiling molding. If the mirror does not completely cover a wall, fill in the balance with curtains, paneling, or built-ins.

• Panels or tiles or a mirror installed in a checkerboard, diagonal, or herringbone pattern, or a mirror with a smoked or antique finish, are more decorative, and tiles are easy for the amateur to install, but they are not quite as effective as space stretchers as solid sheets of clear mirror with the fewest possible seams.

• Silvered acrylic sheeting is flexible and suitable for curved walls, and an aluminum wall, because of its ability to reflect light, gives a spatial dimension somewhat like a mirror.

• Instead of hanging a plain piece of mirror, paint it or frame it. Pick up a pretty frame at an antique or secondhand shop and have a glazier cut a mirror to fit. This is not expensive, and a framed mirror is an excellent substitute for a picture, especially over a couch or bed. Paint or stain a battered frame, or decorate the frame with colored adhesive tape, shells, or buttons, or cover completely with a fabric or a wall covering that is in the room. A design can be painted with acrylic or latex paint directly onto a plain-Jane mirror (paint should be thin when applied, as it has a tendency to "creep" owing to the smoothness of the surface). If the design will not "take," hang the mirror and paint a design on the wall surrounding it.

CHANGING DIMENSIONS

Most of us think of a room as having four sides but, of course, it really has six, and all these can be manipulated to create the illusion of more space.

• *To widen:* Use mirror on the long wall (1); use an advancing or contrasting color on the short wall or an important window treatment to make it come forward (2); emphasize the horizontal elements of the shorter wall, such as a chair rail, a baseboard, and ceiling moldings (3); place the couch or other long and large furniture in the room perpendicular to the long wall (4); use a floor pattern that runs parallel with the width, such as stripes, feature strips, or diagonal squares (5).

• *To lengthen:* Use a mirror on the short wall, the one that is perpendicular to the long wall (1); use a floor or wall pattern that runs parallel to the length (2); place long furniture against the long wall (3); emphasize the horizontal elements of the long wall (4).

• *To raise a low ceiling:* Paint it white or a color much lighter than the wall color (1); use

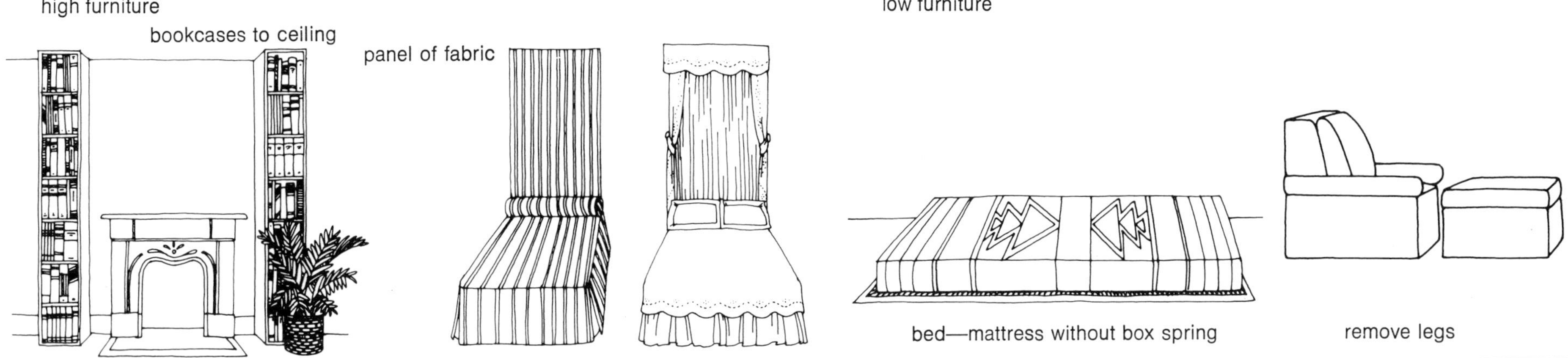

low furniture with low-hung pictures (remove legs of furniture, put mattress on floor) (2); accent the verticals in the room by using a vertical-stripe paper, painting, vertical molding, and by installing the panels and drapes full height to the ceiling; use floor-to-ceiling furnishings such as tall thin bookcases, a bed canopy suspended from ceiling, a fireplace that extends to ceiling (3); call attention to the floor (4) and away from the ceiling. Avoid low-hanging fixtures that "pull" the ceiling down (on the other hand, a chandelier hung from a high ceiling will accent height).

• *To lower a ceiling that appears too high:* Use a darker or brighter color on the ceiling than on the walls or an eye-arresting wallpaper; this effect can be magnified by extending the paint or paper to cover the upper part of the walls. Or actually build a false "dropped" ceiling. By lowering the ceiling of a small room, you can make it appear larger because the ceiling will seem to push the walls out (1); call attention to the lower half of the room by using low-hung lighting and attention-getting floor materials (2); use high furniture, such as high-backed chairs and chests (3); emphasize horizontals by painting chair rails a contrasting color or by adding a dado of wallpaper or paneling (4); do not hang draperies from ceiling but, rather, lower down from the window (5). Try a canopy effect over the sleeping or dining area.

HOW LIGHTING SHAPES SPACE

Don't be surprised to find a section on lighting in this book. So important, yet so often overlooked, lighting can clearly define and masterfully manipulate space. Lights can partition an area into regions, acting almost like a room divider. By turning lights on or off or by lowering them, one section only can be highlighted at the appropriate time; for example, the dining area at dinner time. Similarly, selective lighting can dramatize and accent the strong points in a room and leave the ugly areas in the dark.

In addition to general illumination, an area might have reading and working accent and spotlights.

Few lamps should be used, and these should be as low as possible because low lighting is most flattering to a room, especially a small one. (To make a lamp shine only downward, put a circular metal disk on the shade carrier.)

Indirect and diffused lighting contributes to a sense of spaciousness, particularly if it is hidden and/or built in, eliminating the need for distracting and space-consuming lamps. So consider the following:

• *Uplights.* These square or circular cans shine light upward. They are available in many sizes with three-way bulbs; they cast light on the ceiling and create soft shadows around an area. When reading light is not needed but general soft illumination is, place several uplights on the floor, in the corners of the living room, behind large pieces of furniture such as a couch, or behind plants. (Light behind plants creates a soft shadow that makes an excellent contrast to angular furniture.) This is a magical way to add drama to an otherwise small and insignificant room.

• *Downlights.* Downlights direct a strong pool of light from a cylindrical fixture downward. They can be built into the ceiling, or a strip holding several lights can be installed on tracks applied to the celiing. Downlights can also be attached to walls or bookcases (focused perhaps on something special), and are often used to light a hall or foyer. Pictures and walls lit with downlight seem to expand.

• *Cove lighting.* These concealed strips of lights are generally used to highlight an area with soft light. They might be used behind a cornice to call attention to a window treatment, in a storage unit to highlight a display of sculpture, or even beneath a built-in couch to give it the appearance of floating.

For variety, and to add another dimension to a lighting arrangement easily and inexpensively, install light dimmers.

Lowering the Ceiling

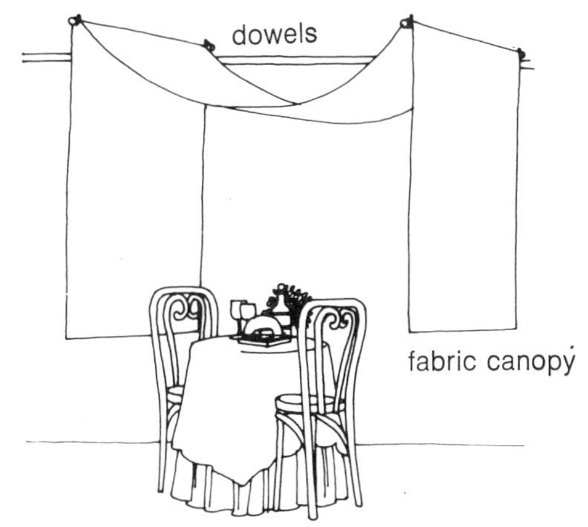

Special Effects with Paint

supergraphic to "furnish" underfurnished room

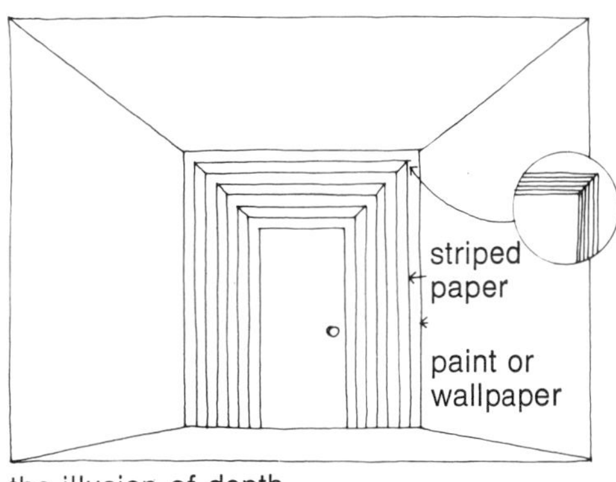

the illusion of depth

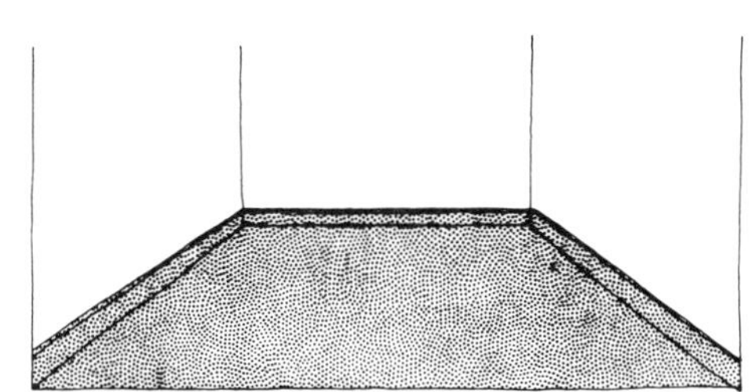

to enlarge floor, paint baseboard same color as floor

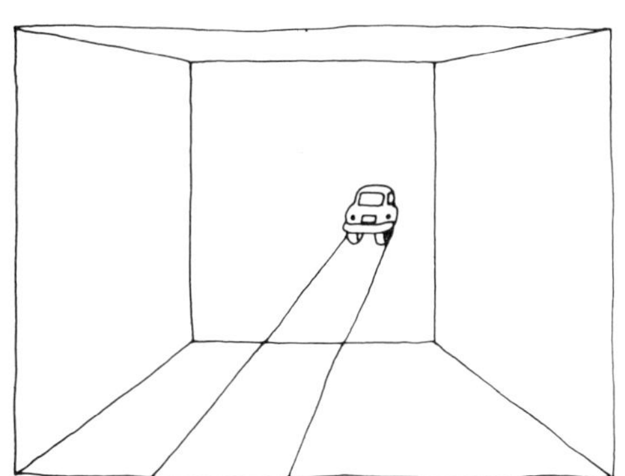

car and road painted on floor and wall of child's room

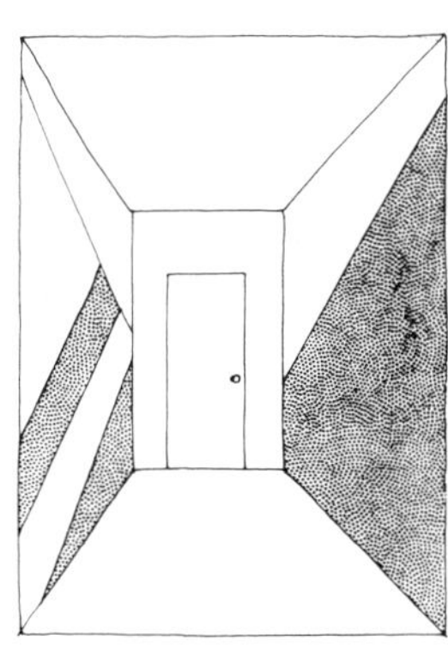

paint on the diagonal widens narrow hallway

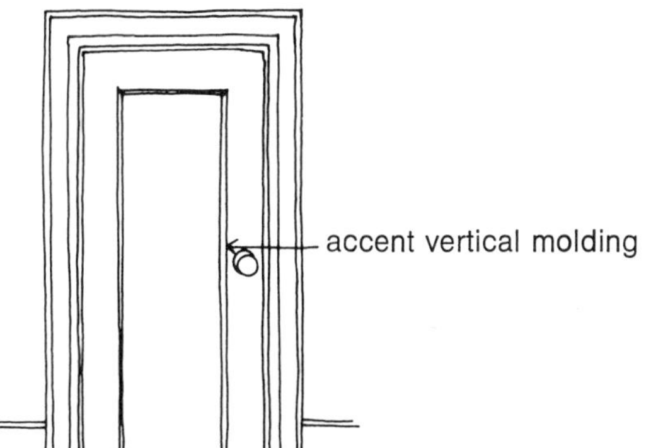

4. ROOMIER ONE-ROOM LIVING

There does not seem to be any greater space challenge on or off this planet than making a one-room dwelling attractive and usable. But even this space can be conquered—with partitions, hideaway beds, and multifunctional furniture that seem almost appropriate for a lunar capsule.

Ingenuity and imagination are important allies here, and often an unorthodox solution is the best one. For example, the smaller part of an L-shaped room need not be set aside for the conventional dining or sleeping area. It could be either designed as a clearly separate area serving a different function such as an office—with space for sleeping reserved in the larger part of the L—or decorated as an integral part of the whole—which would make the total space look that much bigger.

Some subdivision will be necessary for privacy, for directing the movement of traffic, and for the optimum organization of the area. Room dividers—movable partitions, accordion doors, folding screens—are not the only ways of separating space. The arrangement of furniture, a change in color or height, or a sharp variation in wall or floor covering can also serve this purpose.

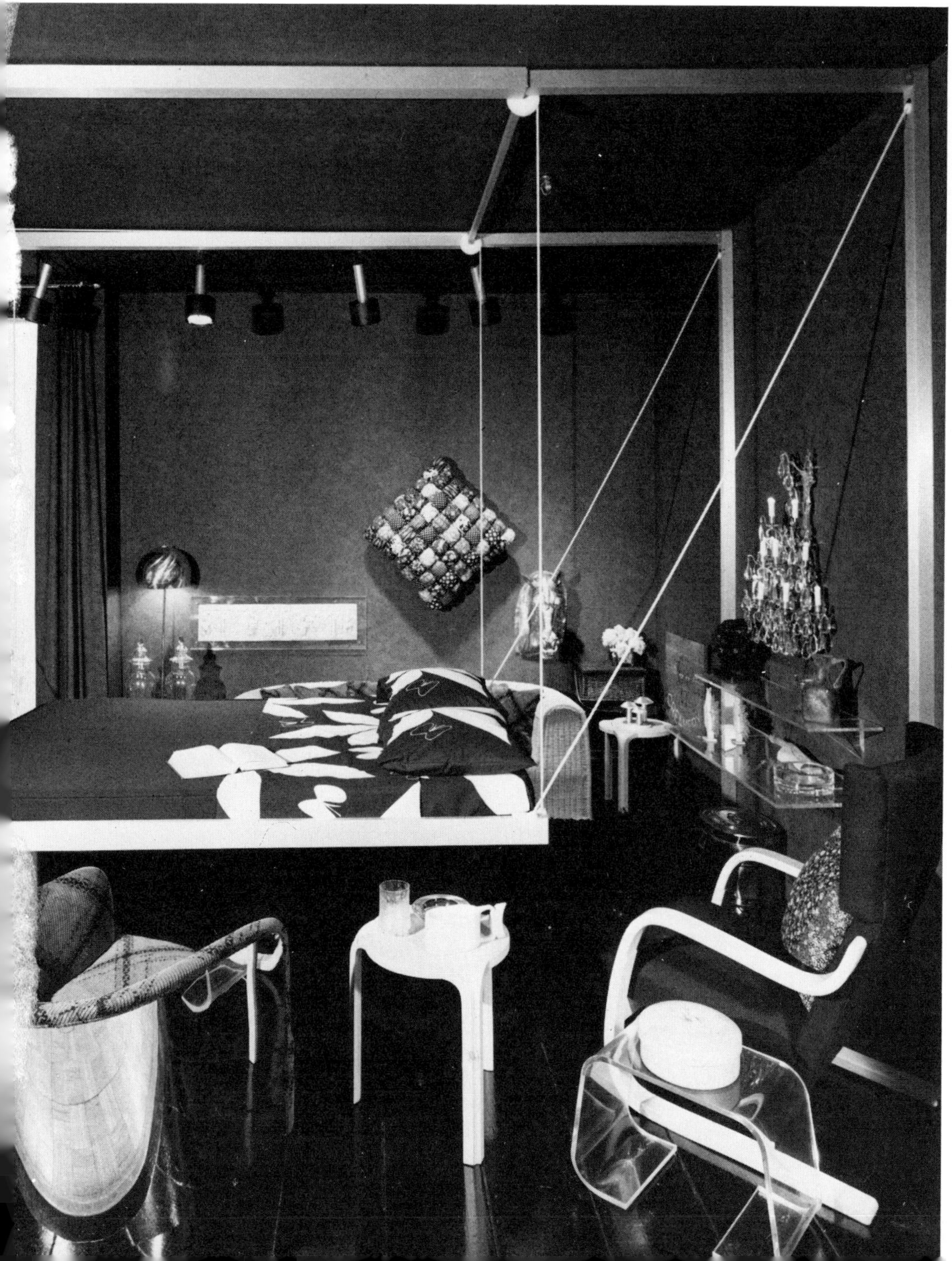

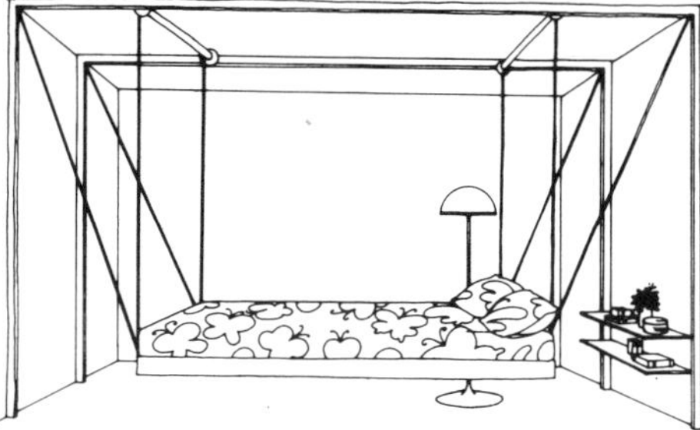

Stored on the ceiling, this bed, which operates on a pulley system, can be lowered at night and hoisted up during the day. The same principle could be applied to any large surface used only part-time, such as a dining or Ping-Pong table, electric trains or racing cars on a board.

sleep and storage unit

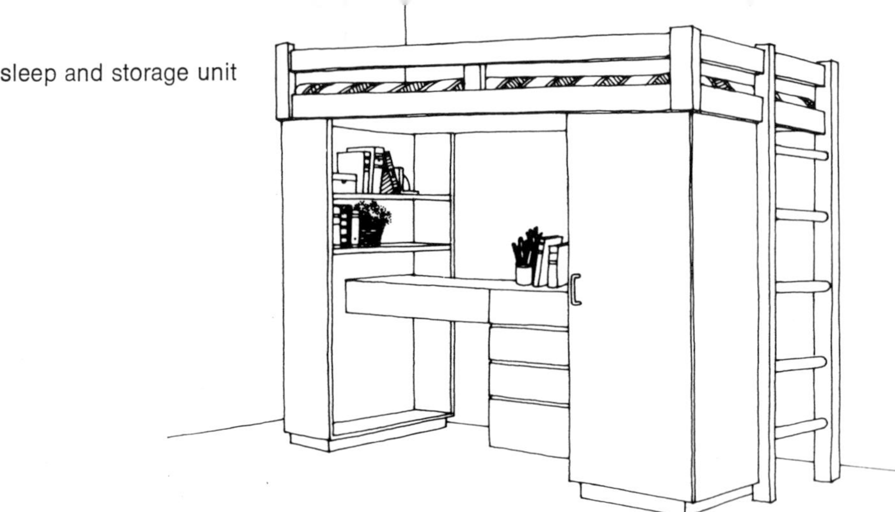

MULTILEVEL LIVING: LOFTS

One of the most effective ways to divide a space is to change radically the height of the floor and to make either a conversation pit or a raised platform. If ceilings are high enough a balcony-like structure, or loft, can be built that will not only double livable space but make a more interesting area. The best place to install a loft is at the narrow end of an area where the side walls can help to support it. Allow about seven feet head clearance for a loft that requires room to stand in, about five feet for seating, and about four feet for just sleeping. Allow room also for climbing in and out. Decorate a loft like a separate room with carpeting and paper or paint. On a sleeping loft use a mattress alone if space does not permit a full bed set with box spring; make sure there is some form of ventilation. If possible, add shelves, storage, an end table, and some lighting.

As with any structural change, time and money must be invested and permission from the landlord granted. If a loft cannot be built, a good alternative is a loftlike unit with bed above, storage and desk below, or variations on this theme that can be bought in a good unpainted furniture outlet.

HOW TO USE FLOOR AND WALL COVERINGS TO DIVIDE SPACE

Separate one area from another through:

1. The use of area rugs. These should relate in pattern and color if they are within eye range of one another.
2. A change in materials, for example from vinyl tile to carpeting.
3. The introduction of wallpaper (or a different color paint) to set off an area such as a sleeping alcove.

One word of caution: The place where the wall or floor treatment changes should make sense. It should be defined by a change in the level of the floor, by the position of a piece of furniture (such as a bookcase that might divide an eating area from a living-room area), or by a change in the direction of the wall. For example, the end of a wall in an L-shaped area would be the place to change the wall decoration, rather than an arbitrary spot in the middle of the wall.

ROOM DIVIDERS

In a way, dividers should really be called room multipliers because "new rooms" or areas can be created with them. An essential part of one-room living, dividers conceal and connect one area and another; attractive dividers can also be an important ingredient in the decorating scheme, if not the focal point.

When deciding on the kind of divider, factors such as whether it should be permanent or movable, see-through or solid must be taken into account. The amount of air and light that circulate through

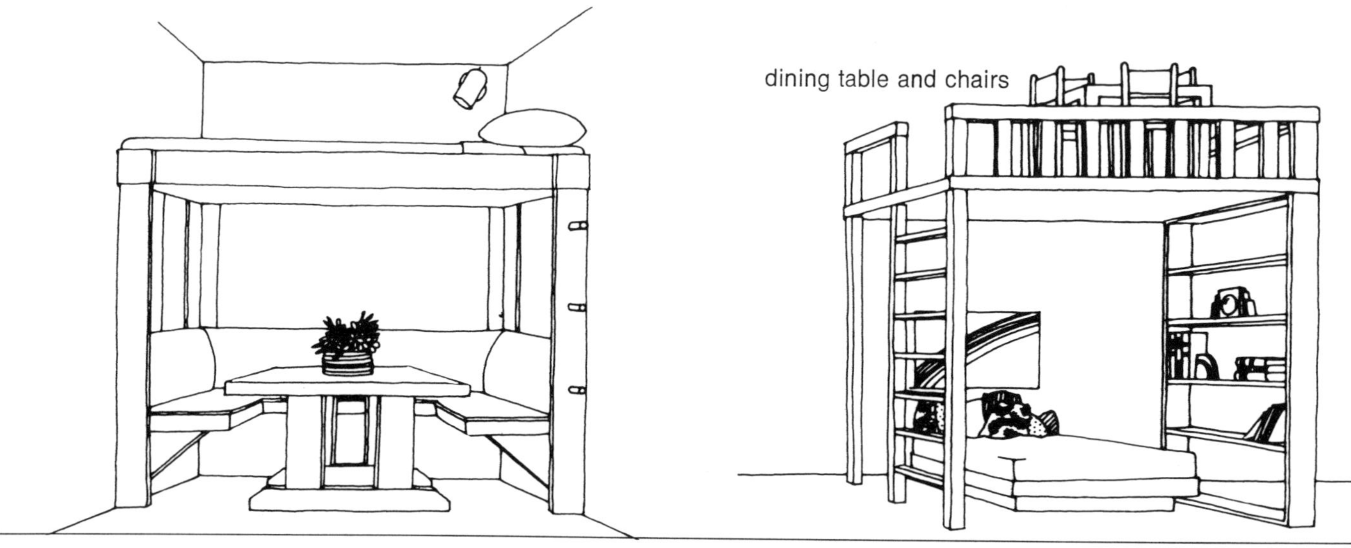

If a loft is built, a separate bedroom can be literally created out of thin air, without using up any floor space.

Bookcase Dividers

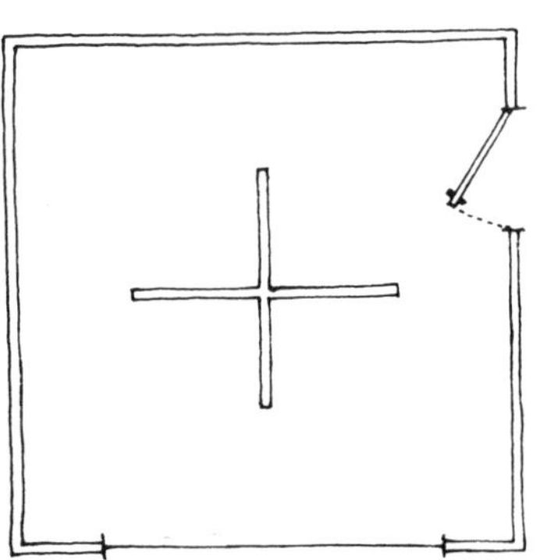

four areas from one:
permanent partition or screen

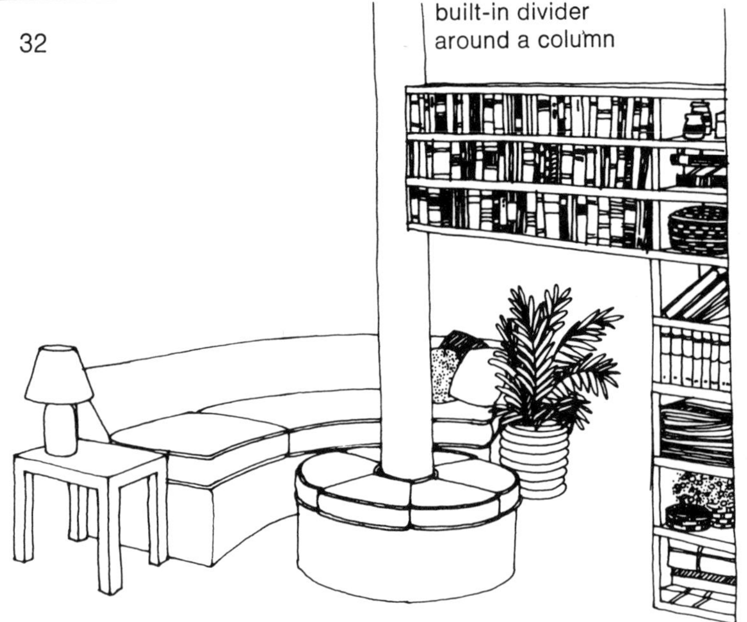

built-in divider
around a column

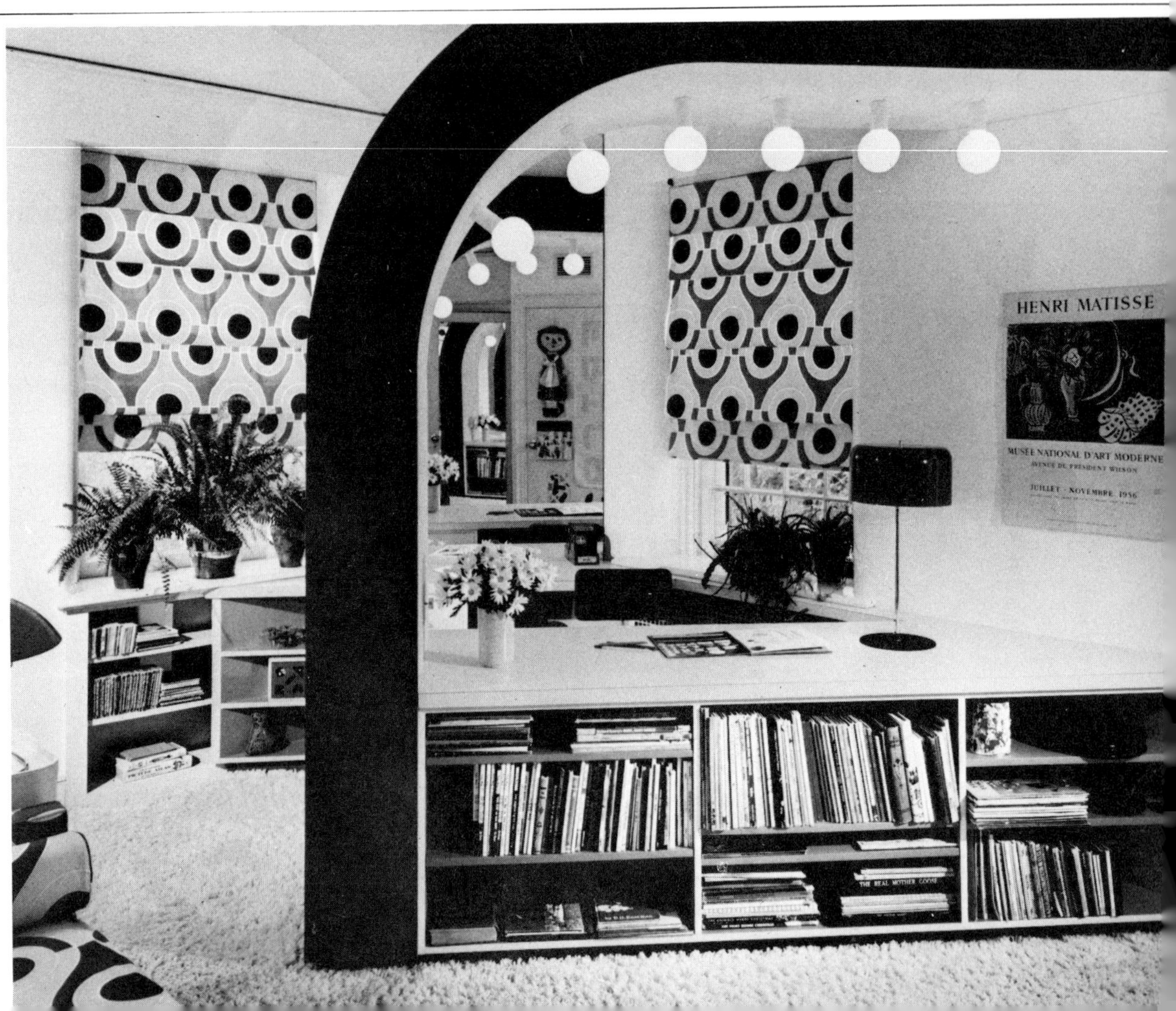

A dramatic arch with oversize bare bulbs is not just a desk-bookcase-divider but a strong architectural element and focal point of the room. It was built on the diagonal to maximize the work and sleep-sitting areas.

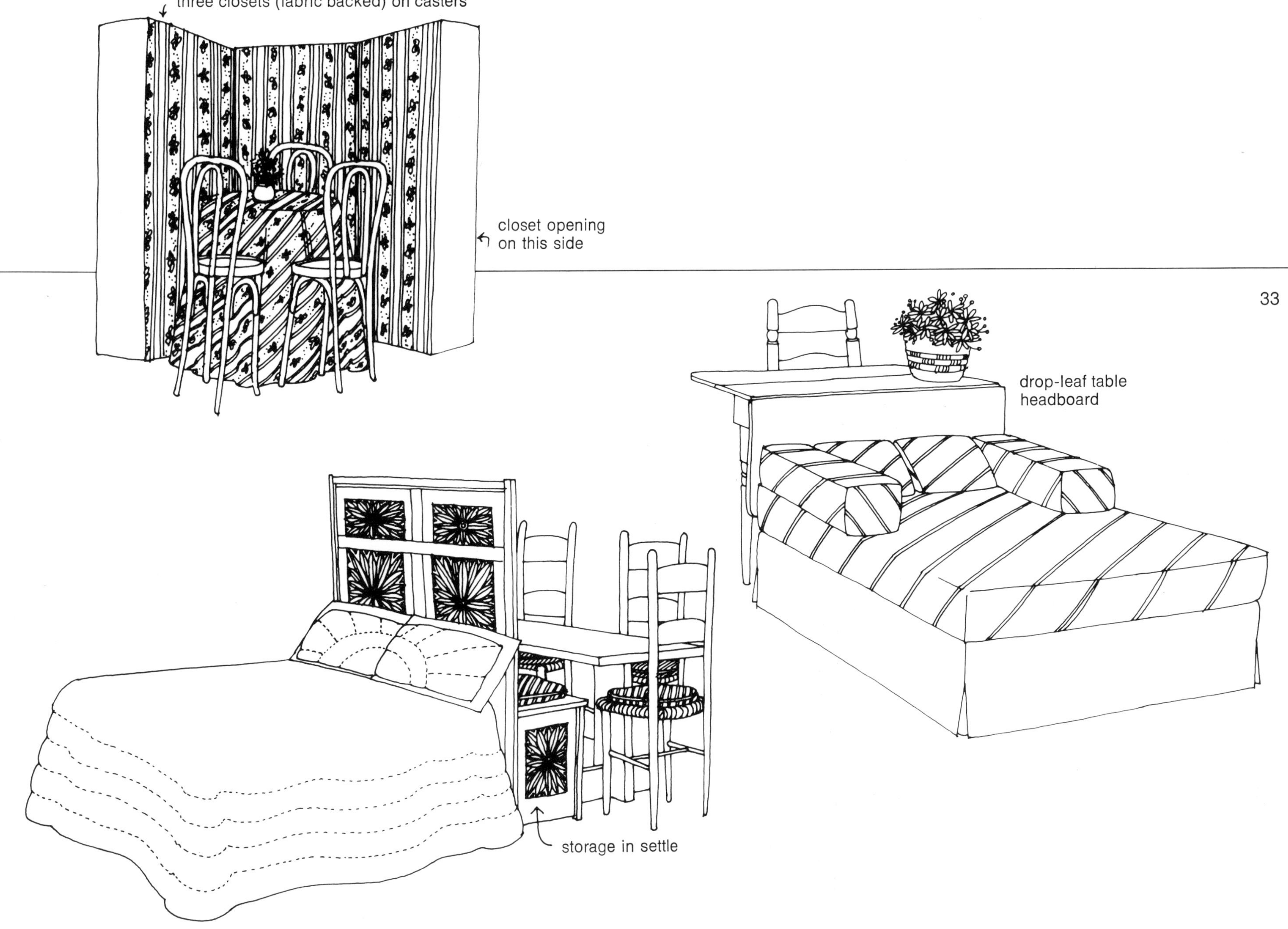
three closets (fabric backed) on casters
closet opening on this side
drop-leaf table headboard
storage in settle

Do-It-Yourself Dividers

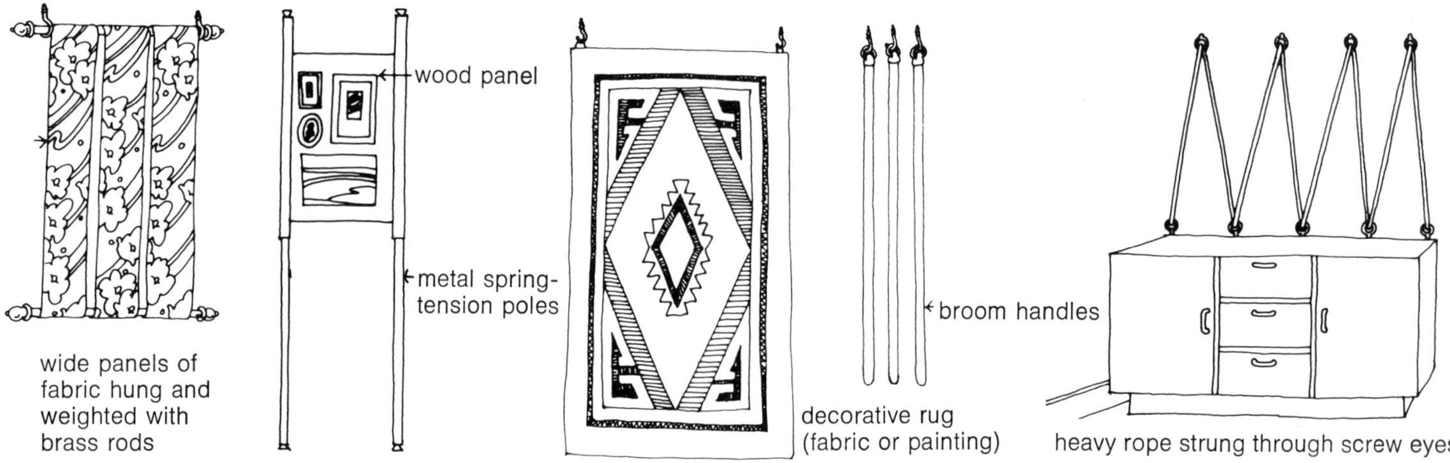

wide panels of fabric hung and weighted with brass rods

wood panel

metal spring-tension poles

decorative rug (fabric or painting)

broom handles

heavy rope strung through screw eyes

a divider can often be altered rather simply. In the example of an open-backed bookcase, this would be controlled by the number of books on the shelves.

If the exposed back of the furniture is unfinished, it can be made presentable with paint or fabric. Alternatively, the unattractive back side can be concealed with one or several plants or a screen.

STORE-BOUGHT DIVIDERS

Stores, of course, sell all kinds of furnishings that can divide a room, everything from spring-pole units fitted with wood panels to shelves and cabinets to folding walls. It is wise when shopping, however, not to restrict oneself to items manufactured expressly for this purpose. Many other things can divide a room and serve another purpose as well, such as one or more metal closets or a bank of storage cubes piled high.

HOMEMADE DIVIDERS

Almost anything attractively assembled can be a room divider, and many of the following are easily made at home. Two important points to remember for this or any other do-it-yourself venture are (1) have enough materials and (2) measure carefully the space to be covered. Measure both the width and the height. The height is usually floor-to-ceiling, but the divider could also run from the top of a piece of furniture or a counter to the ceiling. Allow (add or subtract) a few inches for attaching divider at the top and bottom. Also determine how the divider will be attached—in some cases, with screws, cup hooks, glue, thumbtacks, or staples. When the divider is lightweight, tacks or staples may do; a heavier divider may have to be screwed into a ceiling beam.

To make sure the divider will be perpendicular and hang straight down, drop a plumb line—a long piece of string with a weight or scissors on the end—from the ceiling to line up parts of the divider as it is installed.

- Panels of canvas or other heavy fabric, in a solid color or a pattern, hung from ceiling to floor from hooks or rods make a temporary and inexpensive wall. For a see-through effect, use lightweight or casement material. A large painting or rug can be hung in a similar way.
- Curtains (even shower curtains, Venetian blinds or shades) that extend from floor to ceiling can be installed on a rod or hooks attached to the ceiling. A sleeping alcove can be completely hidden by screening off the bed with a curtain that pulls around, like those used in hospitals.
- Bead or bamboo curtains are attractive and create a subtle division of space. Other things that can be strung or glued onto string include paper plates, or cards, or spools.
- Strips of trimming such as upholstery webbing, ribbons, or cord can be installed floor-to-

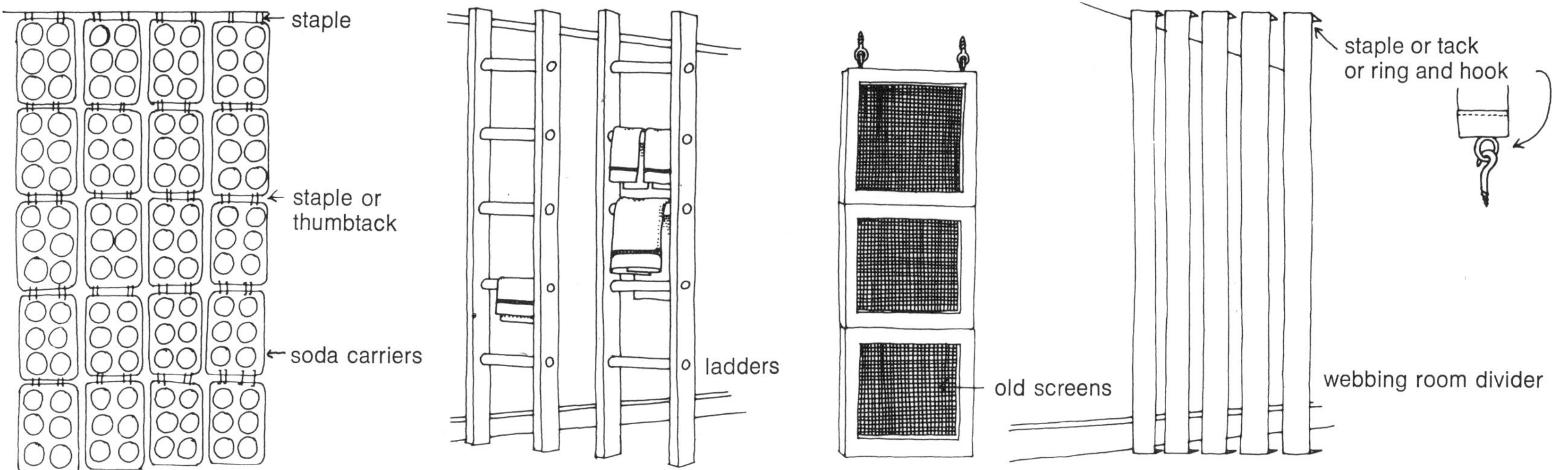

ceiling with staples or hooks and eyes at each end.

- Decorative panels made of filigreed wood or plastic or those made by filling in panel frames with woven ribbons, string, or wool are effective.
- Spring poles with almost any material—cord, wool, ribbon—strung between them are good dividers.
- Tall plants, two or three in a row, are simple but dramatic dividers.
- No-cost dividers can be made from throw-aways such as plastic soda carriers and the three-dimensional molded cardboard panels used to pack eggs. Free and plentiful at the grocery store, these can be stapled or hooked together, painted, and then hung from ceiling to floor. Discarded window screens can be painted and then hung from hooks, and slightly used (but clean) Styrofoam drinking cups can be stacked from floor to ceiling in rows.

FOLDING SCREENS

Easily the most versatile and economical room dividers, screens can also hide an ugly view; conceal an unattractive radiator, beam, or other misplaced architectural horror; create an extra closet or wall; hide the television set, the clothes washer, and messy shelves; make a conversation area more intimate. Extraordinarily flexible, a screen is easy to remove when necessary—for example, to re-establish one large area for a party—and a screen with several double-hinged panels can move backward and forward and can be shaped into many configurations. A low screen will enclose and separate without shutting out light; a high screen will give an illusion of height to an area.

Screens are usually made of three or more panels in almost any material: wood (carved or plain); shoji (rice paper on a wood frame); rattan, metal, leather, mirrored glass, plastic, or covered in cork, felt, wallpaper, or fabric to match the room. It is not too difficult to recover an old screen, and a screen missing legs can be hung by putting screw eyes in each panel and hooks in the ceiling.

Screens are easily tipped over, and the risk of their falling is ever present. So, if possible, place a screen to one side near a wall or next to a solid piece of furniture, or attach one side to a wall (the screen can be folded up flat against the wall when not in use). To install a screen more or less permanently, screw two thin wood strips to the floor to form a channel that corresponds in size and placement to one panel of the screen and slide the panel through it.

SCREENS THAT STORE

- If a screen separates two different areas, each side can be decorated accordingly. For example, pegboard can be put up on the kitchen side of a screen and wallpaper on the dining-

Room Dividers

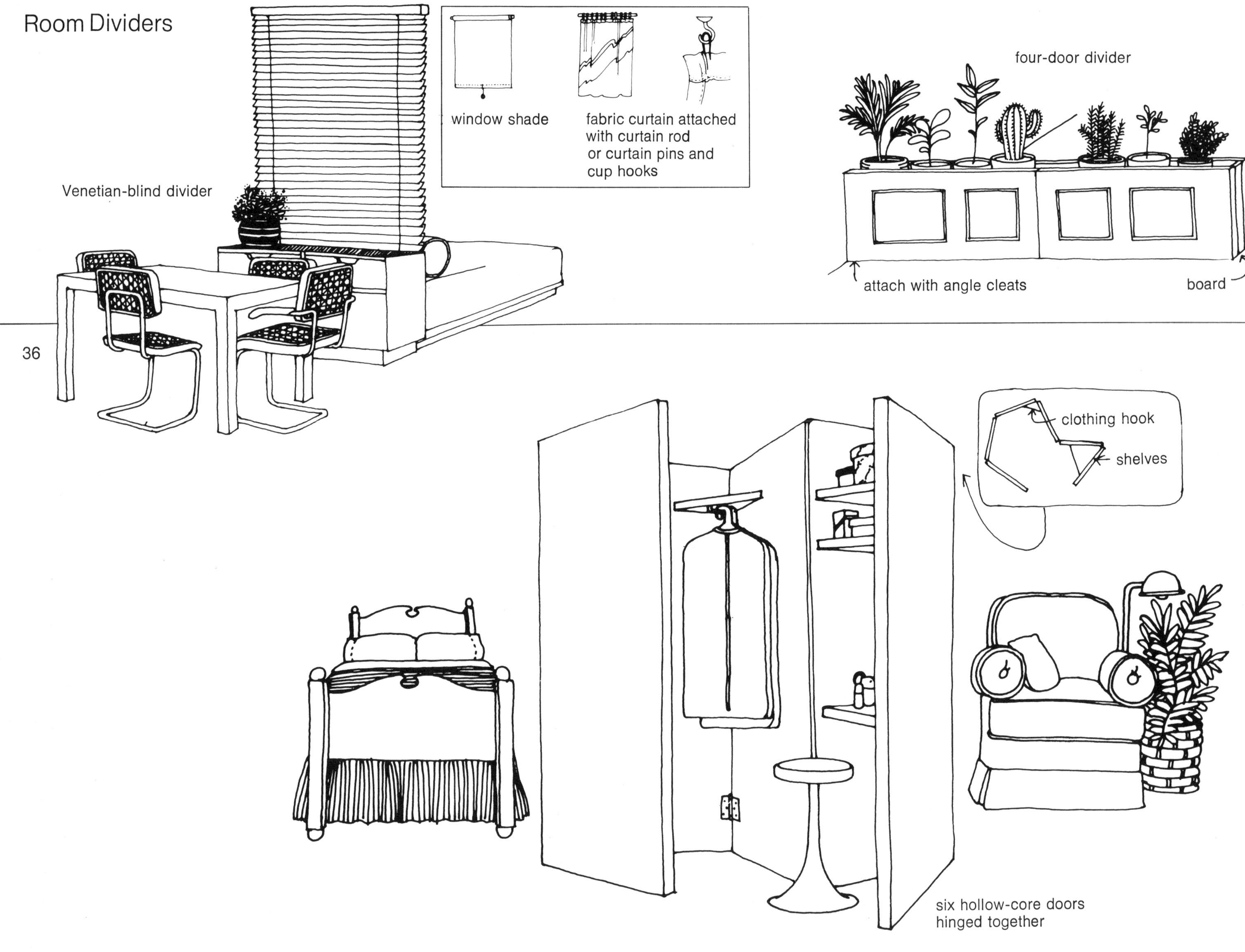

decorative screen at entranceway creates a "wall"

Beds That Disappear

bed alcove

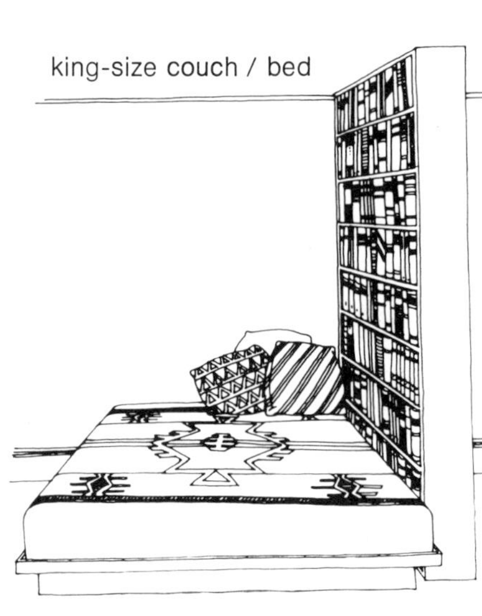

king-size couch / bed

room side to match the dining-room wall.

- A screen can be placed in a bathroom to separate the toilet area from the balance of the room with pockets for toiletries on the sink side and pockets for reading material on the toilet side.
- The TV schedule can be tacked on the inside of a screen that conceals a TV; a rope tie rack and a mirror can be attached on the inside of a screen that forms a dressing area.
- In a family room, a picture gallery of post-cards or posters or family photographs can be put up or pockets for yarn and sewing equipment sewn onto the screen; in a child's room a screen can become a giant bulletin board.

OUT-OF-SIGHT SLEEPERS

Even in Thomas Jefferson's day, radical solutions were necessary in order to solve the problem of where to put the bed. Jefferson pulled his up on pulleys when it was not in use. Although this is still a timely idea, there are many other less complicated options available today. The basic decision to be made is whether to conceal the bed (for example, to fold it away into a closet or to disguise it and dress it up like a couch), or to highlight it in a separate seating-sleeping area decorated with wallpaper, paneling, mirror, or paint. Other important considerations are convenience—how much trouble the bed is to open, whether the linens can remain on all the time (if not, find a place to store them)—and comfort—the firmness of the mattress and the size (for an adult, at least 33″ wide and 72″ long).

As in the case of all furniture that expands, a clearing must be left for a bed that opens, with no heavy furniture that is hard to move (like a coffee table) in the way.

- *The Murphy bed:* Invented in the twenties, the Murphy bed is an old standby and a practical space saver. Through a mechanical device, the bed folds up flat against a wall. Unfortunately, the cost of installing and constructing the concealing cabinet or closet can make it expensive. Although the bed is supposed to stay made up, the linens may slide off as the mattress makes its ascent upward. The Murphy bed can also be hidden in a wall or behind a sliding panel, a screen, a mirrored wall, or even behind a large wall sculpture or wall hanging.
- *The foldaway bed:* One modern variation of the Murphy bed is a bed that drops down from the wall in somewhat the same way as a drop-down shelf.
- *The platform bed:* If, in order to establish a division of space, part of the floor has been raised in a room, a bed unit can be constructed

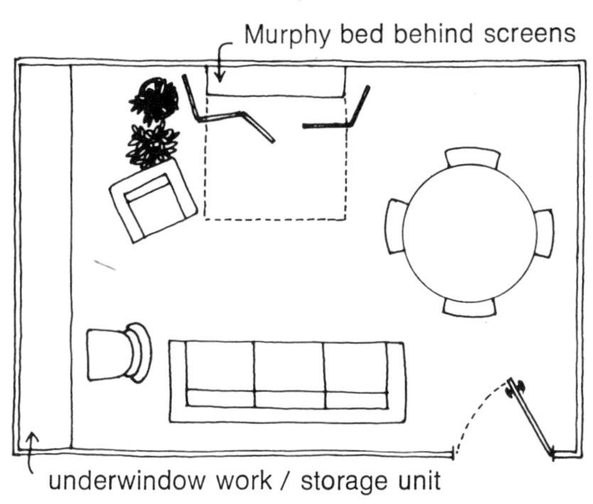

Murphy bed
view 1

to slide out from this platform like a drawer.

• *Box springs and mattresses:* It's all in the cover-up. A box spring/or mattress can be dressed up and transformed into a perfectly respectable, moderately priced "couch":

1. Consider eliminating the bed frame or the legs if the bed does not have to be moved. This will make a trim-looking unit that is also lower—closer to the height of a couch. The box spring can also be eliminated and the mattress placed directly on the floor, a good idea where ceilings are low.
2. Sew a mattress cover of sturdy fabric like cotton duck, velvet, or corduroy (avoid boudoir colors and fabrics) in the style of a contour sheet, with elastic in corners. Cover the box spring with fabric, using white glue, double-faced tape, or a staple gun.
3. Buy an attractive throw, or improvise with a Mexican blanket, an Indian rug, or an antique quilt.
4. Conceal sleeping pillows with fancy covers that supply decorative interest at the same time; add a bunch of accent pillows to fill in and decrease the depth of the bed and make sitting more comfortable.
5. Combine a mattress alone with a storage piece of similar size; put it on top of several chests of drawers, or trunks, or wooden boxes, or one large wooden box with top or sides that open for storage.
6. Add a headboard and footboard upholstered in the same material as the "spread" and, again, many pillows.
7. Place a large bed in a corner or alcove to make it look smaller.

• *Half-hidden beds:* A bed can be semi-hidden in an alcove that is partially covered with curtains or sliding doors. It can slide out from within a piece of furniture such as a deep bookcase unit or a corner table, or even from within the wall itself.

• *The sofa bed:* One of the most popular and practical aids to one-room living is the sofa bed, and a newer variation, the ottoman bed. Of the several different styles, some are more suited to part-time, occasional use and others to full-time use. The most common kind has a concealed mattress (innerspring or poly-urethane foam in a range of widths from twin to king) that pulls or folds out from the seat all made up.

• *The studio couch:* The studio couch or day-bed is basically an upholstered mattress and box spring. Some styles have an additional mechanism that converts the couch into two beds. Bed linens may be concealed by the studio cover or they may have to be put on at night, depending upon the model.

view 2

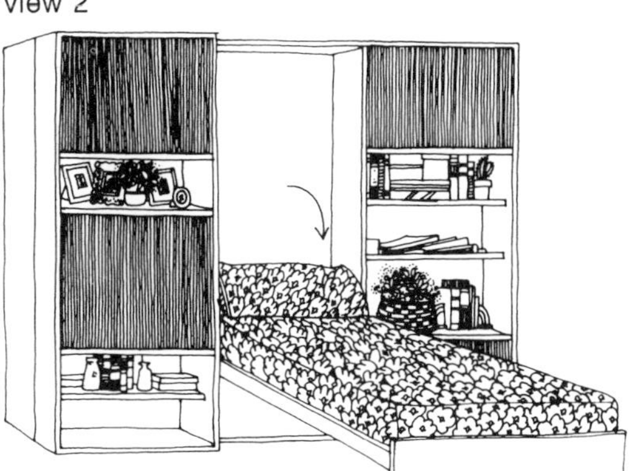

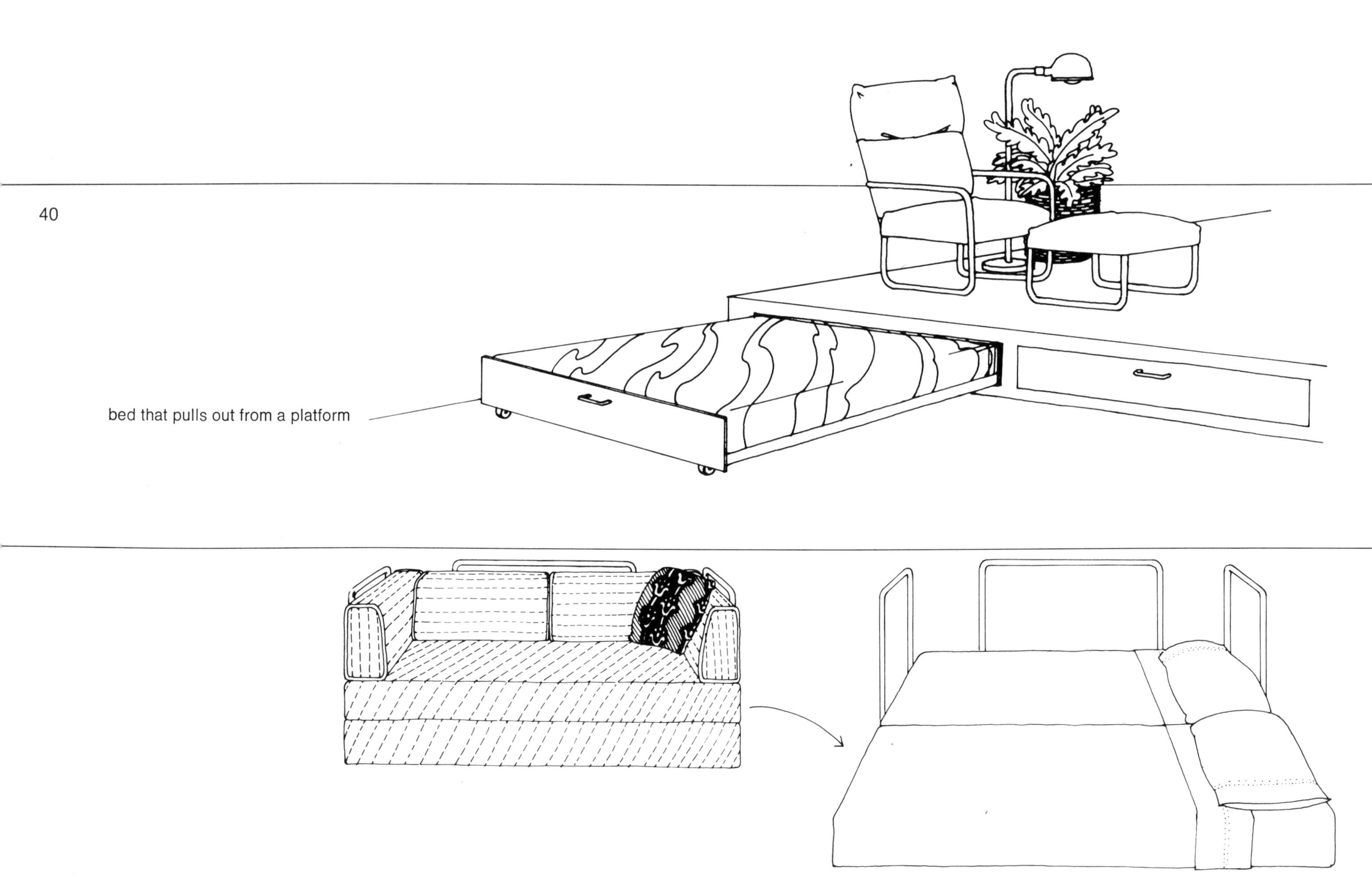
bed that pulls out from a platform

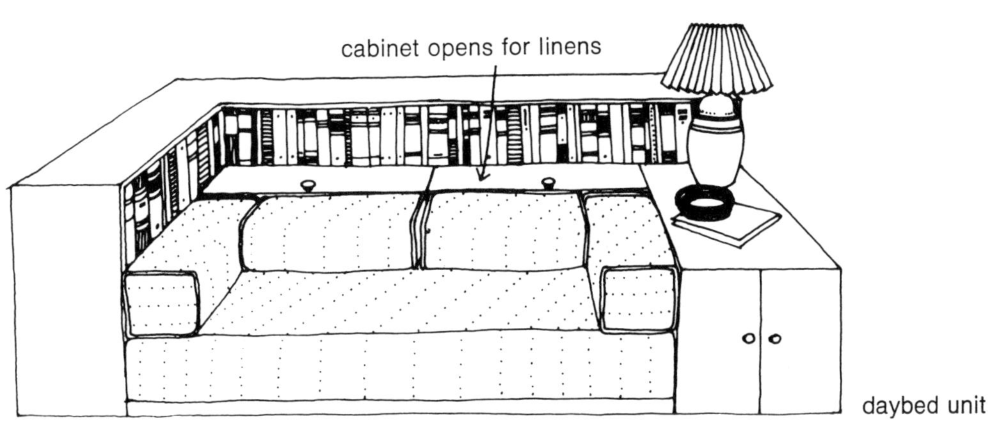

daybed unit

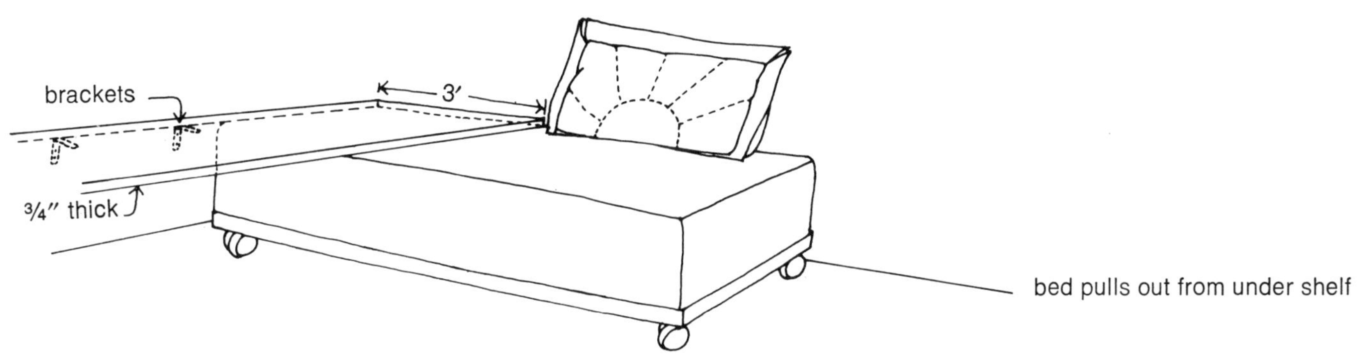

bed pulls out from under shelf

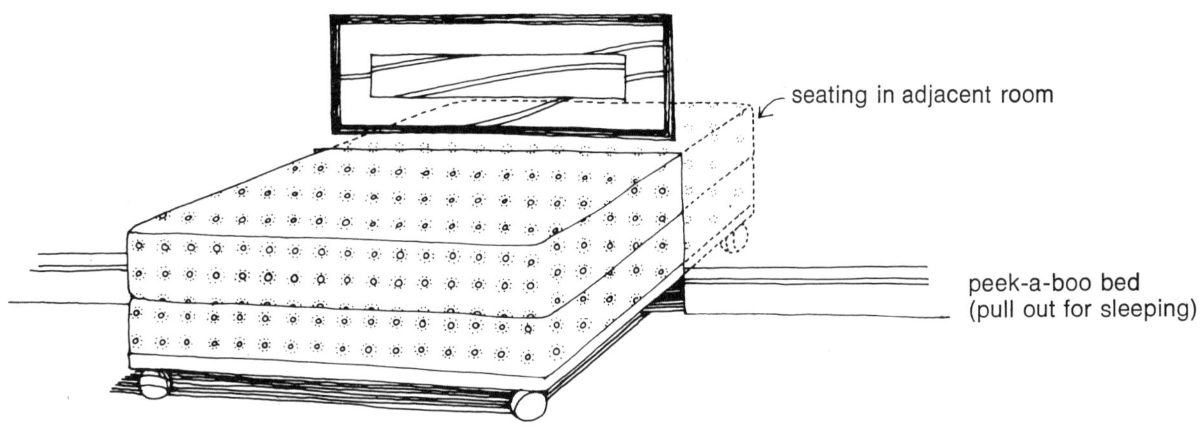

peek-a-boo bed
(pull out for sleeping)

5. Spacious Sleeping Spaces

Bedrooms come in every size. Even a very small or low area can be pressed into service without sacrificing comfort. A big bed can be placed virtually wall-to-wall into a vest-pocket room looking more like an attractive bed alcove than a cell-like bedroom. Since standing-up space is not necessary, attics and eaves can be converted into charming sleeping spaces.

The placement of the bed usually determines where everything else in the room will go. Traditionally, one large bed or two twin beds (set side by side) were centered on a long unbroken wall and that was all there was to it. Now, beds can go where they look or work best, with space left over, perhaps, for a sitting or office area. A room will look luxuriously underfurnished and spacious if one large bed is placed in the center of the room and all but essential furnishings are eliminated or put in the closet. On the other hand, a large bed will appear smaller if it is off in a corner or tucked under a window with part of its bulk concealed beneath pillows. (But be sure the bed has wheels or casters so that it can be moved away from the walls to be made up.) To gain floor space, twin beds can be arranged end-to-end or perpendicular to each other around a corner. There are no conventions. Utility and comfort are the key considerations.

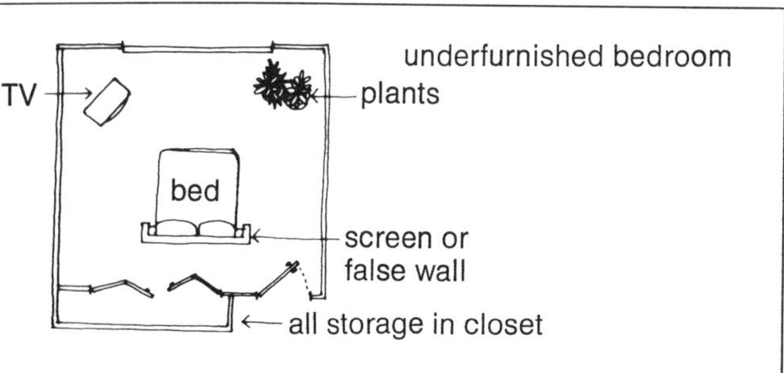

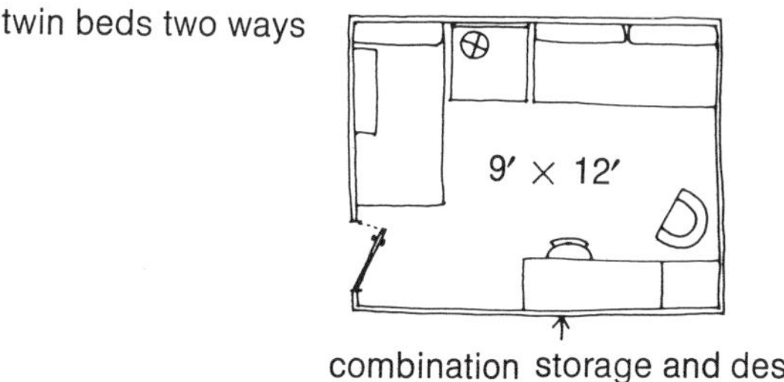

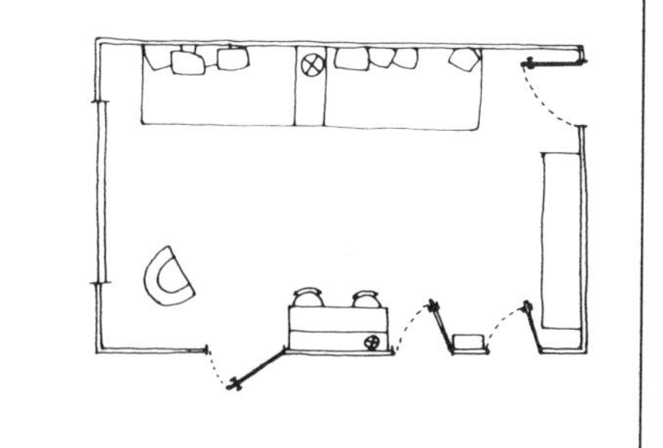

Large furniture is placed defiantly in a small bedroom, arrayed along the walls and dominated by a draped bed in the corner.

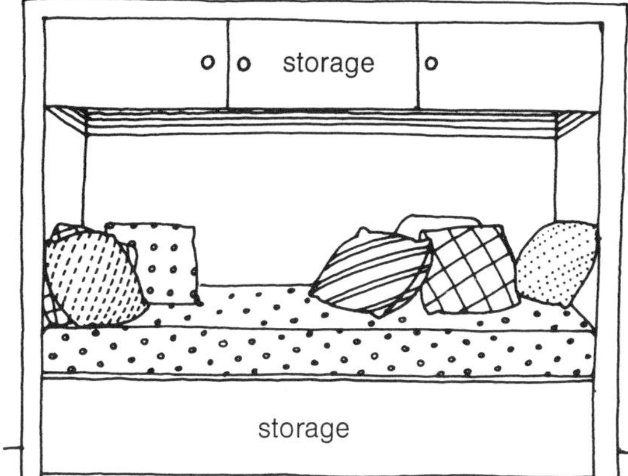

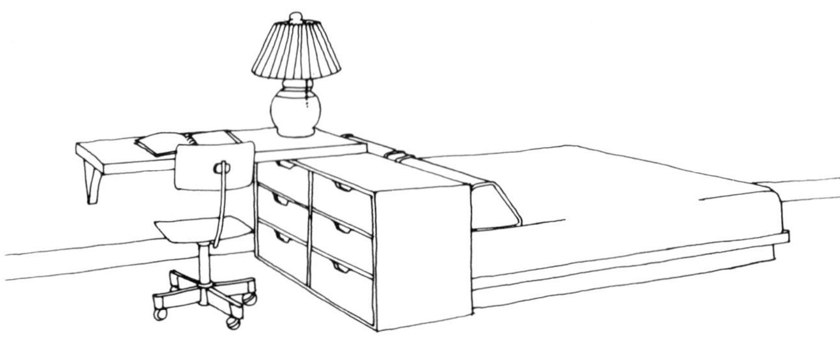

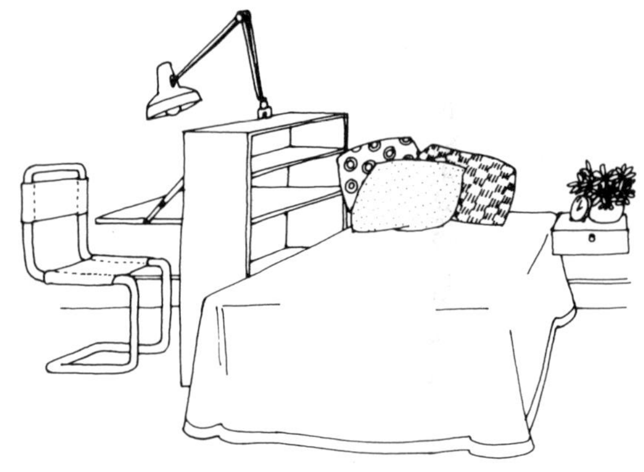

MULTIPURPOSE BEDROOM FURNITURE

Bedroom furniture can serve many functions:

- A bookcase or chest of drawers or corner cabinet, when placed against a bed, can also be the headboard.
- A storage unit can be built around a bed with provision for shelves and lights and headrest.
- A desk can be the bedside table, and with a mirror placed above it, a dressing table as well.
- A blanket chest can store a great deal and be equally useful as extra seating.
- A breakfront can hold clothing in drawers below and books on shelves above.

ROOM FOR GUESTS

With daybeds or banquettes, convertible sofas or foldaway beds, extra sleeping spaces can be created almost any place: in the living room or the dining room, in an alcove, down a wide hallway, or behind a screened-off corner. Just make sure there is a measure of privacy and quiet—and access to a bathroom.

Selection of an area for a guest bed should depend on whether one expects long-term roomers or only an occasional visiting fireman.

A den may be available on almost a semi-permanent basis during school vacations when a college-age child is home (with a permanent place for his possessions), while a dining room or home office might be space to spare on a more limited basis. And your husband's boss might make do a night or two on the convertible couch in the living room or the built-in banquette in the hall, but lack of privacy for a longer period would create an uncomfortable situation for everyone.

Within an existing bedroom, additional sleeping space can be provided by installing two or more beds in the space usually taken by one. A bunk bed or trundle bed (a combination of both for two extra guests) are meant for just this. Disposable beds that disappear when no longer needed and are particularly suitable for younger visitors include: cots (metal with mattresses and canvas army cots), sleeping bags, air mattresses, hammocks, and foam cushions pinned together for the night.

WELCOME ADDITIONS

- A small storage space for folding clothing or at least one empty drawer of a desk, dresser, or cabinet.
- A fold-down rod attached to a door or a small folding coat rack, or a clothes tree or several large wall hooks, if no closet space is available for hanging clothing.
- A place to put such amenities as a clock, radio, ashtray, magazines, mirror, books, paper, pencil, hot plate, toaster oven—even a small, quiet refrigerator.
- A special spot for toiletries and towels, perhaps an old washstand if the guest shares a bathroom.
- A folding luggage rack.

bed and storage wall

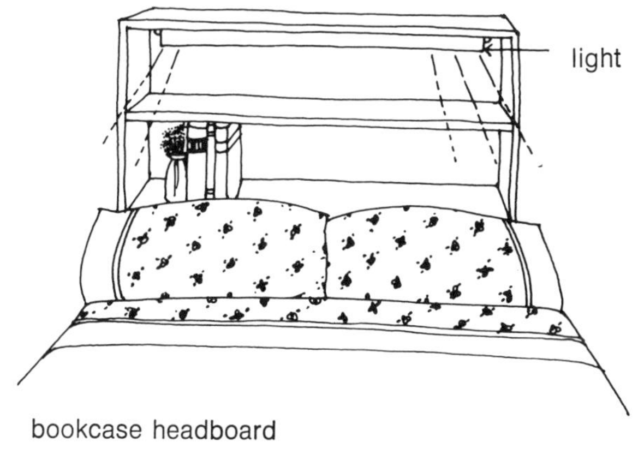

bookcase headboard

hanging cube with clamp-on lamp

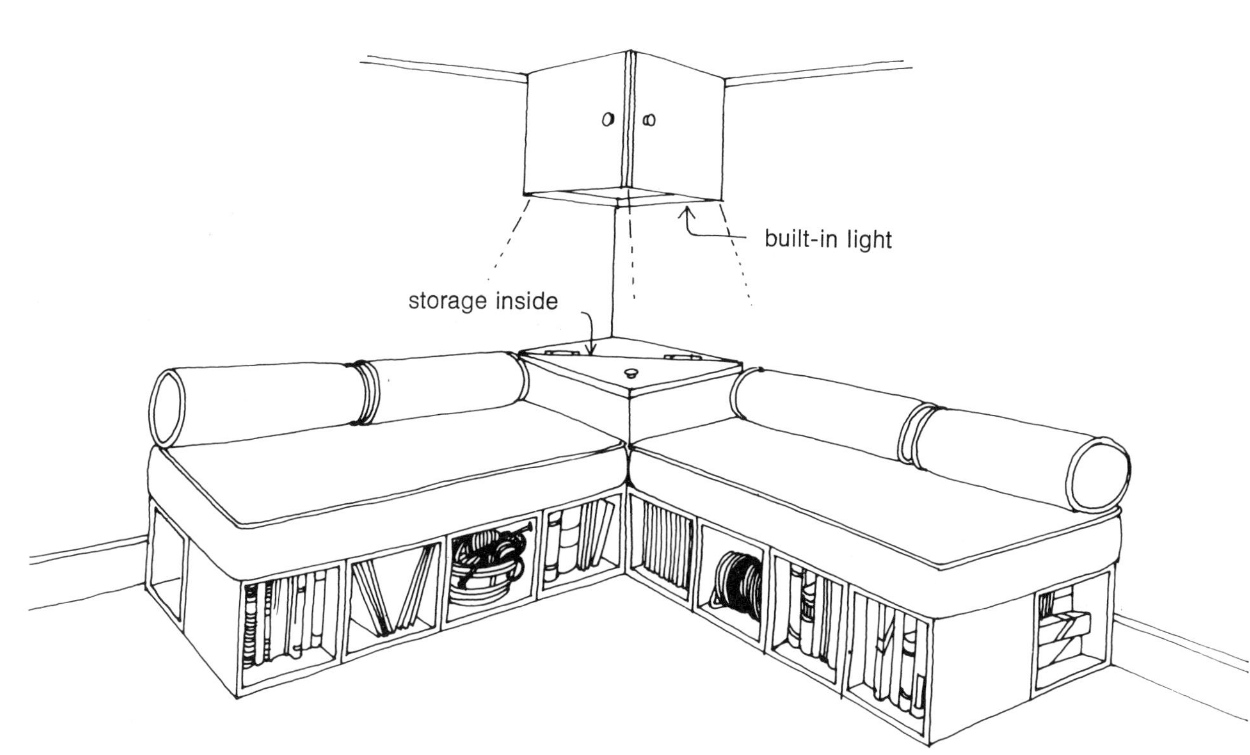

The carpeting and the placement of the chest of drawers divide this bedroom into office and sleeping areas.

In this bedroom all the storage is in prefabricated and formerly unfinished modular furniture, combined and modified to include custom built-in lighting (behind valance) and clothes closet. The dresser unit at the foot of the bed holds a television set on the back.

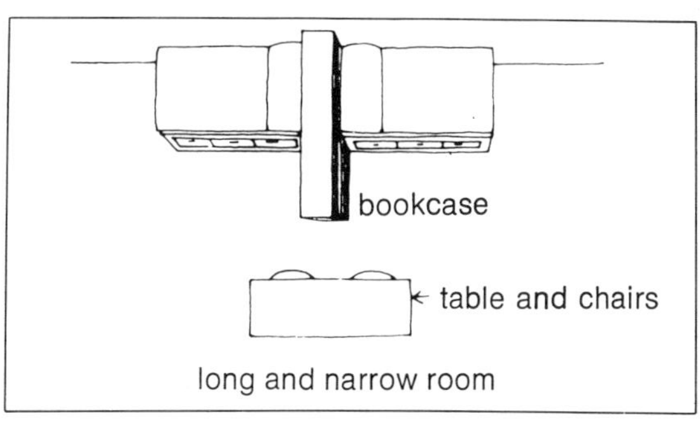

long and narrow room

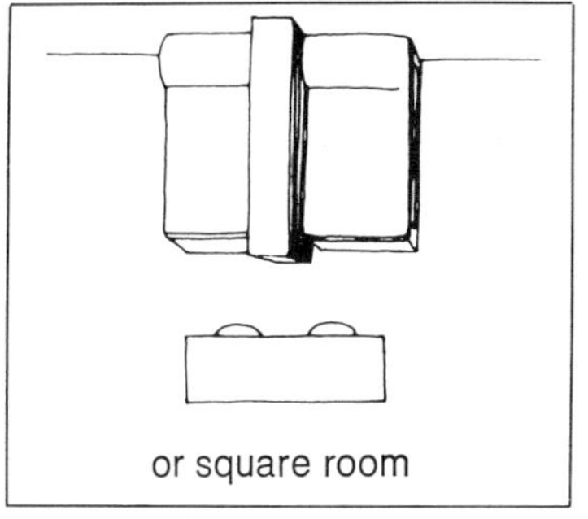
or square room

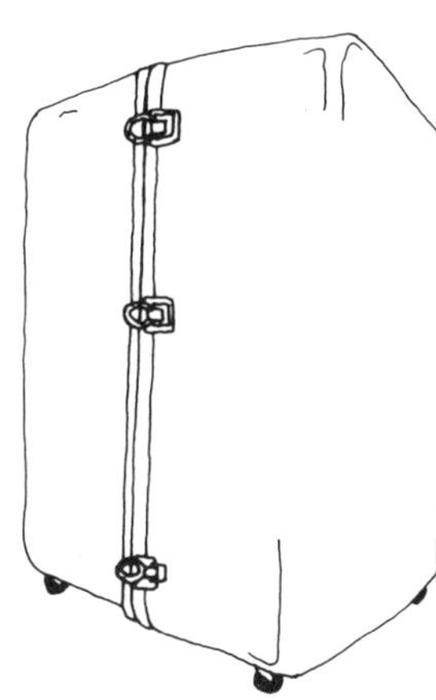
Here is a self-contained bedroom in a suitcase that can be easily wheeled around the house or moved around the country. The Fiberglas unit has a foldaway bed, shelves, a closet, and other storage.

Curtain-off a corner for a dressing area, convert a closet into an "office" and, like magic, a new room appears! Attics and alcoves, hallways and high-ceilinged rooms all have hidden potential. So instead of adding on or moving, fully explore the space that already exists.

FIVE UNDERUTILIZED AREAS

• *In alcoves:* Frequently found in older homes, these can be workshop, laundry, or pullman kitchen, concealed behind folding doors, curtains, or shades. (See Chapter 9.)

• *In closets:* By removing fittings such as the rod and shelves, and adding, as necessary, lighting, shelves and cabinets, and plumbing, closets can be converted into work, music, guest-sleeping rooms or a darkroom, library, or washroom. Use the inside of closet doors for storage, put up pegboards and narrow shelves, but cut down on claustrophobia by removing a door that is not needed to hold or hide things.

• *In lofts:* Double-decker living is now quite common, and it is not unusual to see a sleep area or office-library area created from un-

A small office, with a bar and storage below, was built by the owner/architect in the upper portion of a high hall. The transom of the abutting doorway becomes the "window" of the work area, affording not only ample light but also a beautiful view through the window in the library–dining room beyond. The couch was placed in the living room to serve as an entry screen to the front door and to define the foyer area more clearly.

Sleeping Shelf

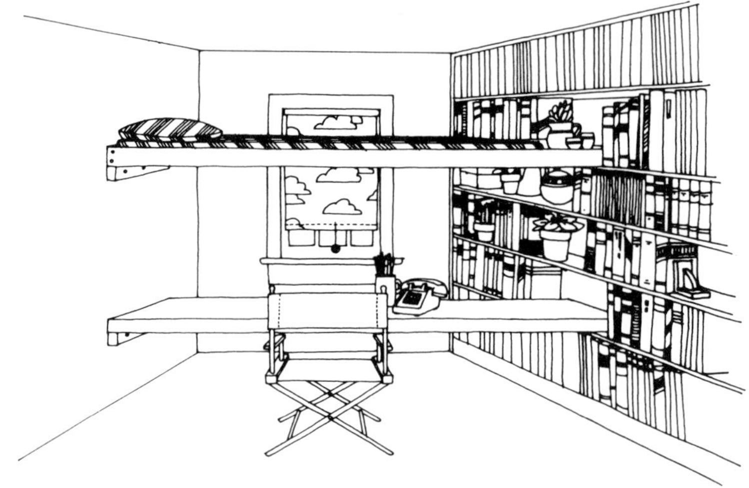

occupied air space. So, look up and see if the space above the closets, the hallway, the living room can be put to work (see section on "Multilevel Living: Lofts" in Chapter 4).

• *In basements:* This large, usually underused area is perfect for storage, for a playroom, laundry, workshop, or den, or any combination of these. Just watch out for dampness in walls and floors and solve moisture problems before installing floor or wall coverings. Then, to brighten a dark basement, add a window, bright colors and patterns, a lot of lights, and white paint.

• *In attics:* An odd shape with too many corners and awkward sloping walls and ceilings, the attic area can have great character when well decorated. First, however, find out if the attic floor is structurally stable or if it must be reinforced. Some attic floors are built only to be the ceilings of rooms, not to support heavy loads of furniture. Then consider adding a small window or a skylight, or increase the size of the present window. (Keep in mind how this window will look from the exterior.) The decoration of an attic should be coherent: one-color paint, one all-direction pattern on everything to disguise irregularities. The slopes and slants where walls and ceilings meet should be treated as one area. Fabric to match the wall covering supplements this effect. A painted wall graphic will "cancel out" the eaves; bright-colored paint on the short wall of a long, narrow attic will make that wall advance and thereby improve the proportions of the space. (See Chapter 3.) Floor mattresses, low seating, cabinets, or shelves lend themselves to the narrow space under eaves where ceiling meets wall. But the simplest kind of furnishing can be no furniture: just a big pile of large pillows arranged as needed. If the attic area is strictly for storage, suspend rods across rafters or put hooks in rafters for hanging such items as garment bags or sports equipment.

PRECAUTIONS

When considering converting an area into a new room, remember to evaluate whether the space is suitable for the intended function. Depending on the purpose of the space, think about the following:

1. Proximity to heating and cooling systems.
2. Ventilation (either a window or a vent for sleeping and cooking).
3. Lighting and electrical outlets (in workshop or office).
4. Plumbing (for darkroom, laundry, bathroom).
5. Dampness (particularly in attics and basements).
6. Privacy and quiet (for guests, work, or sleeping).
7. Accessibility (is a sleeping space near a bathroom? Are the steps of a ladder too steep for children?).

Work "Rooms"

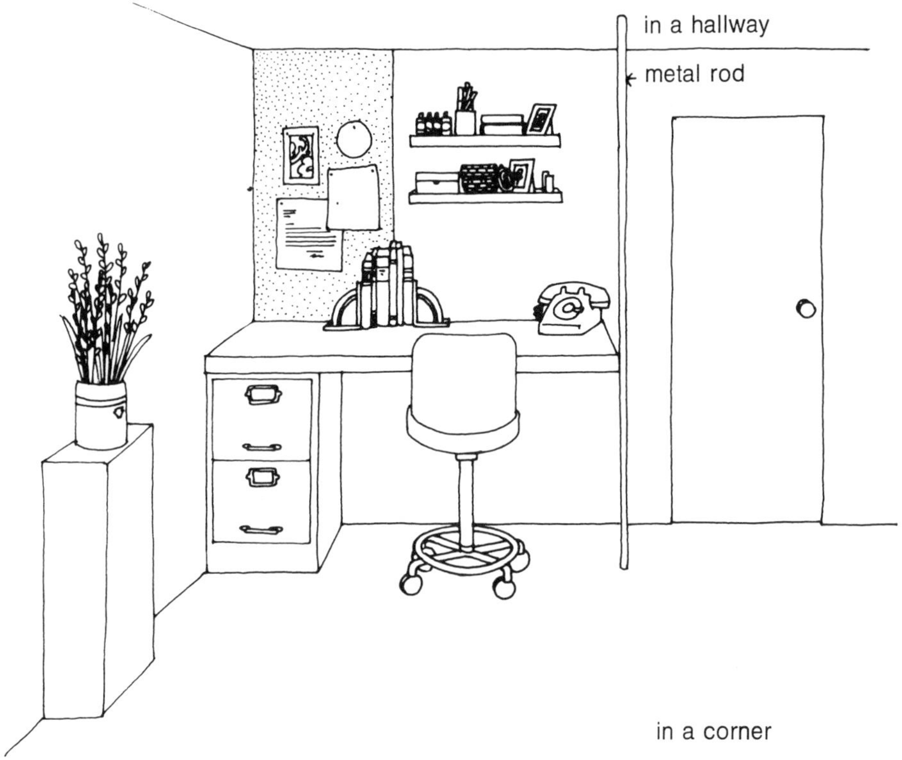

in a hallway
metal rod

in an alcove
kitchen cabinets

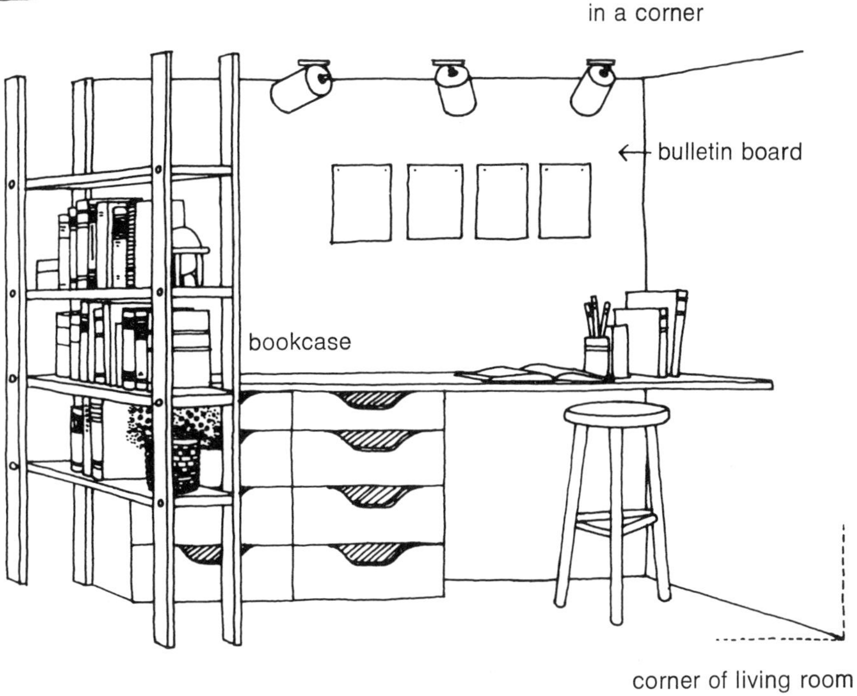

in a corner
bulletin board
bookcase
corner of living room

in a bedroom
four hollow-core doors
fasten with metal mending plate or loose pin hinges

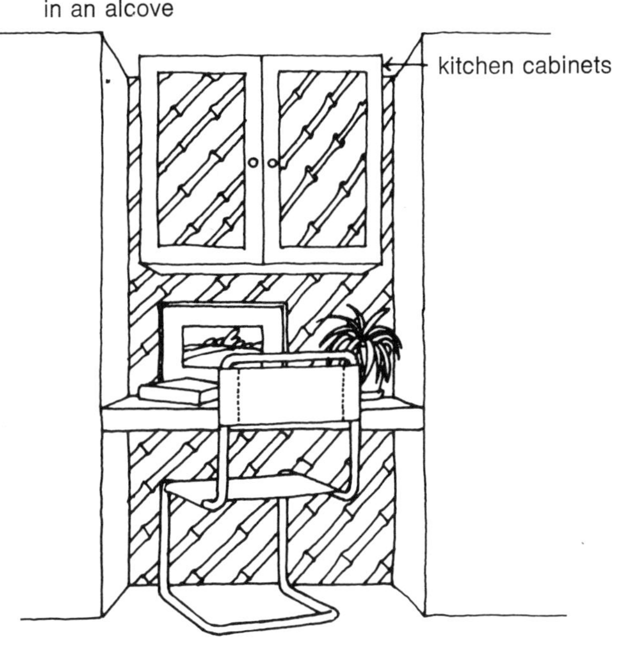

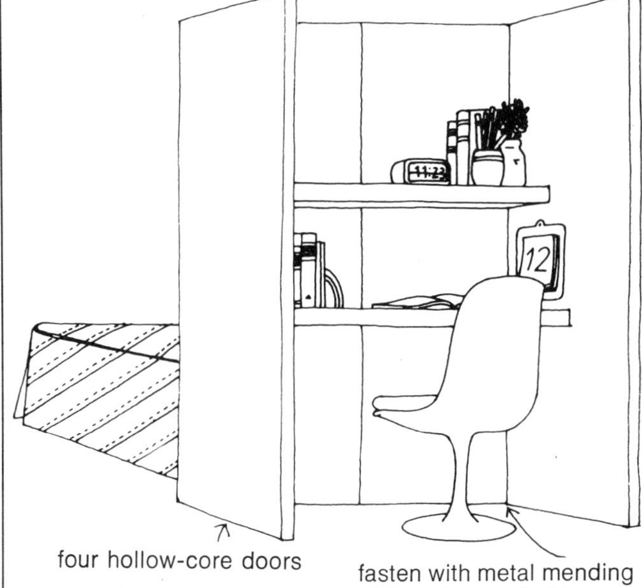

Under the Eaves Sleeping and Sitting Spaces

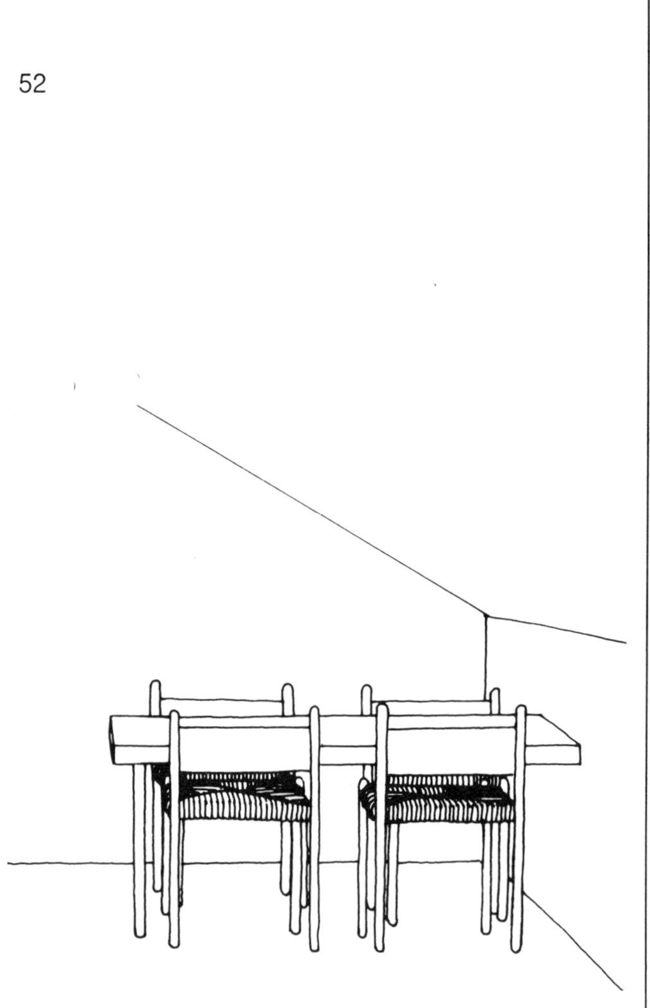

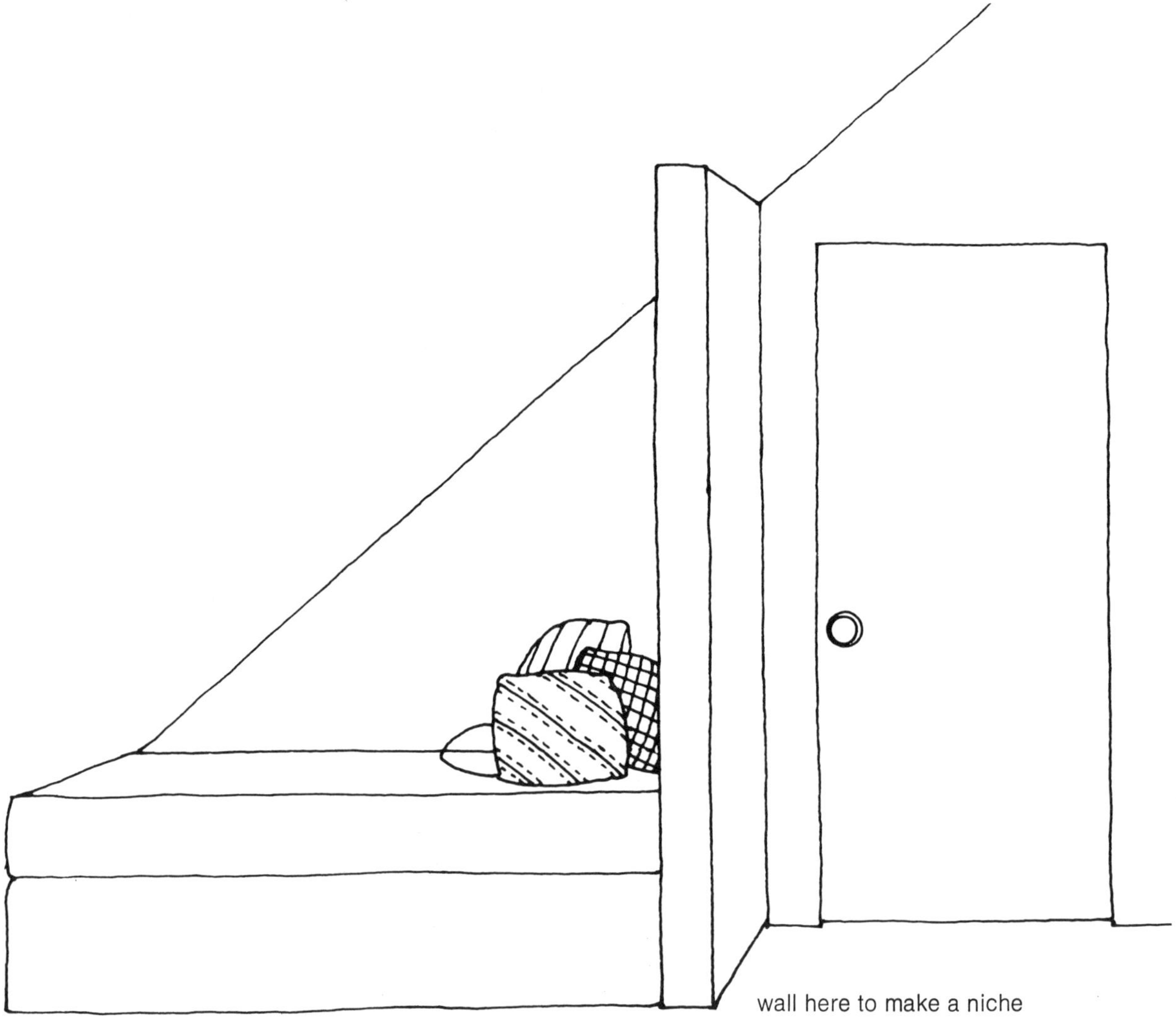

wall here to make a niche

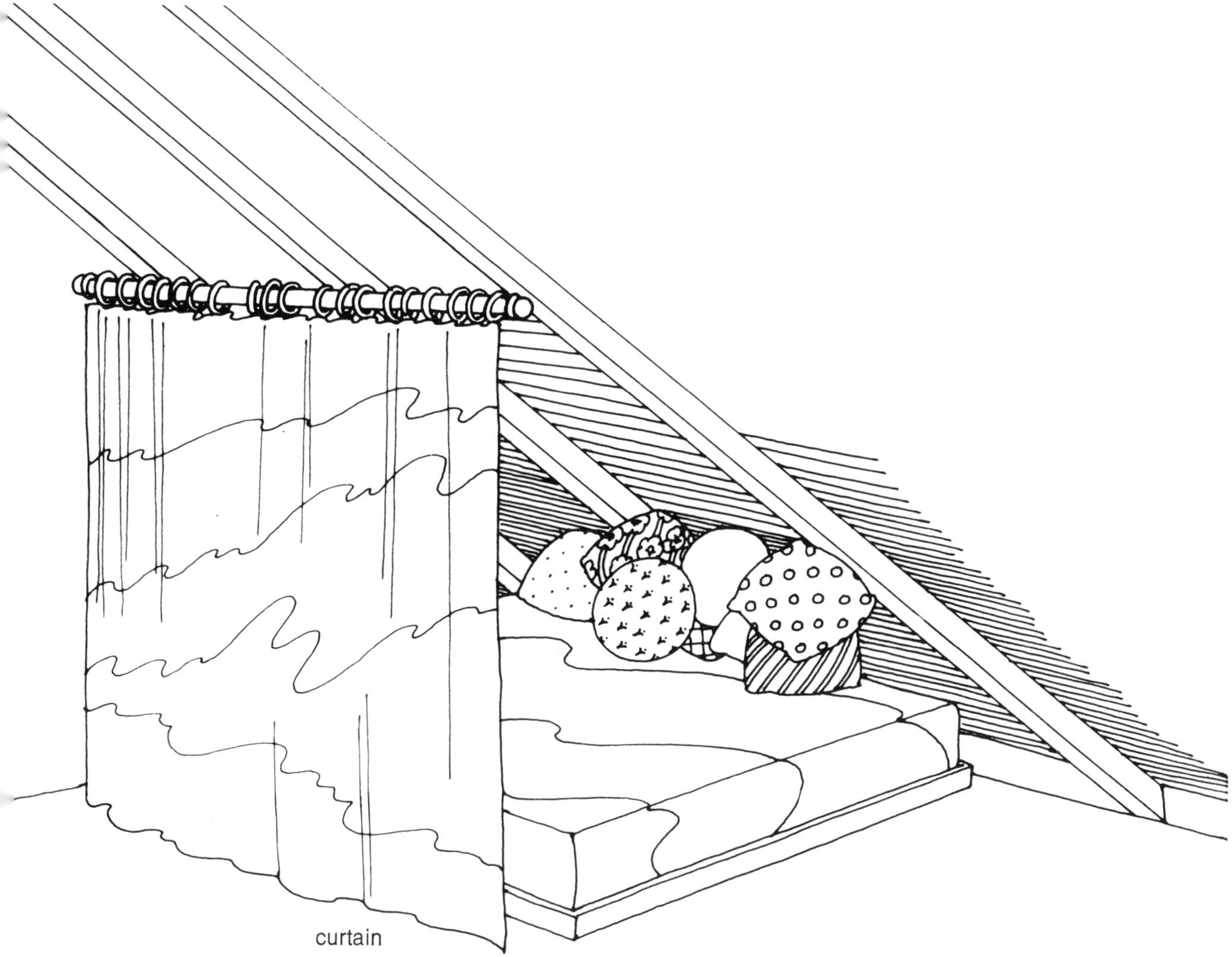

curtain

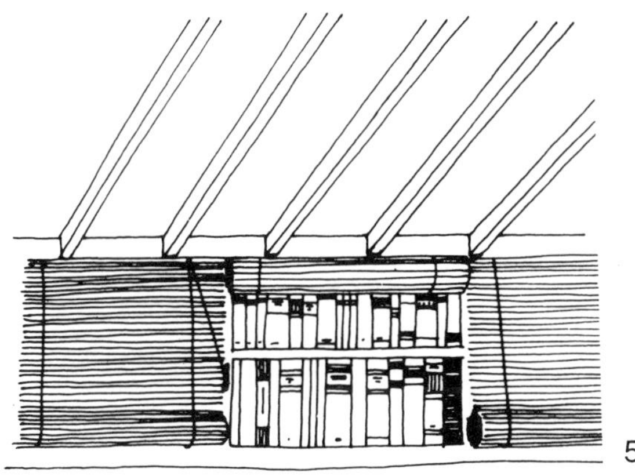

shelves

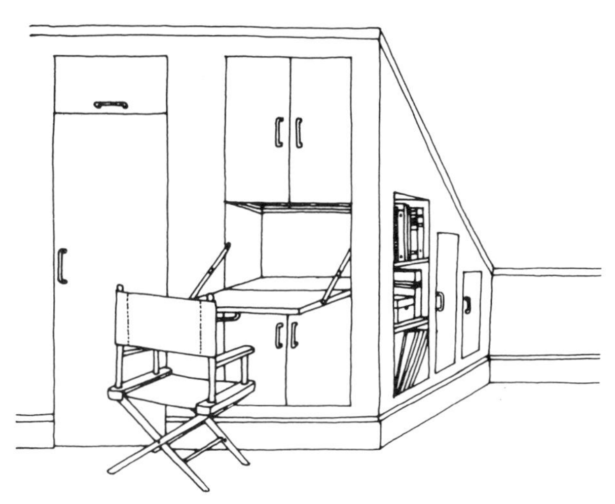

Extra space for sleeping was found under the eaves of a cathedral ceiling. For privacy, the balcony was partially enclosed with window shutters, low enough to permit the circulation of light and air but high enough to block the view from the living room below. The bold and large-scale wallpaper confers distinction on an otherwise dull space, while delicate and small-scale furnishings fit perfectly into the tiny area.

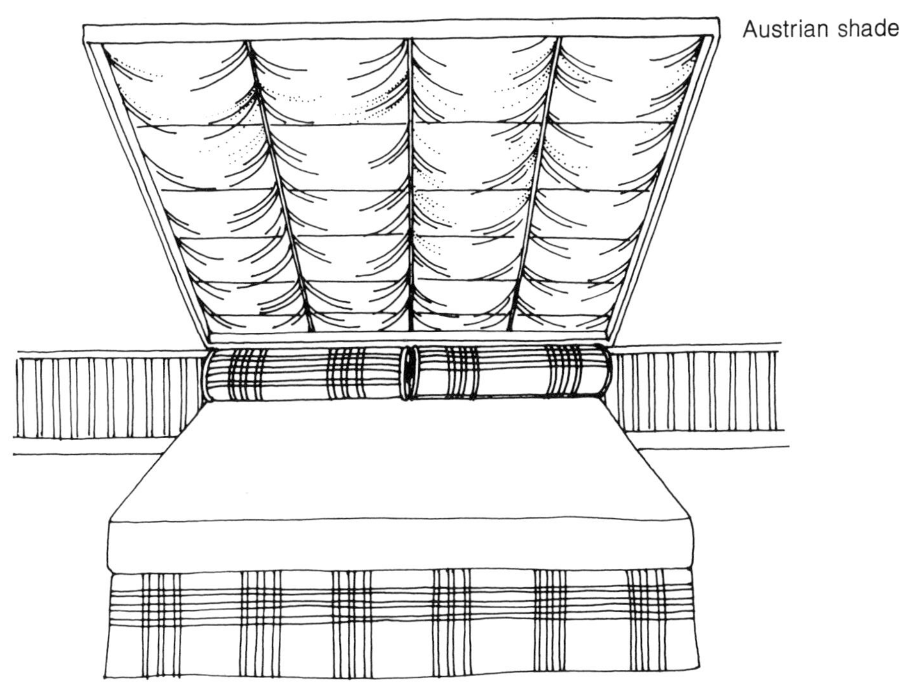
Austrian shade

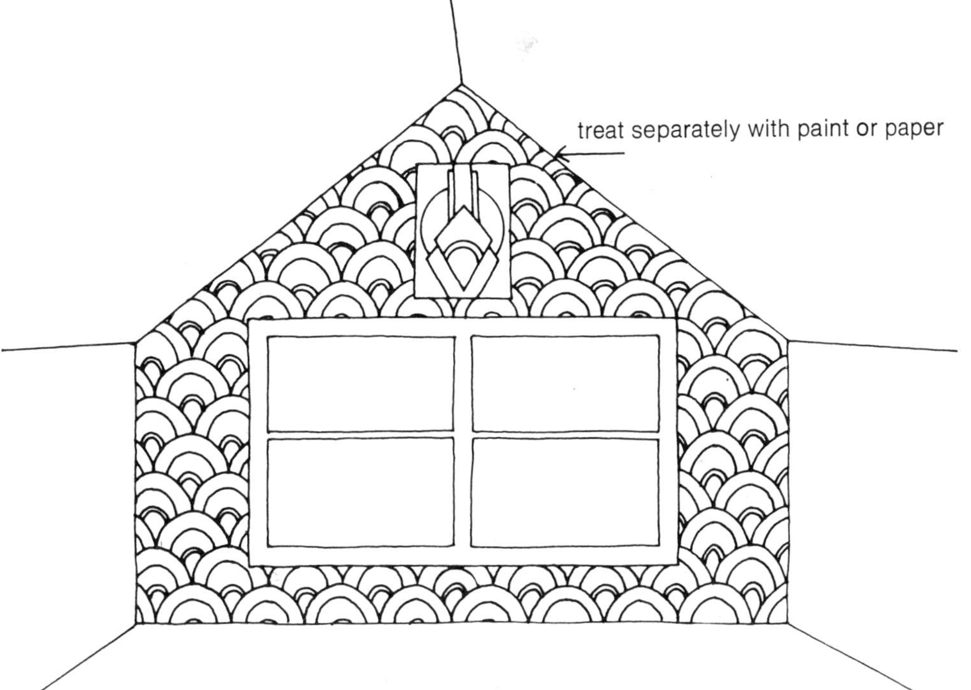
treat separately with paint or paper

gable ends covered with shelves

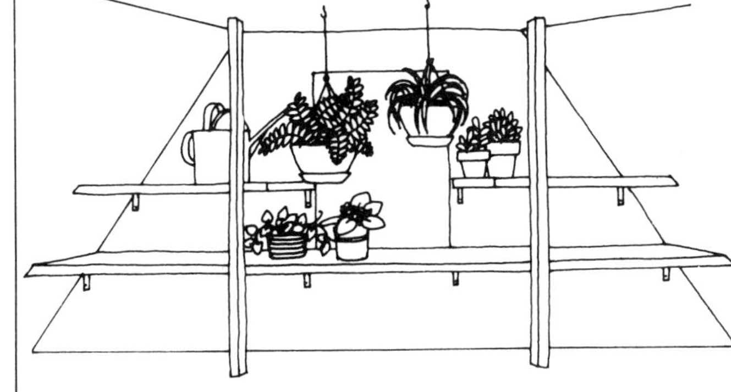

7. STRETCHING STORAGE

Drawers stuffed to overflowing, closets that won't close, not enough shelves, these are the artifacts of modern society. But it doesn't have to be that way. First, eliminate—sell, trade, throw away or, if worthwhile, commercially store—unnecessary items and oversize heirlooms. Then analyze and reorganize the remains, taking into account the following:

• How frequently are items used? All the time or only seasonally, like winter clothing or summer sports equipment? This will determine whether storage need be live (readily accessible) or dead.

• Should the storage unit reveal or conceal? Be open or closed? Protected from dirt? Sloppy shelves hidden? Should the storage unit and its contents be a decorative focal point as, for example, the use in a small dining area of pretty open shelves with plates that are color accents?

• Is the storage unit temporary or permanent? If free standing or attached with screws, the unit may be easily removed. If permanent, built-ins can probably not be used again.

• Where is storage located? Is it rationally related for greatest convenience: pots near the stove, boots near the back door?

Generous storage space is concealed in the carpet-covered sleeping and sitting platform and in the dining banquettes of this one-room apartment.

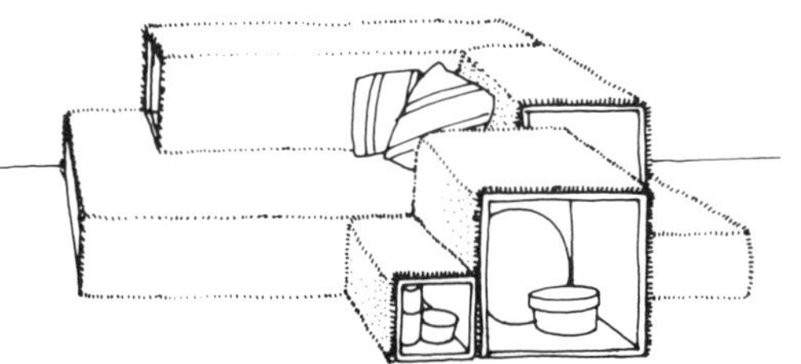

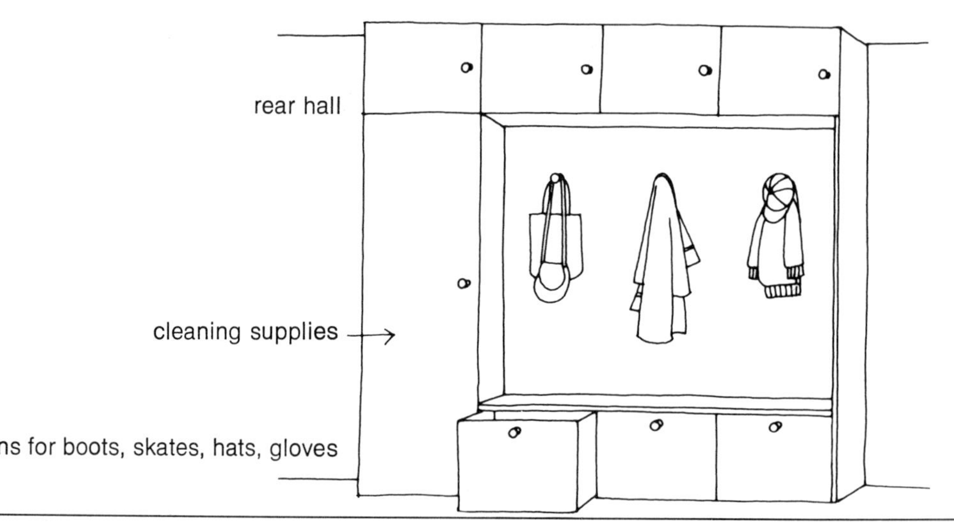

STYLES OF STORAGE

• *Storage walls.* Make more storage space by covering a wall from floor to ceiling and from wall to wall with shelves, cabinets, bookcases, cubes, even orange crates. Although a storage wall can be quite narrow, it is advisable to measure those things to be stored before beginning construction. A television set or stereo system, glasses or plates can be deceiving in size. A storage wall can do double duty as a room divider. In some instances, a wall partition, generally about 4″ to 6″ deep, can actually be replaced with a storage wall about 12″ deep with a loss of only a few inches and a gain of generous storage space.

• *Wall-hung storage.* Terrific savers of floor space, storage units that are attached to walls offer yet another place to put your possessions. Be sure walls are sturdy and screw unit into a stud in the wall. To plan out the arrangement of more than one wall-hung unit, cut out paper (newspaper, brown paper) patterns of the units. Move these around on the wall until the desired configuration is achieved; then lightly tape pattern to wall and trace around it. Bulletin board and pegboard could also be considered in this category. Pegboard, a marvelous material for wall storage, is a perforated wallboard with an almost unlimited variety of hooks and accessories, including bottles, manufactured to hang from it.

• *Shelves.* Open shelves are the most economical type of storage, and a well-planned arrangement can both solve storage problems and add design interest to an area (see Chapter 11). Shelves can be covered or concealed with thinly slatted blinds, window shades, panels of fabric and curtains; one door, or many folding doors on a ceiling or floor track (try large dime-store mirrors installed on a track like sliding doors).

• *Drawers.* Drawers should be low enough to see into and deep enough to hold something, but not too deep that things become lost or the drawer becomes too heavy to pull out. Allow enough room for drawers to open all the way. Drawers that are store bought or those that are improvised from aluminum baking pans or plastic tubs can, with the addition of runners, be put under counters, cabinets, tabletops, and shelves. Alone or in groups, drawers from a secondhand chest can be hung or stacked on the floor. These can also be incorporated into shelf and storage units, thus saving the money it costs and time it takes to make drawers or to have them made. Drawers can be compartmentalized with dividers homemade from the tops and bottoms of flat boxes.

• *Boxes and bins.* Boxes of fiberboard, wood, or plastic can be placed on shelves, under beds, in closets. Those "boxes" that are visible on shelves, counter tops, tables, and desks

Grouping Storage Units

coffee table (small chests and cubes with top added)

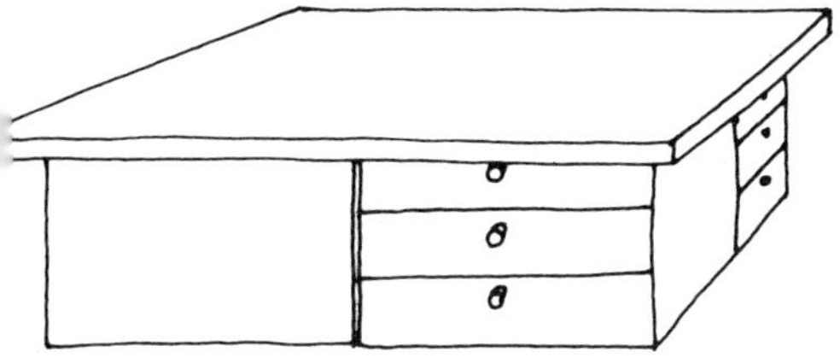

slide units together to make a dining table

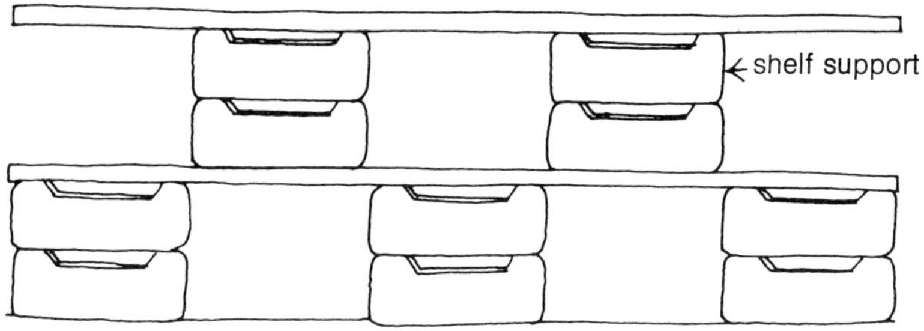

shelf support

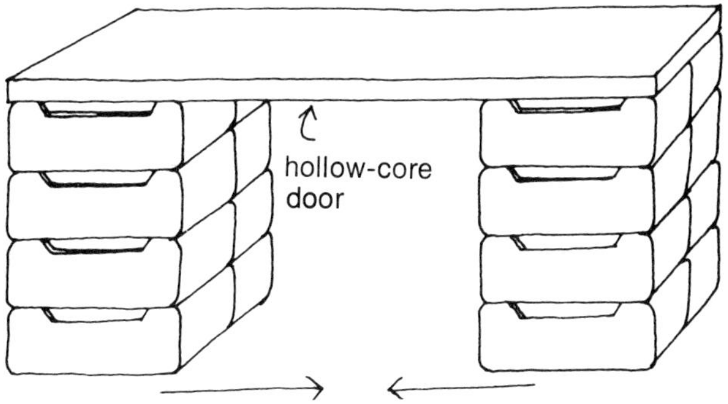

hollow-core door

Grouping Chests

horizontally

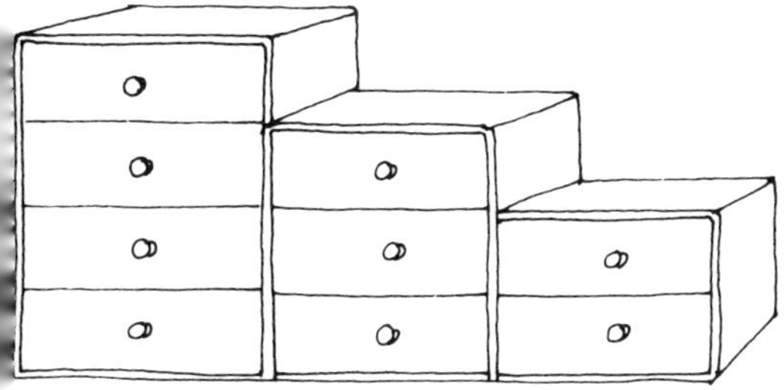

vertically

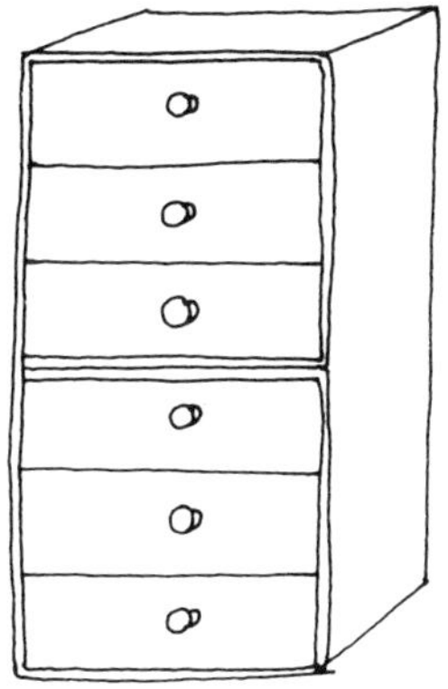

back to back

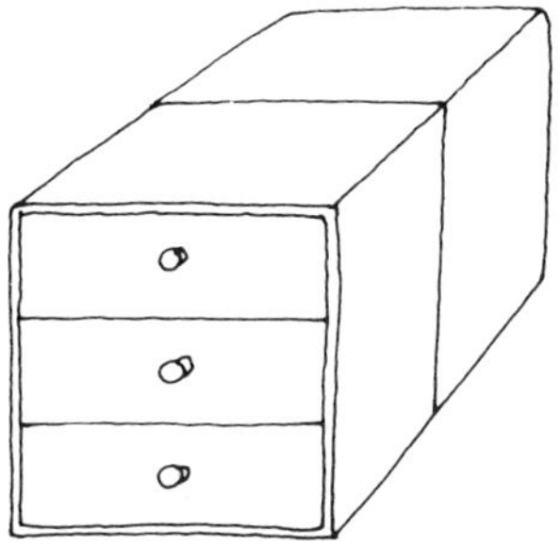

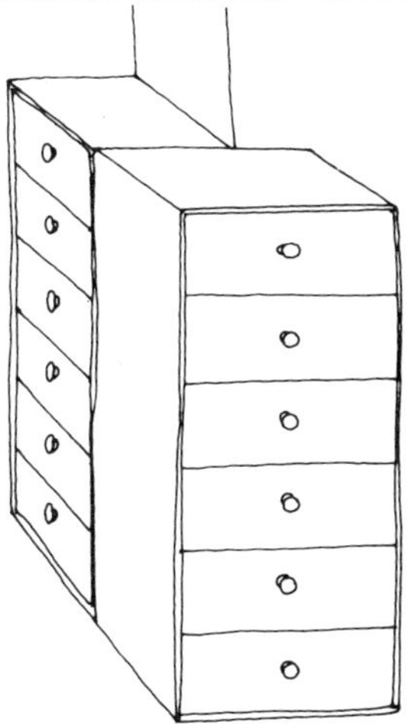

around a corner

Drawers

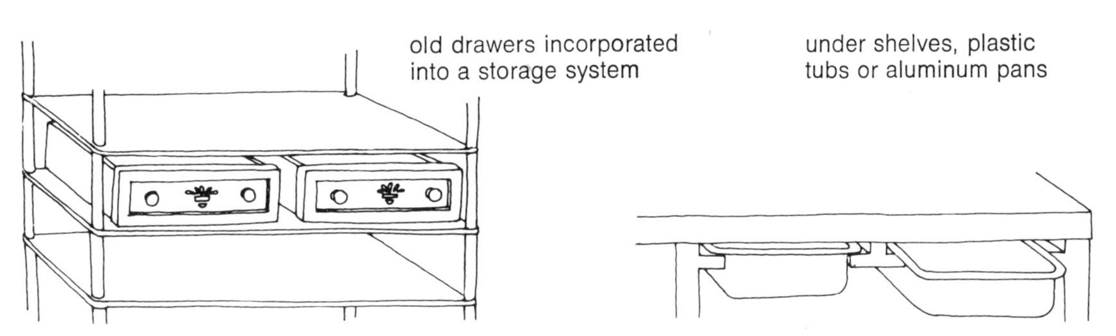

old drawers incorporated into a storage system

under shelves, plastic tubs or aluminum pans

shallow boxes divide drawer

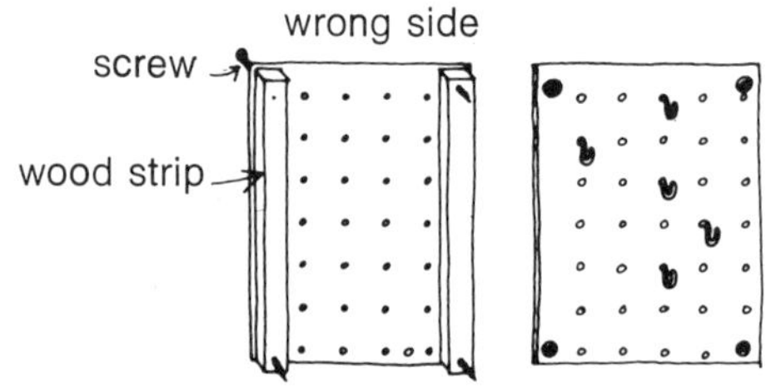

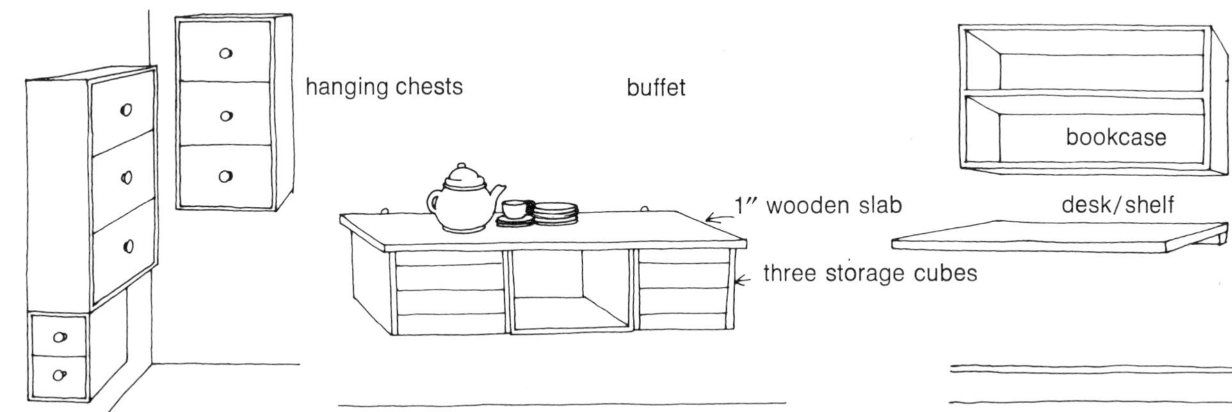

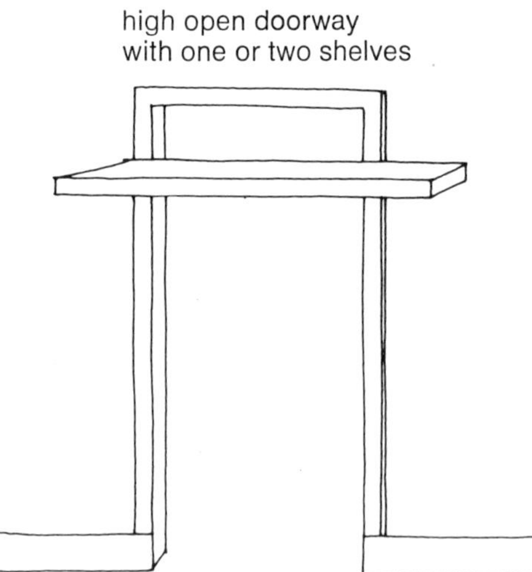

should be decorative—colorful plastic bins, pretty baskets, antique tin cans.

• *Round containers.* Magazines, maps, wine, boots, towels can all be rolled into tubelike forms of different diameter such as mailing tubes, tin cans, pails. Small tubes are perfect for keeping electrical cords untangled. Table linens can be stored wrinkle free by rolling them around the outside of large cardboard tubing (or dowels) and pinning.

SOURCES FOR STORAGE FURNISHINGS

It goes without saying that the most common kinds of storage furniture—wall units, bookcases, chests, sideboards, and storage beds—are available at department stores and at regular- and unfinished-furniture stores. But there are other sources, less obvious, where functional furniture and accessories can be found.

• *Hardware, home improvement, and variety stores.* Products such as the following are attractive, well-designed, and readily available.

1. Storage cubes: Singly or stacked in groups to make an end-table storage wall or room divider; used open end up as wastebaskets or planters; used open end down as a pedestal and with a top and cushion added as seating; about 14″ or 15″ square, made of fiberboard, molded plastic in bright colors, wood finished and unfinished; some come with horizontal or vertical dividers or drawers and with hardware to hold several cubes together.
2. Miniature chests: Either small stacking drawers or chests with many small drawers can be placed on shelves, counters, and desk tops for the storage of such diverse items as cosmetics and paper clips; especially useful to the home hobbyist in a workshop or for collections of many miniature items, like stamps or coins.
3. Larger fiberboard or metal chests of drawers. Originally intended for closet storage, attractive enough now to make a public appearance in the room.
4. Wall storage units of molded plastic with sections for assorted items—useful hung in work areas and in kitchens and kids' rooms.
5. Folding organizers for temporary use—a coat rack, luggage stand, wine rack.
6. Special storage aids like ski racks or boxes that hold many years' worth of old magazines.

• *Stationery or office-supply stores.* Cheap and sturdy, most office furniture is adaptable for home use. Two of the most versatile and popular products are:

1. File cabinets used as they are or decorated with paint or paper; high ones in closets and corners; low ones as end or night tables, arranged in groups to make a desk or incorporated into a storage wall. Since file drawers are very deep, they hold a great deal and are especially useful in children's rooms for the

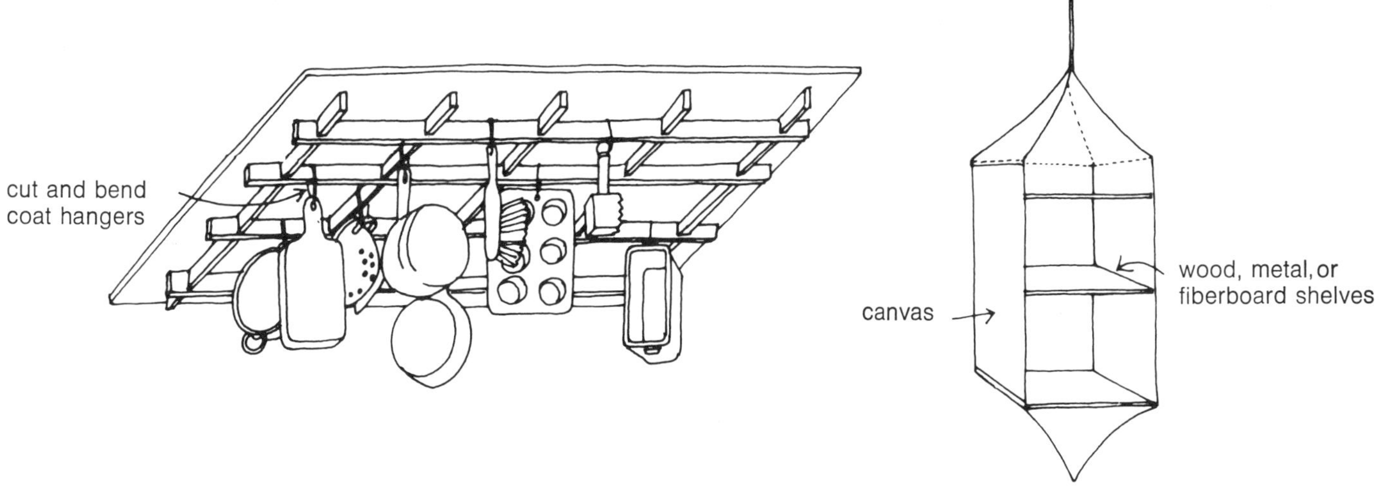

storage of toys. Usually metal, file cabinets can also be fiberboard, wood, or plastic.
2. Shelf systems are very simple in design and very simple to put together, in a wide variety of sizes and shapes that will fit anyplace. Mostly metal and usually an ugly gray or green, these shelf systems are easily spray painted with a cheerful color.
• *Building supply houses.* Odd items that with imagination can be transformed for storage include: flue liners (stacked or singly) for books, magazines, wine; bricks with holes for pencils; masonry blocks to make bookcases.
• *"Antique" and secondhand stores.* Be open-minded and experimental. Approach each interesting antique or old item with an eye for its storage potential and decorative appeal. For example, use:
1. an old dentist cabinet for silverware, place mats, other flat items;
2. an old display cabinet from a store to show off a collection;
3. old library card files singly on a table or several stacked to make a coffee table or along a wall;
4. an old trunk for storage, seating, as an end or coffee table;
5. an old-fashioned glass-enclosed bookcase;
6. use the old door(s) from a broken piece to cover a narrow wall-hung shelf unit (stain or paint the shelf unit to match the doors).

• *The town dump.* With more imagination than money you can create storage pieces from next to nothing. The following, salvaged from town dump or grocery store, garbage heap or city streets, can be decorated with paint, paper, or fabric: soda crates (their small sections are perfect for storing spices or tiny toys); orange crates (placed on the floor or wall, individually or in groups); Styrofoam used for packing large equipment; old furniture (save parts such as drawers and doors from otherwise unusable pieces); bags, barrels, and all manner of boxes.

STORAGE FOR HOBBIES

Hobbies can be carried out wherever there is adequate space and storage for the equipment involved. (The surroundings should be protected where necessary and particularly messy hobbies should be performed in a kitchen or another easy-to-clean-up area.) For example, you can sew or type in the dining room using a nearby breakfront to keep the supplies and to store the sewing machine or typewriter, and a sturdy dining table or a shelf that drops from a wall storage unit as a work surface. And many new products are indispensable aids for the home hobbyist with limited space. One of the most useful is a folding workbench.

Collections can be kept in small storage boxes such as tackle boxes or toolboxes. If they are attractive—shells and scarves, old tools and toys—

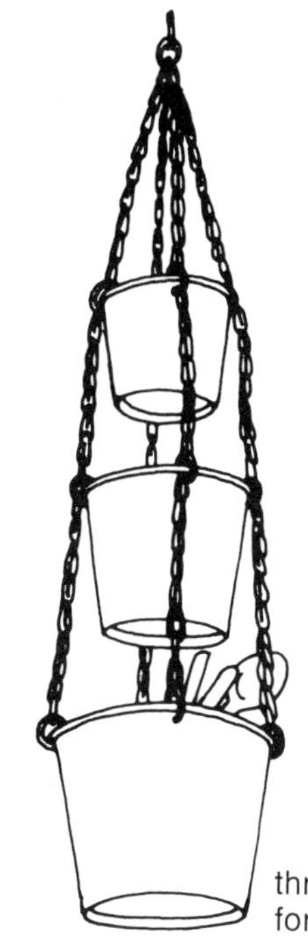

three buckets on chains for odds and ends

Small-Scale Storage

odds and ends chest

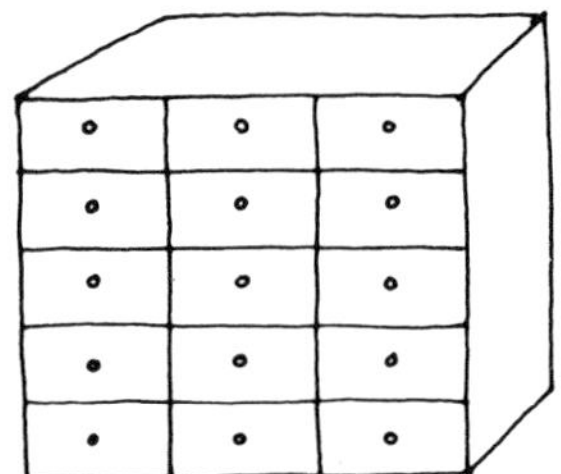

shoe bag

62

screw jars under shelf

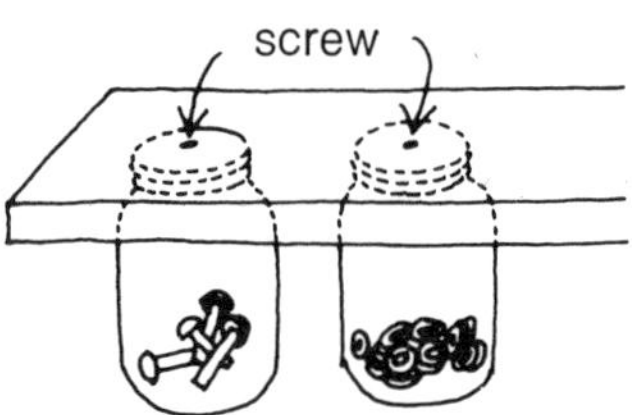

tackle box

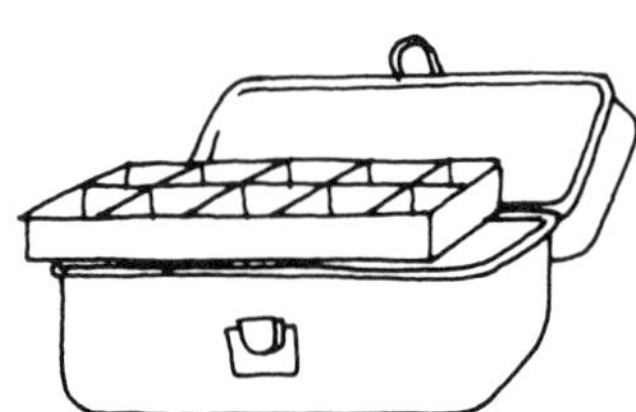

Rolled Storage

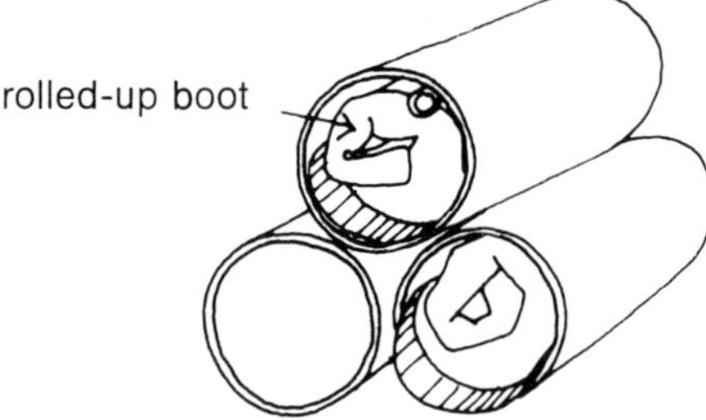

cardboard tubes
bolted or glued together

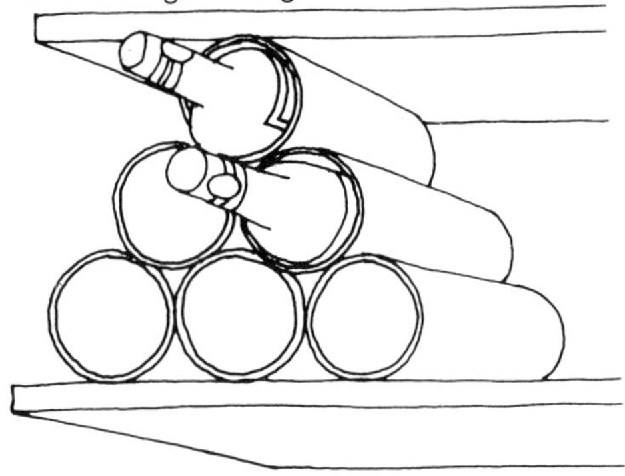

plastic pails on bathroom door

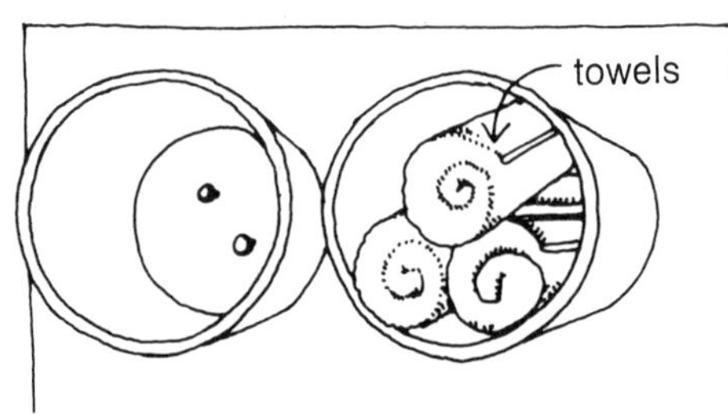

Free Storage Furniture

broken top of furniture

kitchen cabinet on its side (cushion on top)

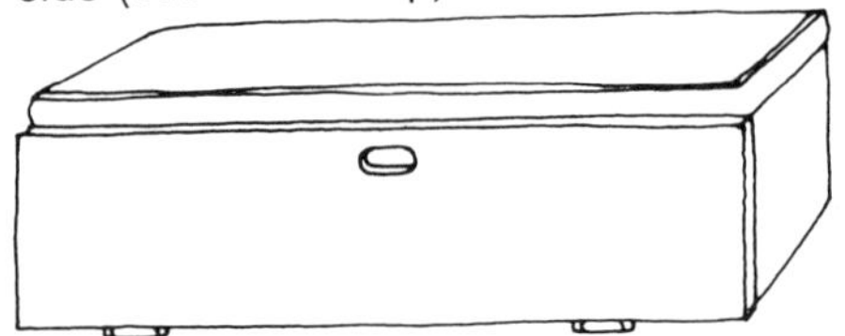

bookcase from old dresser drawers or singly as a hanging shelf

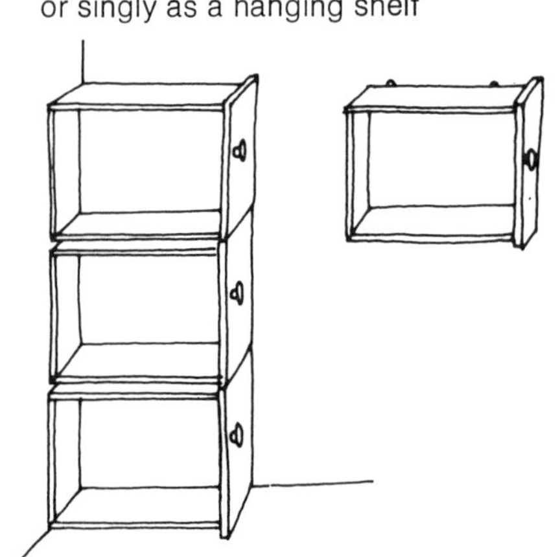

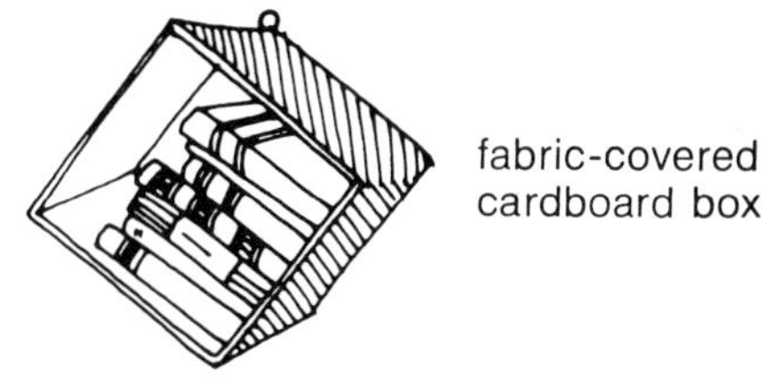
fabric-covered
cardboard box

spice rack
(soda crate)

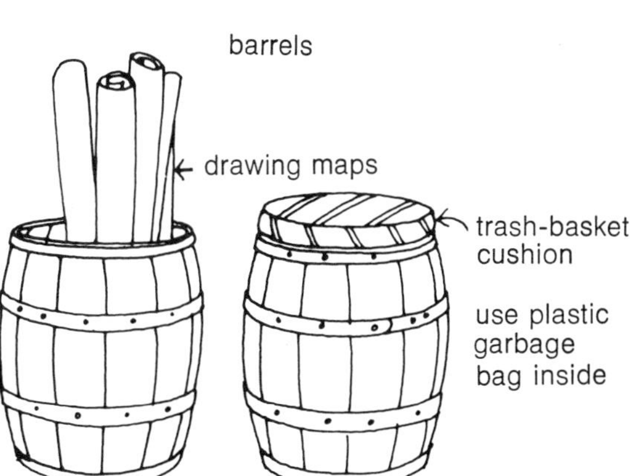
barrels
drawing maps
trash-basket
cushion
use plastic
garbage
bag inside

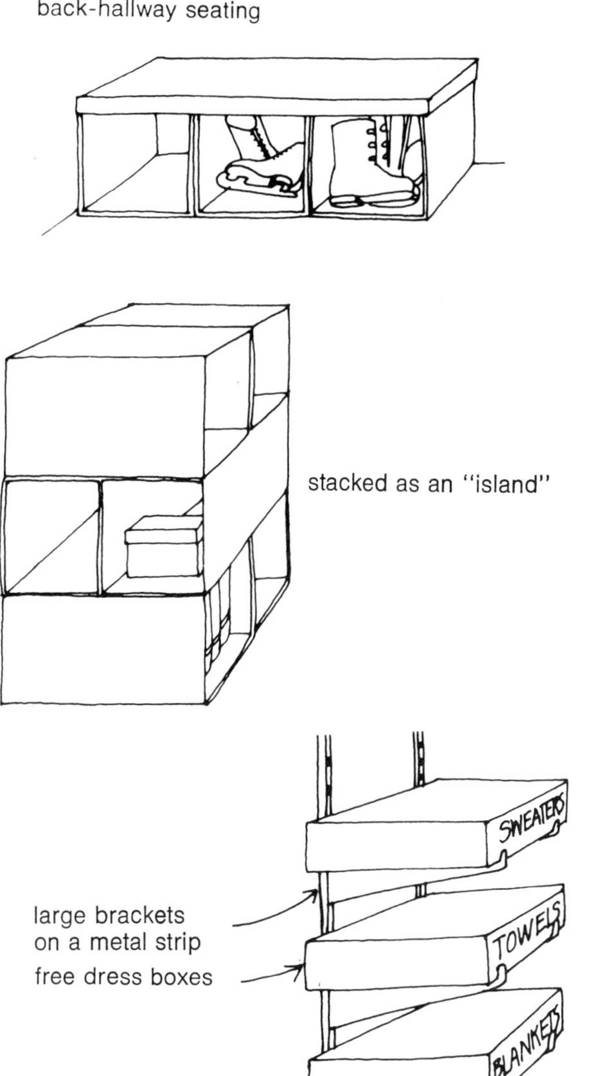
back-hallway seating
stacked as an "island"
large brackets
on a metal strip
free dress boxes
SWEATERS
TOWELS
BLANKETS

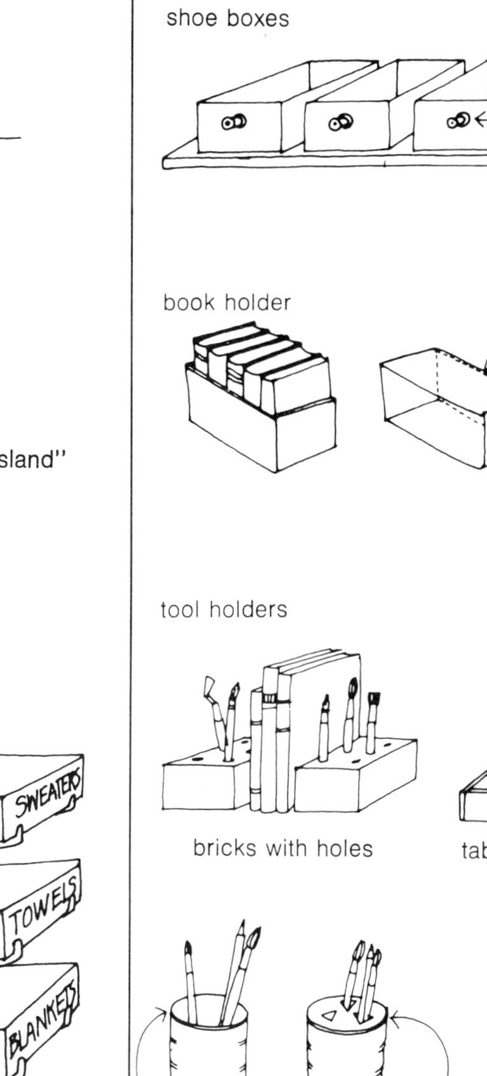
shoe boxes
spool pulls
book holder
cutaway
tool holders
bricks with holes
tableware holder
remove one end or
punch hole with church key
glue

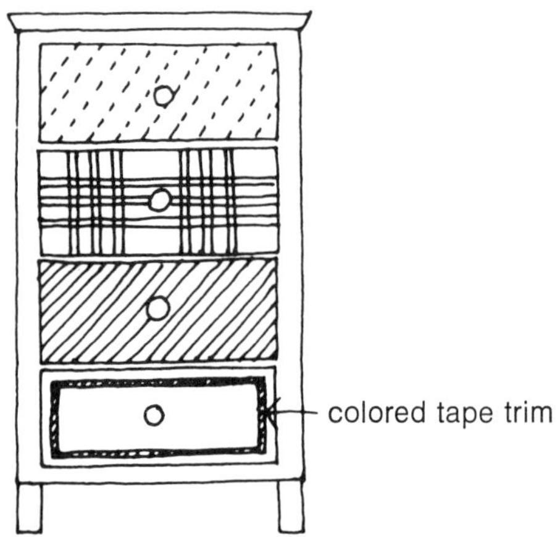

each drawer a different color or pattern

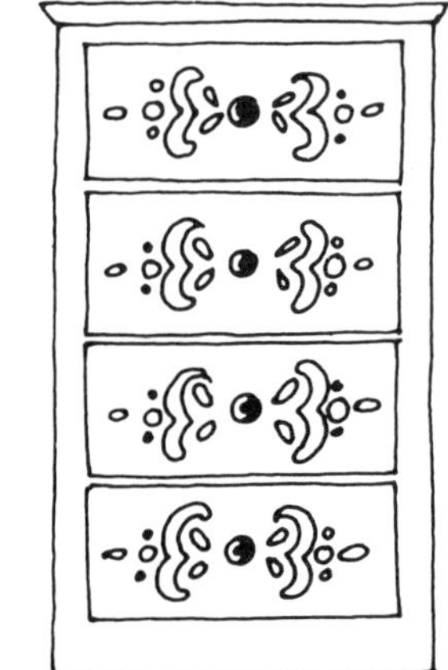
paper cutout or stencil design

collections can be displayed on shelves and hung on walls, not stored away.

Ideally sports equipment should be stored outside in a garage or toolshed. In an apartment put equipment near the back door in closets or cabinets, barrels or baskets, or in large laundry bags hung on hooks.

DECORATING STORAGE FURNITURE

Many storage pieces that are old may be structurally sound and simply in need of a face lift or new finish. Briefly, here are a few hints. These apply in some cases to new, unfinished furniture as well as old furniture:

• Before refinishing, reglue and brace rickety pieces (remove old glue before regluing, if possible) and fill in dents or holes with woodfiller.

• Smooth filled-in holes, bumpy or peeling areas, and rough surfaces with sandpaper. A shiny surface that is to be painted should also be roughed up a bit with sandpaper to make the paint adhere better.

• All furniture being finished should be dry, smooth, and clean, free of wax, grease, and dirt. Sometimes a good wiping with a clean cloth and mild soap, a quick retouching of scratches with crayon, eyebrow pencil, or Scratch Cover, and a thorough waxing are all that is needed to fix up an old finish.

• Paint a chest or cabinet in this order: (1) remove hardware and drawers and paint drawers separately; (2) paint chest top; (3) then lay chest on its back and paint sides, front, legs.

• In addition to a plain painted finish, it's fun to try an antiqued, splattered, mottled, stenciled, or a freehand effect.

• Unfinished furniture is usually painted or stained, but it can also be left natural with a coat of polyurethane or paste wax added to protect the surface, without hiding it.

• A penetrating oil stain can be used on unfinished furniture or furniture that has been stripped down to the bare wood. Just follow the manufacturer's directions. Since this is a messy, smelly job, the area should be protected and well ventilated. An easy and neat alternative "stain" is liquid shoe polish in a sponge bottle dispenser. Protect this and other stain finishes with wax or polyurethane.

• Cover chests, cabinets, boxes, tables, shelves, inside doors, inside and outside of drawers with wallpaper or fabric, including inexpensive remnants of expensive ones, to match the room. For odd shapes such as the inside of a drawer or breakfront, make a paper pattern first, then cut fabric or paper from this.

• Make the folding or sliding doors of a storage wall or closet look like a decorative screen by covering them with: a large picture or map, a photo blowup, a mural, or a bold painted or papered supergraphic design.

Storage That Opens and Closes

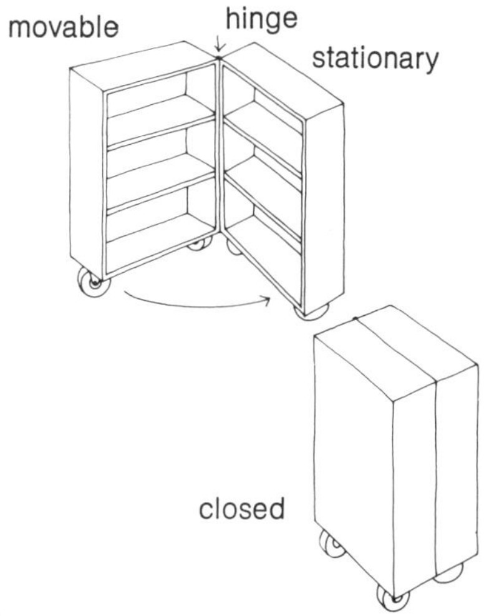

movable
hinge
stationary
closed

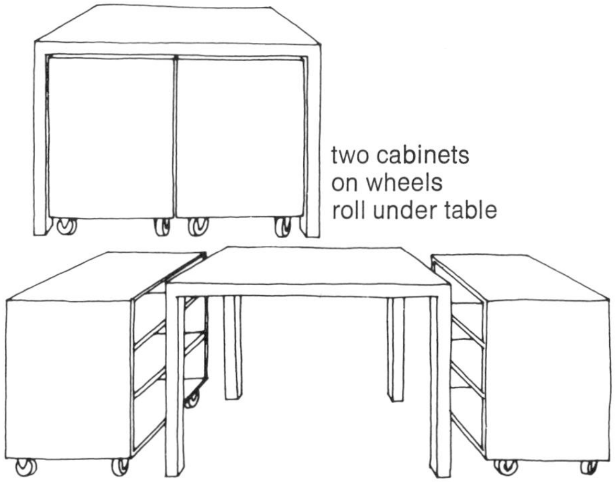

two cabinets
on wheels
roll under table

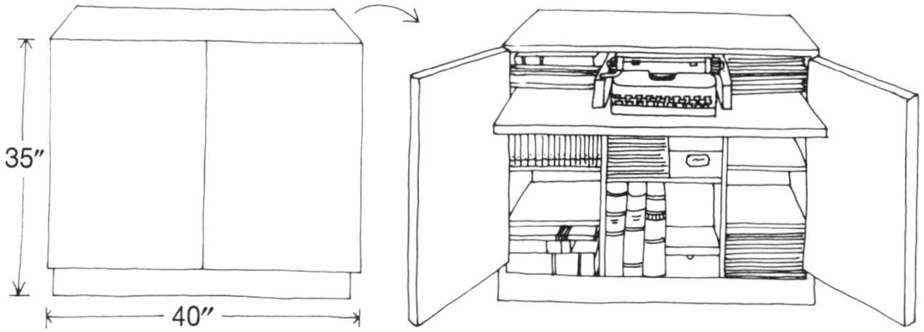

35″
40″

One need not be neurotic to have a neat closet. Closet organization can be an acquired skill.

The average closet is 2′ deep and 3′ to 6′ wide, and usually comes with one pole and one inaccessible shelf. To stretch this space, sort out closet contents, putting out-of-season items some place else, in boxes or empty suitcases, in the attic or under the bed. Reappraise the function of the closet. A linen closet may be eliminated by putting supplies and linens on bathroom shelves. A foyer closet may be cleared by removing all excess outerwear that accumulates over a long winter and by hanging current outerwear on pegs in the entry or back hall.

Size, as well as location and convenience, is an important factor in deciding which closet to use for what purpose. So, plan for and measure what should be stored; for example, the length of clothing, the width of bridge chairs. If possible, allocate the roomiest closet for sports and leisure-time equipment—card table, movie screen, luggage, skis. Utility and linen closets, on the other hand, can be quite small and shallow, whereas closets for adult clothing should be larger and at least 24″ deep.

Left: An ordinary closet was transformed into a cozy dressing room by removing the door and substituting tie-back curtains, installing carpet and fabric shirred on rods, and selecting furniture with a light feeling. *Above:* A closet converted into a work and storage area by removing a useless rod (the young boy occupant had few clothes that required hanging) and filling the space with a desk, lamp, bulletin boards, and a Styrofoam shelf unit (made from packing material).

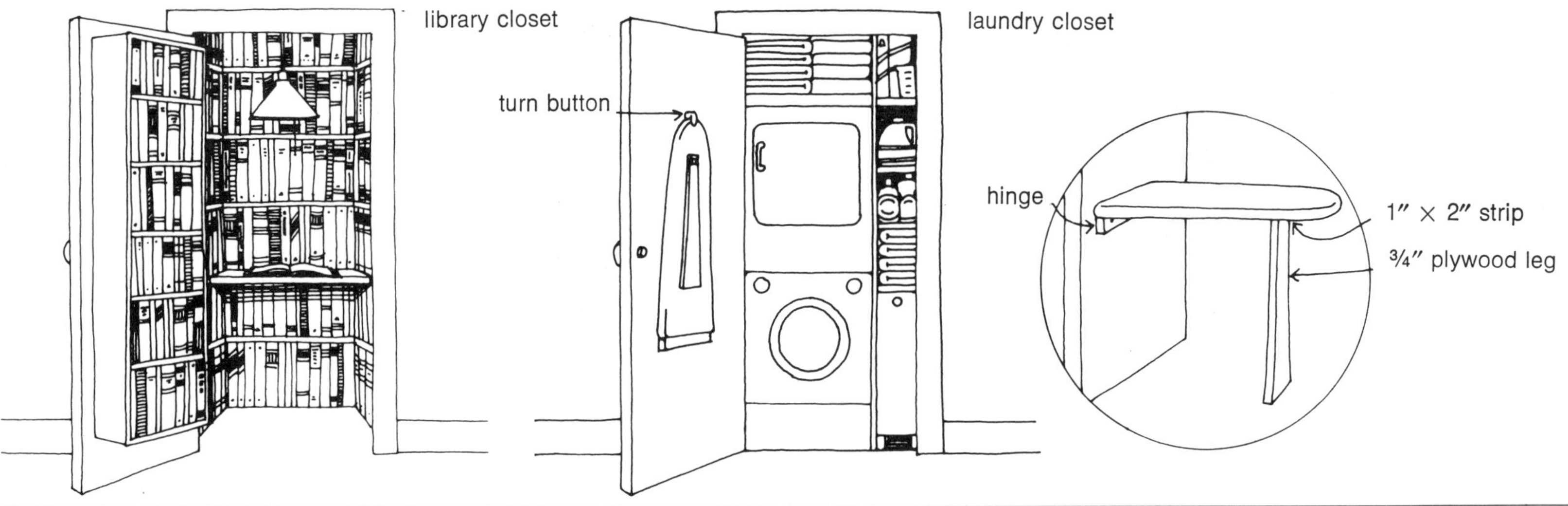

PLANNING AND EQUIPPING CLOSETS

Well-stocked hardware stores or the closet shop of department or variety stores sell excellent gadgets that help to make full use of closet space—special hangers and hooks, racks and rods, even a complete kit with all fittings necessary to redesign a closet. Consider adding one or more of the following to make a more efficient and attractive interior: extra poles and shelves; pretty matching boxes (especially clear plastic); built-in drawers (possibly all the way up to the top of the closet) or a small, inexpensive secondhand chest; a light with a bulb of about 75 watts.

On swing doors hang pegboard, hooks, racks, narrow shelves, a mirror, or a shoe bag (not just for shoes but for socks, stockings, and other small storage). Seven feet is about the highest the average adult can reach, and this figure is, of course, much lower for a child, so delegate as dead storage anything on higher shelves.

• *The clothes closet* should be designed to accommodate the size and type of clothing to be stored. To do this, first estimate the amount (width and height) of hanging space needed. Put clothes in groups roughly by size, length, and width, ideally allowing about 2″ of width for each garment. Determine the height of the hanging space by measuring from the rod to the floor, or, in the case of a high hanging rod, to the top of the next rod or to built-ins—chests or shelves. Add on a few extra inches for clearance.

Since wardrobes and styles vary so much, it is hard to recommend standard sizes. The following figures are included only as a rough guide:

jackets, suits, skirts, shirts, blouses, folded trousers: 36″–40″
street dresses, slacks, topcoats: 52″
long dresses, robes: 72″.

Chests, shoe racks, and so forth can be put under the space left by shorter clothing. Upper shelves should clear the rod by about 2½″ to 3″ and ideally be about 10″ to 12″ deep. If shelves are very deep—18″ or more—an excellent idea is to put articles of clothing on trays that can be pulled out. Then clothing will not "get lost" in the back. If possible, grade shelves in size from narrowest at top to widest at bottom. The space between shelves should be about 9″ for shelves that hold shoes and 10″ for shelves that hold pocketbooks. But again, the distance from one point to another should be determined by individual storage needs and shelves could be adjustable as those needs change.

Tie and belt hangers, shoe bags (the see-through kind that keeps about eighteen pairs in 5″ of hanging space) and a pocketbook bag that operates on the same principle, blouse and skirt trees all help make the most of vertical space. Ties, belts, shoes, bags, umbrellas, and more can be stored

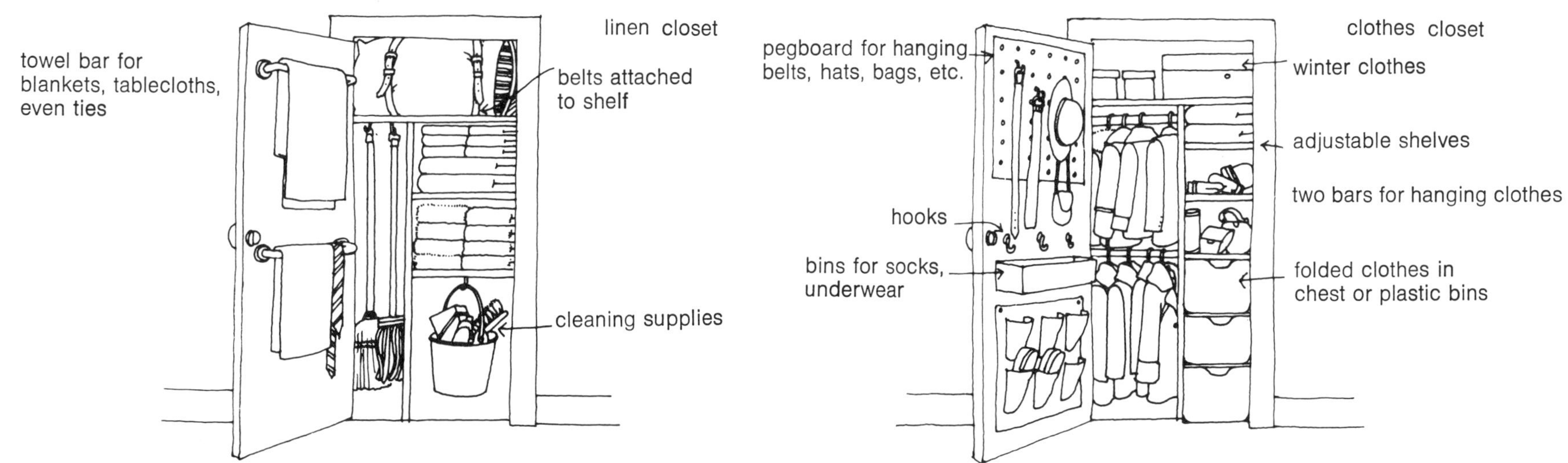

on a standard swing door but about 5″ of space must be allowed.

• *The linen closet* should be planned to hold some or all of the following: towels, bed and table linens, soap, pillows, blankets, toiletries, hamper, and assorted household appliances such as a hair dryer, vaporizer, or sewing machine. Blankets and tablecloths can be hung on large towel bars attached to the inside of a door, and if shelves are shallow, pillows can be strapped on face out.

• *The coat or guest closet* should provide a place for hats, umbrellas, pocketbooks, a mirror, a small shelf, perhaps a telephone (in addition, of course, to coats).

• *The utility/broom closet* might have room for mops and brooms, the vacuum cleaner, a shopping cart, cleaning supplies, and light bulbs. Tools can be put on pegboard on the door, odds and ends in small cardboard or plastic chests of drawers on shelves.

ENLARGING CLOSETS

Extra space can sometimes be found by opening up the side walls of a closet and installing shelves or drawers between the studs, assuming no wiring or plumbing will interfere. Similarly, the interior roof of a closet that is directly beneath an open attic space can be removed to add storage space above, and also to gain access to the attic, if necessary.

Greater visibility of and easy access to the interior of a closet add considerably to the amount of usable space. This can be achieved by substituting the following for a standard swing door: sliding doors, folding doors (accordion or bi-fold), a pocket door (the door slides into an actual "pocket" in the wall); or curtains made of cloth or beads. This is a bit of a trade-off because the storage space available on the back side of a swing door is lost.

In a new home or renovation, cabinets can be designed for the air space between the top of the closet and the ceiling.

DECORATING CLOSETS

Once organized, it is nice to decorate a closet to harmonize with the adjoining area. The walls, storage boxes, shelves or chests, and, believe it or not, the floors can be covered with fabric, paint, or paper. Colored tapes, cloth trim, and wood molding can be added to give the closet a professional touch. Protect paper that is not plastic and fabric applied to floors that get some foot traffic with a coat of polyurethane paint.

The outside of a door can be covered with mirror, decorated with trim or colored tape, or completely covered and transformed into a work of art—a collage or painting—with wallpaper, fabric, or paint (paint each panel of a folding door a different color).

Sleeping Closets

Substitutes for Closets

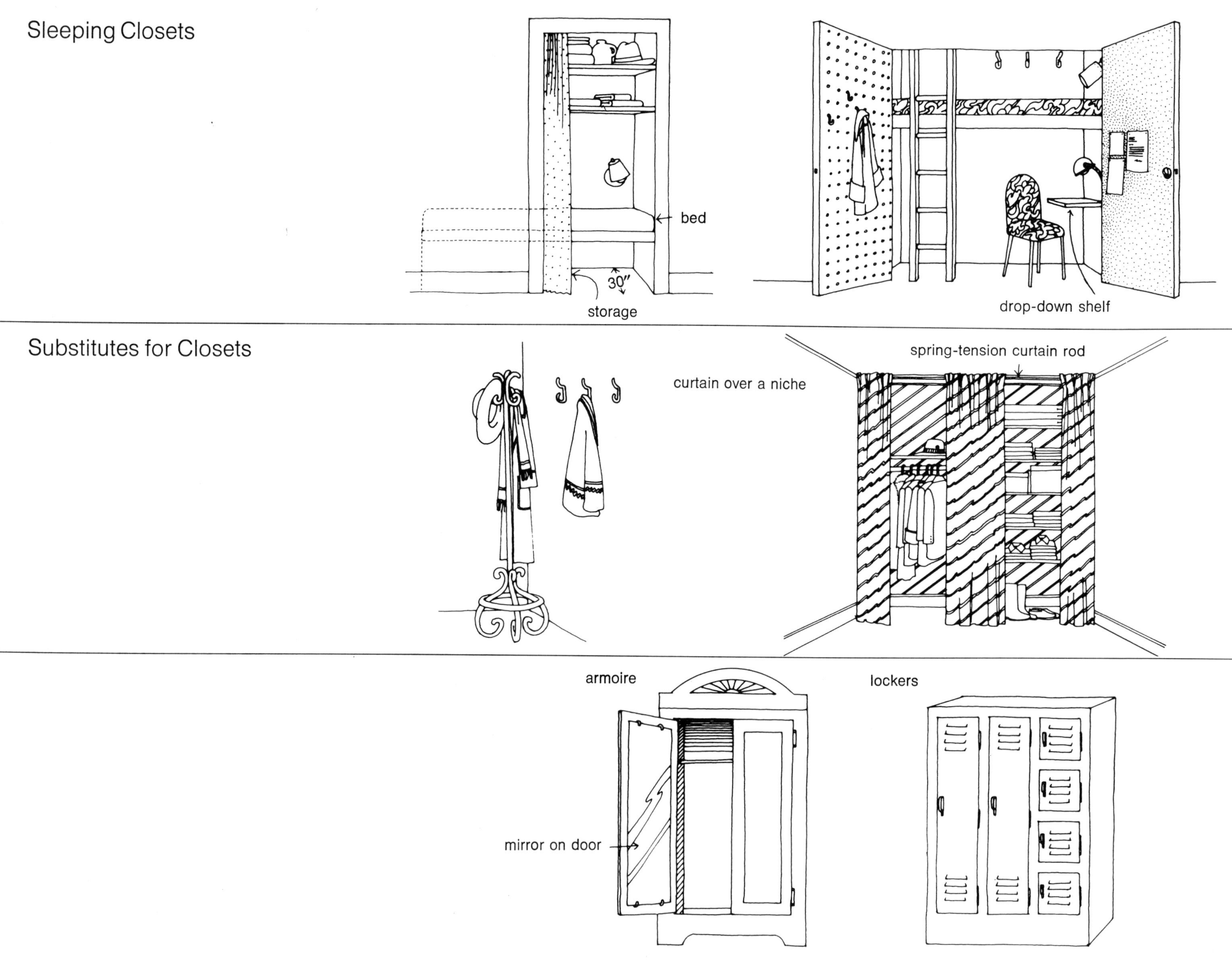

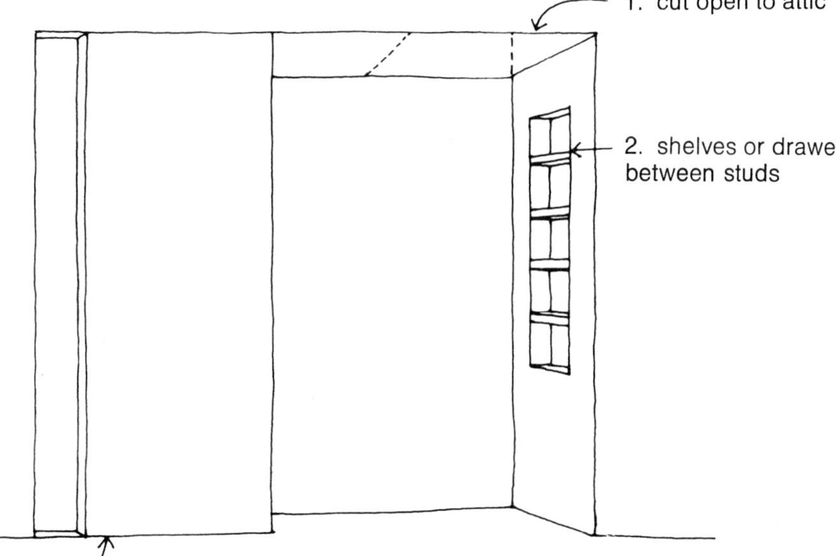

EXTRA CLOSETS

If closet storage space is still at a premium and additional closets are needed, buy inexpensive cardboard or metal closets or even lockers. One or more can function as a room divider as well. Or splurge, buy an antique armoire, which can be both extra closet and dramatic focal point. Large and hard to fit in many homes, old armoires can often be bought for a reasonable price; not surprisingly, a custom-built closet, which lacks value and decorative interest, can cost more. (If space permits, hang mirrors on inside doors.) Interesting old clothes poles or Victorian wall-hung racks can pinch-hit as a hall closet or a temporary guest closet.

9. MAKING THE MOST OF WASTED PLACES

To find neglected space, conduct a thorough search of the house. Look up, look down, look all around. Don't rule anything out.

Wallpaper, paint, and carpentry can work wonders with even the most inconsequential and unattractive area.

• *Down hallways.* Make your hallway into more than a passageway: in wide halls, storage units such as cabinets, shelves, and closets can be constructed wall-to-wall and floor-to-ceiling. Even if the hallway is narrow, storage units can be installed on the wall high enough to permit a tall person walking by to clear them (about 6½′ above the floor).

• *Around windows.* The area around a window is too often overlooked. Why not use the space below the window by building a window seat with storage space inside and pillows for sitting on top? If built-ins are beyond your budget, one or more low chests or hassocks would be a less expensive alternative. Shelves, cabinets, and cubes can be hung on the wall surrounding the window, and shelves can be attached to the window frame itself. Clear plastic- or glass-shelf units with plants are particularly attractive when hung in front of a window that does not have to be opened too often. Wall-to-wall draperies are perfect for hiding large flat objects such as folding tables and chairs. Just install the draperies or cur-

There are no wasted places in this living room: a sculptured staircase leads up to a den area created from unused air space; beneath it, a large seating area with slim shelves fits snugly into a corner. The walls hold a collection of photographs and musical instruments.

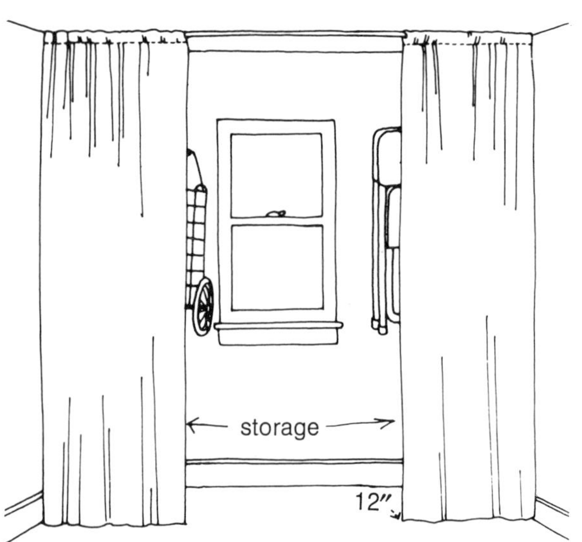
storage
12″

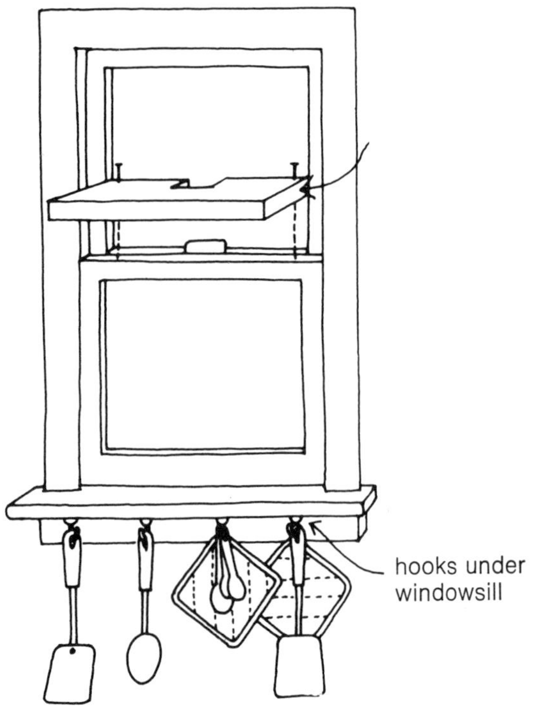
window shelf 1″ × 4″ board cut to fit inner casing, notched around lock and nailed into top of frame
hooks under windowsill

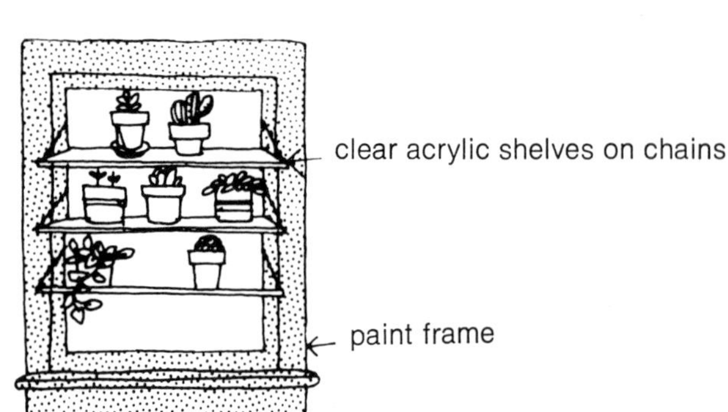
clear acrylic shelves on chains
paint frame

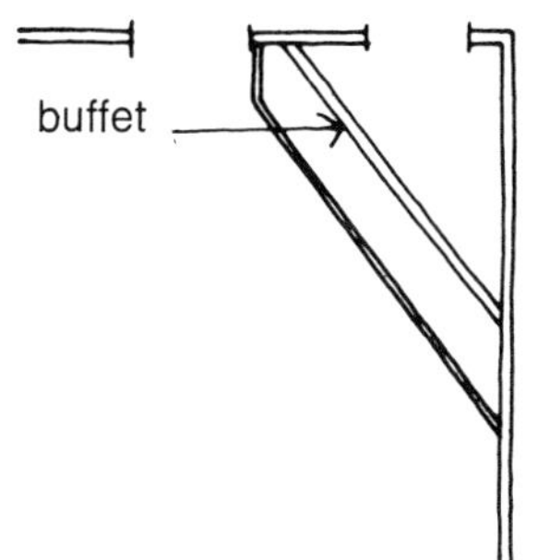

curtained off for a dressing / make-up room

or screened off

corner sink in bath

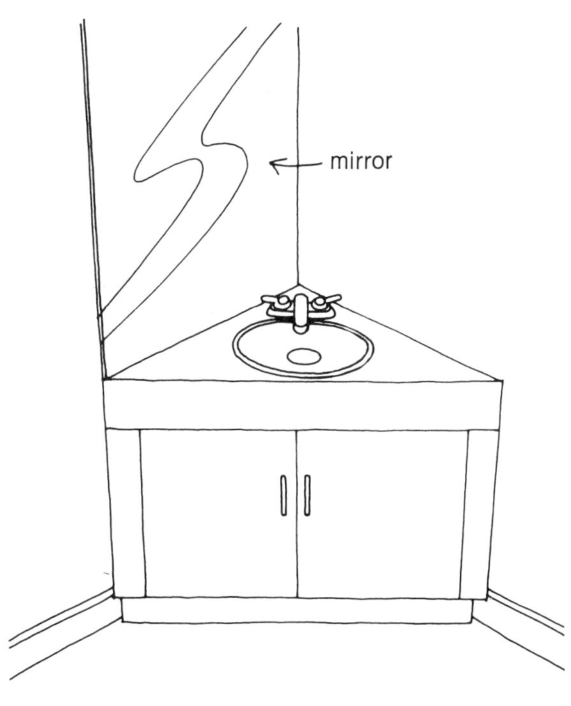

In Corners

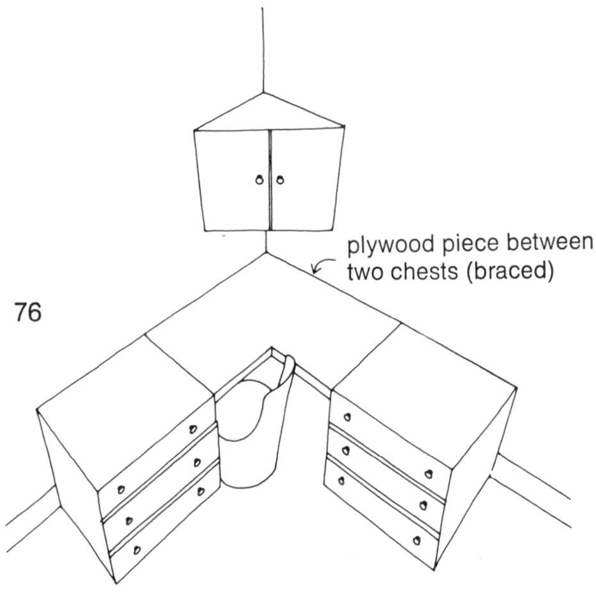

corner library and reading retreat

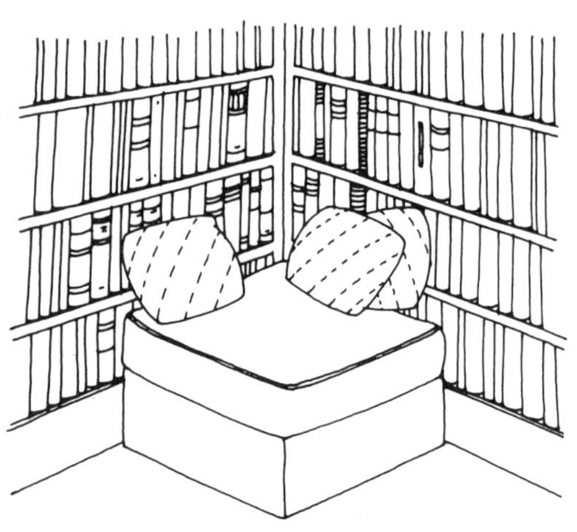

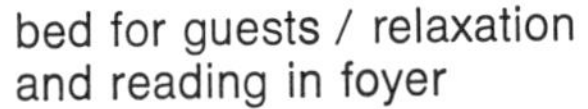

bed for guests / relaxation
and reading in foyer

corner study unit

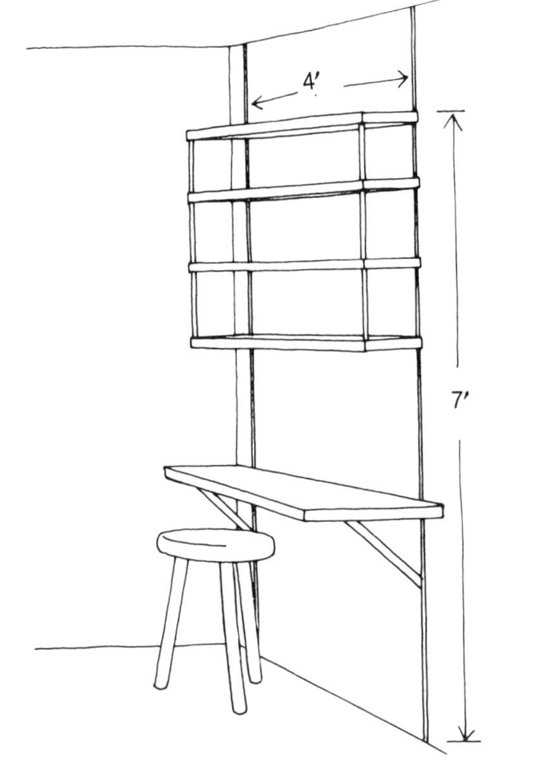

office corner

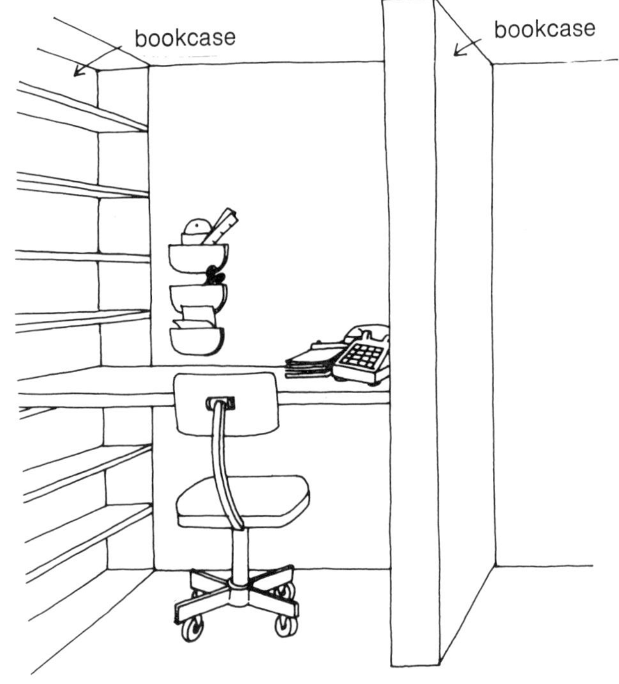

Up Above

bicycle hoisted on pulley up to ceiling

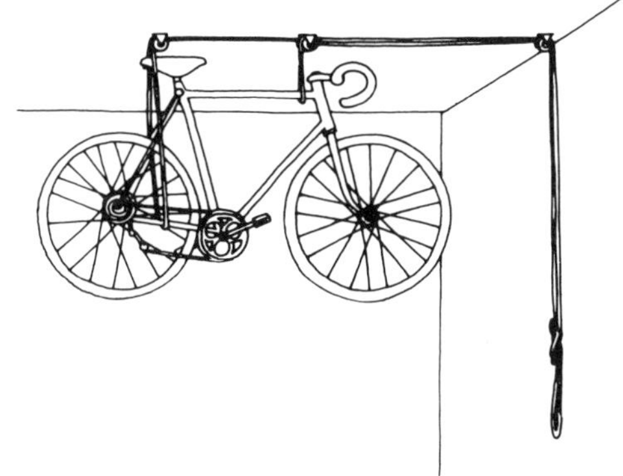

shelf hanging from ceiling

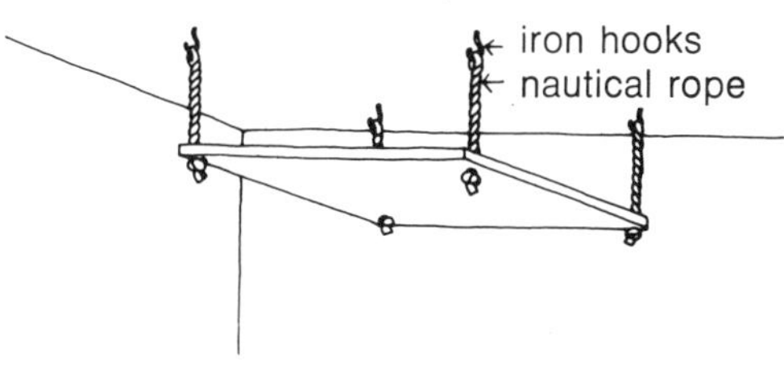

cabinets with sliding doors

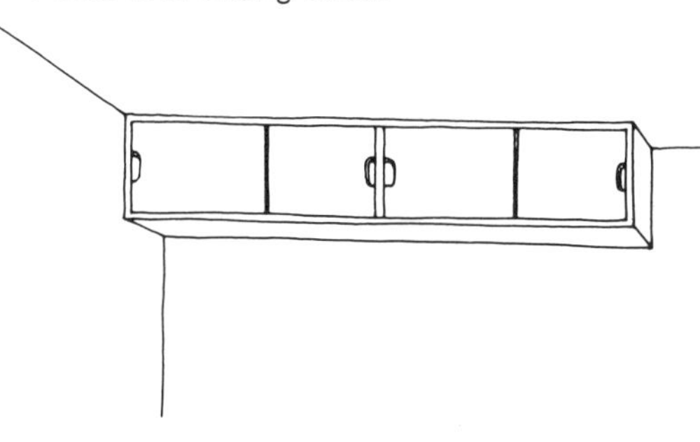

Down Below

beneath a bed

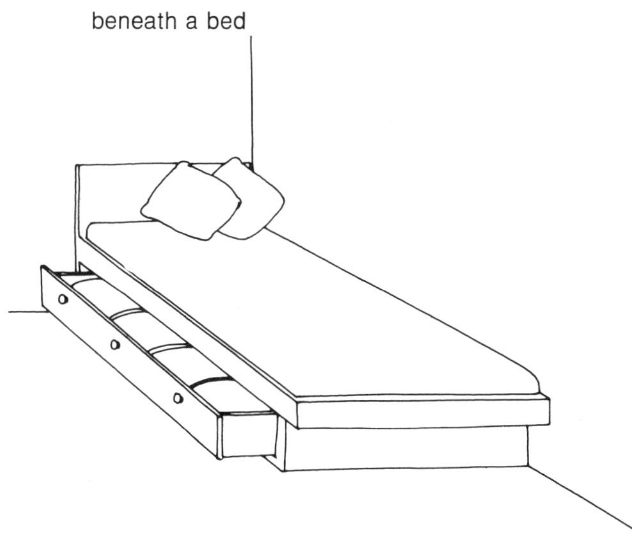

beneath a platform

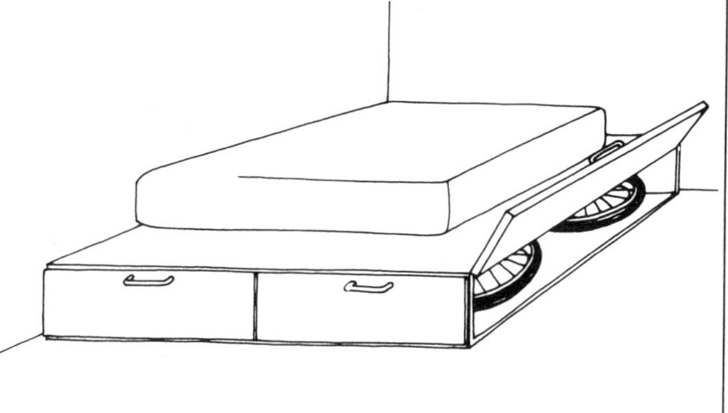

Alcoves

eating alcove

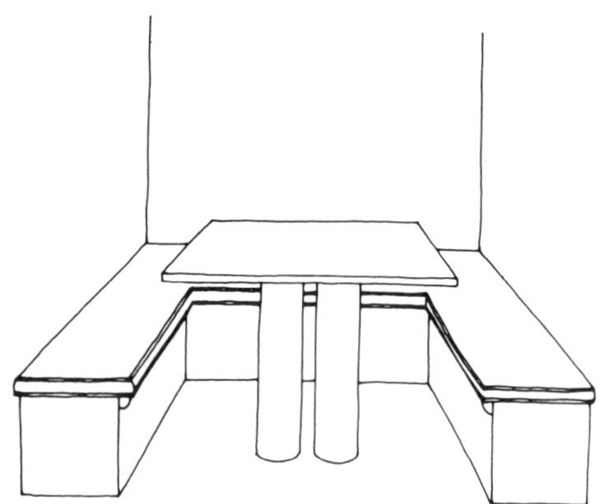

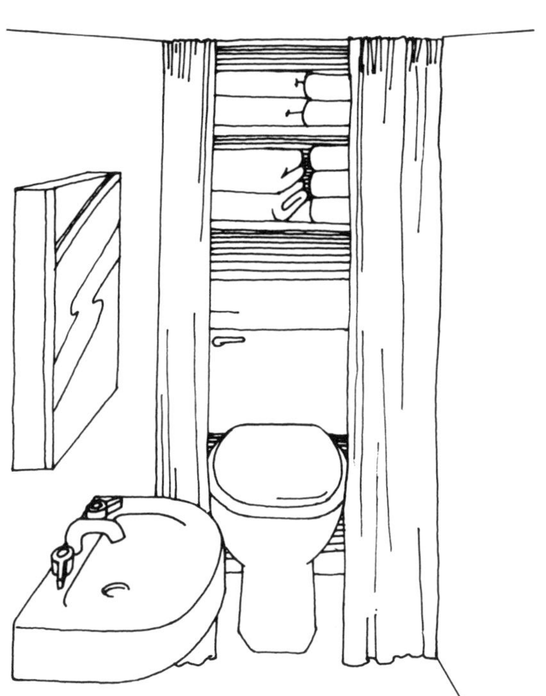

Alcoves

laundry alcove

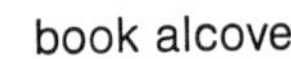

book alcove

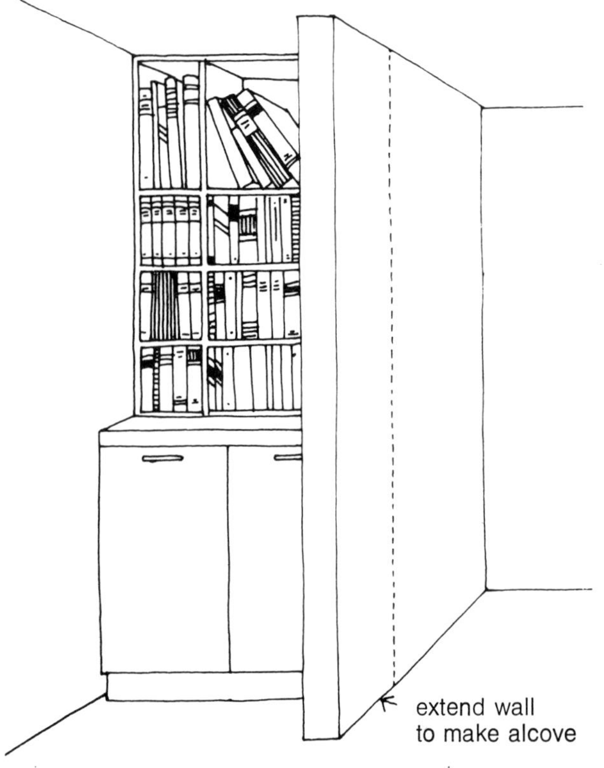

between two closets

Niches

storage niche between studs

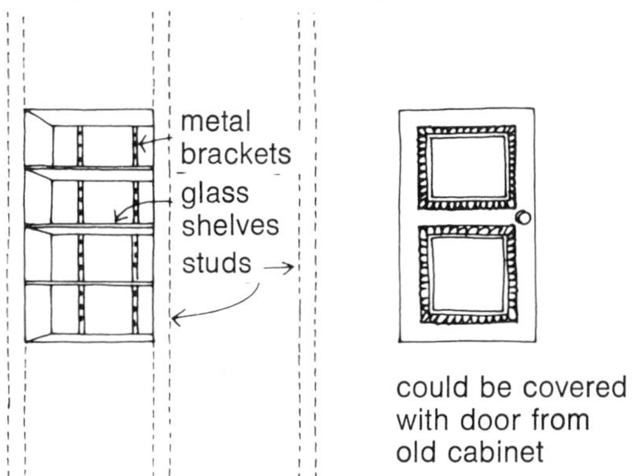

could be covered with door from old cabinet

narrow cabinets in niche behind door

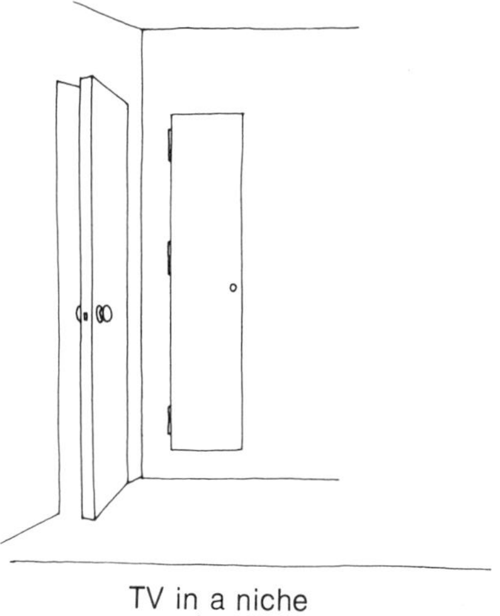

TV in a niche

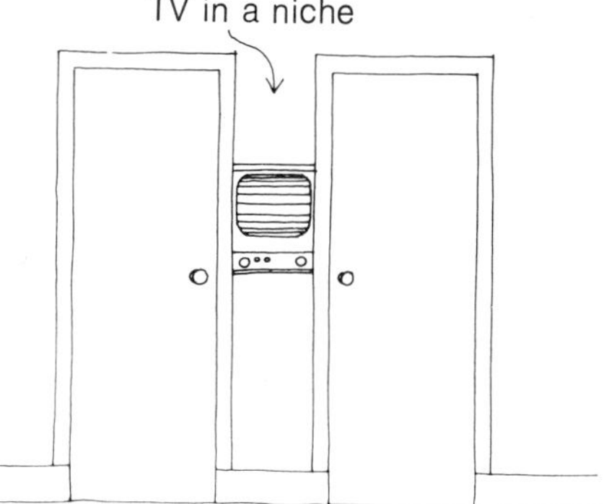

On the Landing

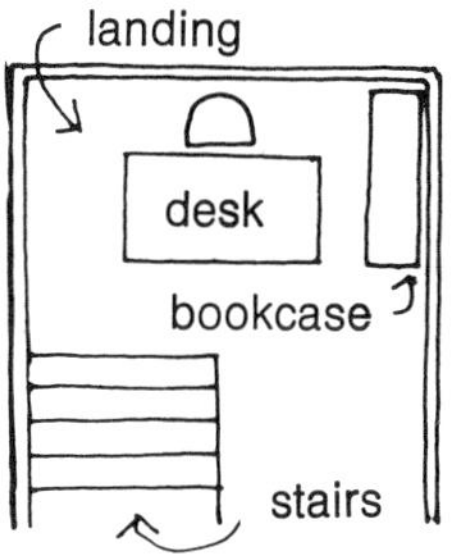

pillows for seating

storage for records, phonograph, books

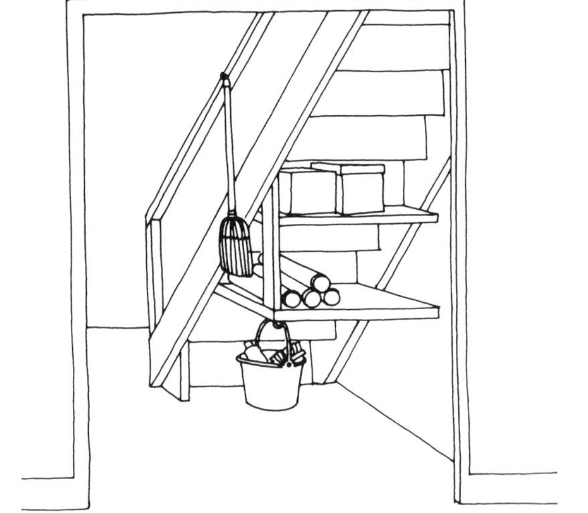

tains at least one foot away from the wall to leave enough space for this purpose.

- *In corners.* Corners are deceiving. They are larger than they look and quite a bit of furniture can fit into them. By adding a banquette, comfortable chair, or small couch and shelves, a little library can be created in a corner; by adding a chair, table or desk, and good lighting, a private place for work or for making up can be created. A corner is also a good place to put a closet. Some furnishings, including chairs, cabinets, and sinks, are designed specifically for corners.
- *On doors.* Doors also have hidden space: the entire back or front of a swing door can be covered with narrow hanging shelves, perforated hardboard (pegboard), shallow storage units or many nails and hooks for just hanging things.
- *Up above.* Unused air space abounds in most homes, so reclaim it for the following: cabinets and shelves installed near the ceiling; baskets, buckets, and large shelves hung from the ceiling; shelves beneath high archways; storage space above kitchen cabinets, closets, toilets, and tubs. A pulley system can be used for hoisting bulky things skyward, like baby carriages, bicycles, and big games such as Ping-Pong tables or boards with electric trains or racing cars.
- *In niches and alcoves.* Within the walls themselves there is usable space. A niche—or recess—can be carved by cutting into a plasterboard to expose the 14½″ space between studs. Assuming this space is clear and not bisected by pipes or wires, it can be filled with shelves or a narrow cabinet, like a medicine cabinet. For privacy, the shelves can be concealed behind a window shade or small door (perhaps louvered shutters or "antique" doors removed from a discarded old cabinet). Or left uncovered, the shelves can be used for the display of sculpture and other decorative objects. Niches are also handy end "tables" in bedroom or living room. Alcoves are like large niches. They are cozy places to tuck a bed, couch, or desk. A wall can be extended to make one, or a fake beam can be built to match one that already exists, with the alcove created by the space between.
- *Down below.* There may even be empty space right under your feet. If a raised platform is high enough and the inside accessible, large possessions like bicycles and luggage can be stored beneath it. Other storage space can be found under sinks and beneath beds and couches.
- *Around stairways.* Homeowners who have stairways will also find that they have some space to spare. Underneath, there may be room

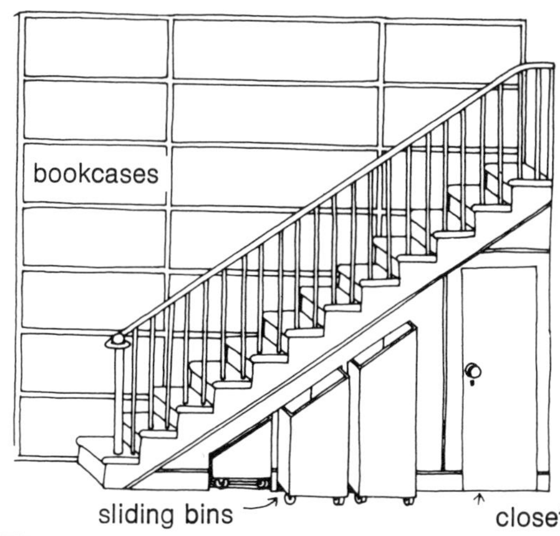

for a small guest bathroom, laundry room, a telephone "booth," closet, storage bins, shelves, and cabinets (including file cabinets). On the staircase wall, pictures, pegs for clothing, shallow cabinets, and bookshelves can be placed and large carpeted landings can be used as a sitting area with pillows added. The top landing may be ideal for bookshelves, desk, or couch.

• *On radiators.* The space around a radiator and the radiator itself can be used as long as the vents and access to controls are not blocked. A shelf can be added above a waist-high radiator to serve as a desk, a buffet, or hall "table"; an enclosed radiator can shelve a display of decorative objects or be transformed into a "table" with the addition of paint or paper topped with a piece of marble, wood, or glass.

• *On walls.* Now, if you are still hung up on where to put possessions, hang them as the Shakers did. Frequently ignored as a place to put furniture, walls can support practically anything legless—chests, desks, even pianos—provided they are properly installed. This is a good way to gain more floor space. And if the objects are pretty as well as practical, such as an unusual assortment of kitchen tools, plates, baskets, or trays, a decorative wall treatment will be an extra dividend.

Up the Stairway

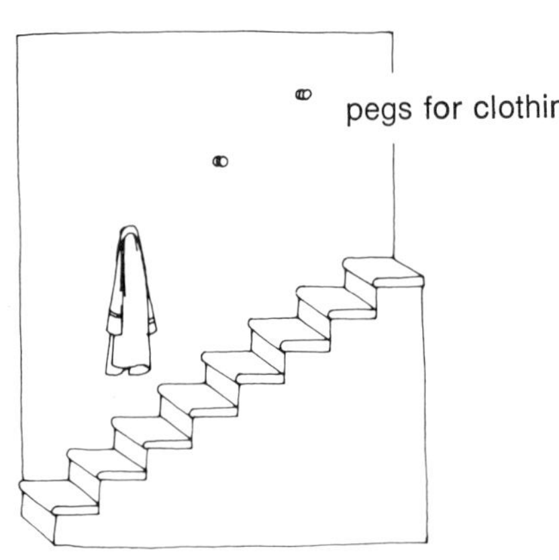

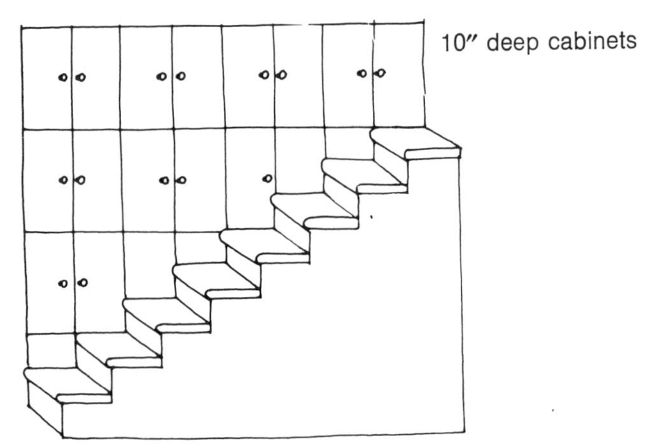

On the Radiator

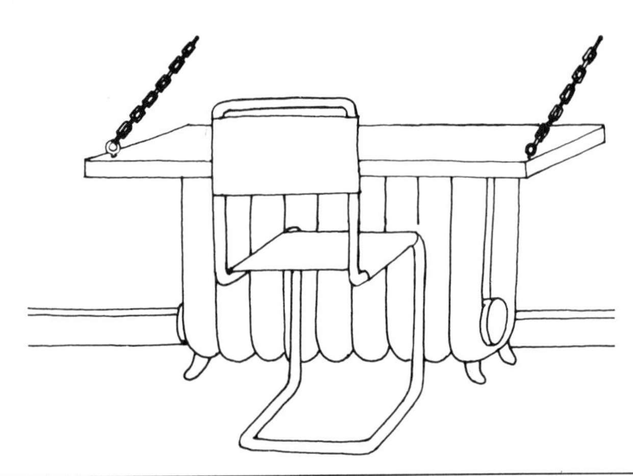

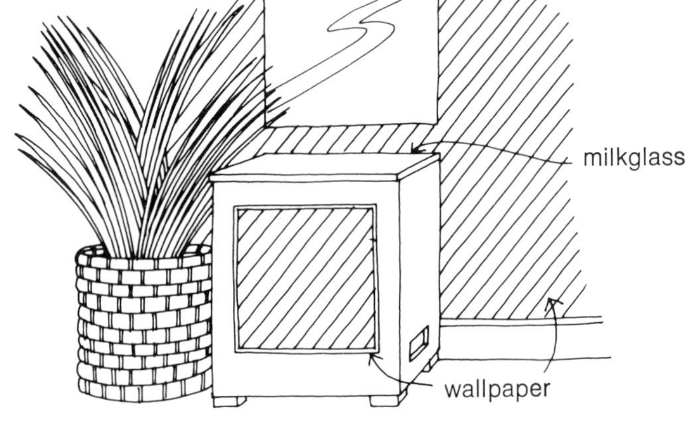

Behind the Furniture

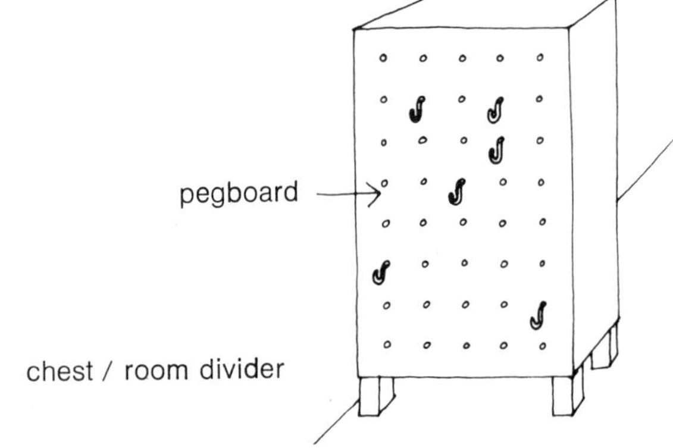

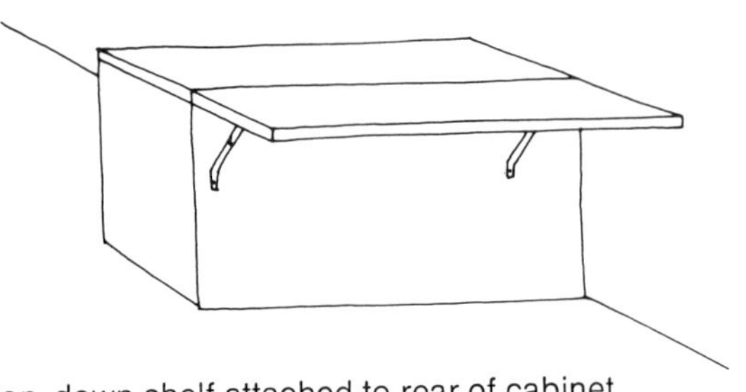

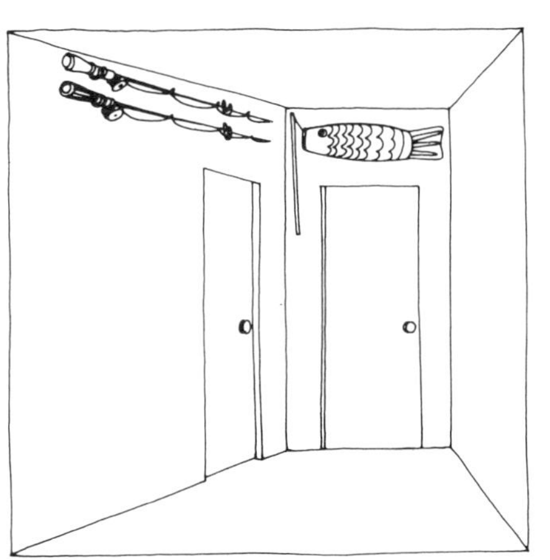

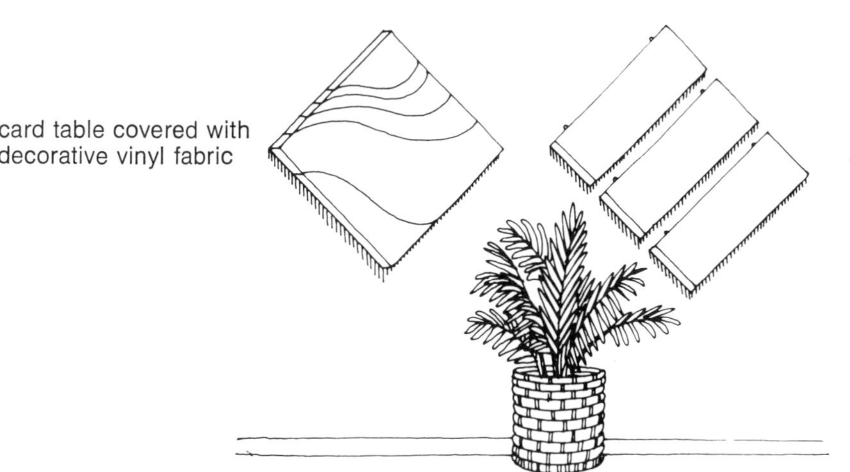
card table covered with
decorative vinyl fabric
colorful leaves of table

bike hung on clothes hanger
(bracket screwed into studs)

hanging chest

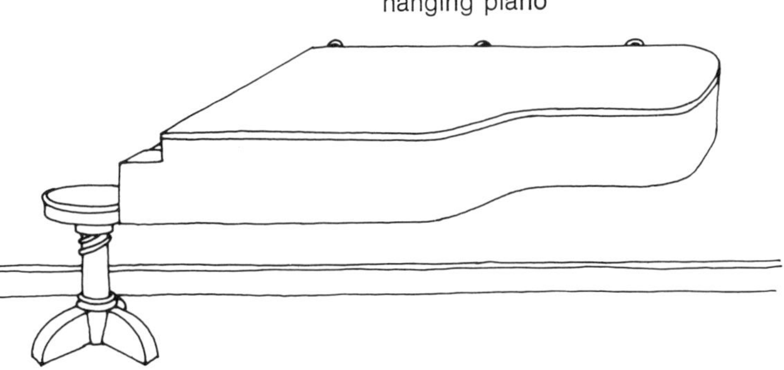
hanging piano

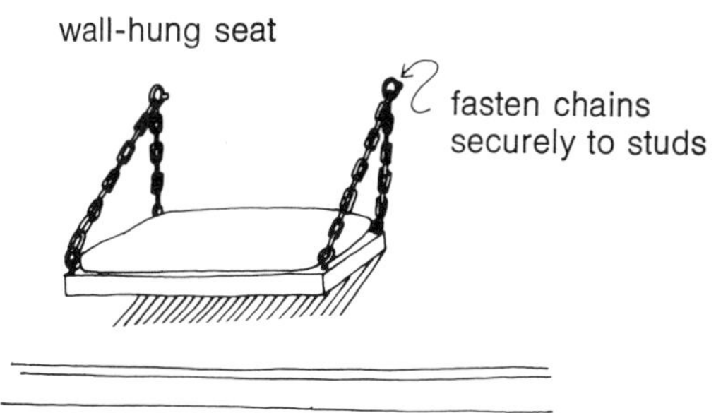
wall-hung seat
fasten chains
securely to studs

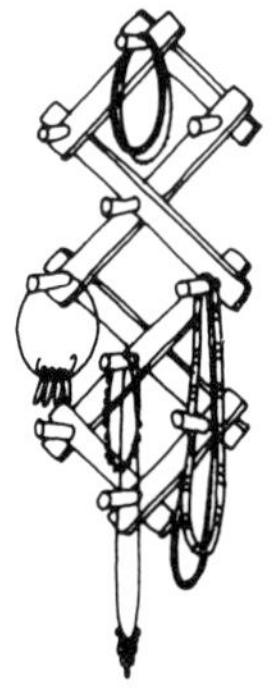

In many ways trying to find and organize space in a child's room is an unending assignment. Not only do children's possessions grow bigger as they do, but very often one small given area must accommodate more than one child for sleeping, playing, working, and, often, eating. The space and the furniture must be adaptable to both changing needs—toys now, books later—and changing sizes.

Fortunately, the basic furniture needed after infancy remains essentially the same, and this might include a selection from the following: for sleeping—a bed, a night table; for sitting—chairs at desk or table, a comfortable lounge chair, giant floor pillows, a window seat; for working (or eating)—a table or desk (near natural light if possible); for storage—bookshelves, toy chests, and cabinets (a wall-to-wall, floor-to-ceiling unit incorporating these features and also a desk is ideal). Furniture for young children should be washable, sturdy, and safe (no sharp corners, no lead paint, and so forth). And it all should be arranged so that some empty area of floor space is left free for playing.

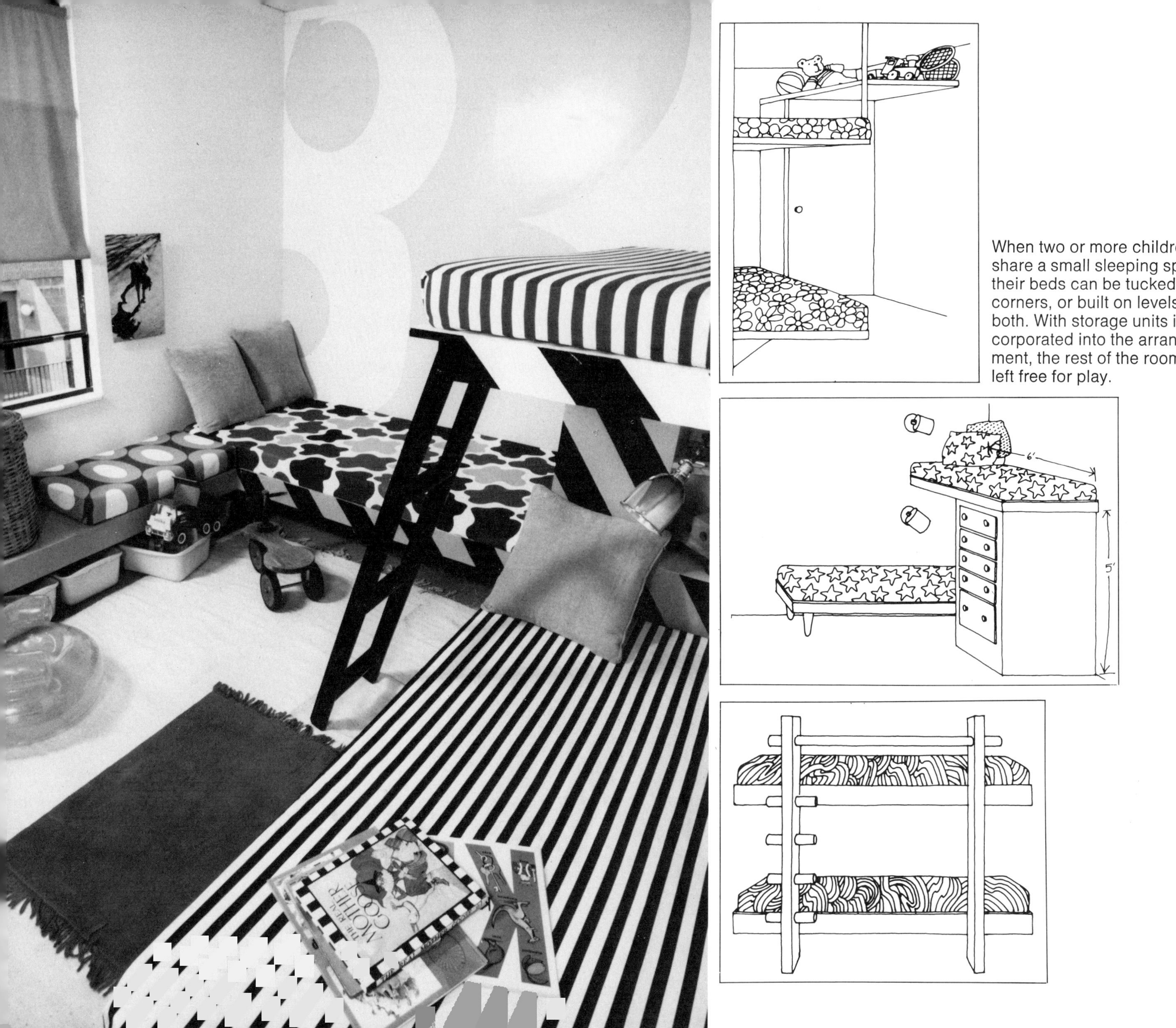

When two or more children share a small sleeping space, their beds can be tucked into corners, or built on levels, or both. With storage units incorporated into the arrangement, the rest of the room is left free for play.

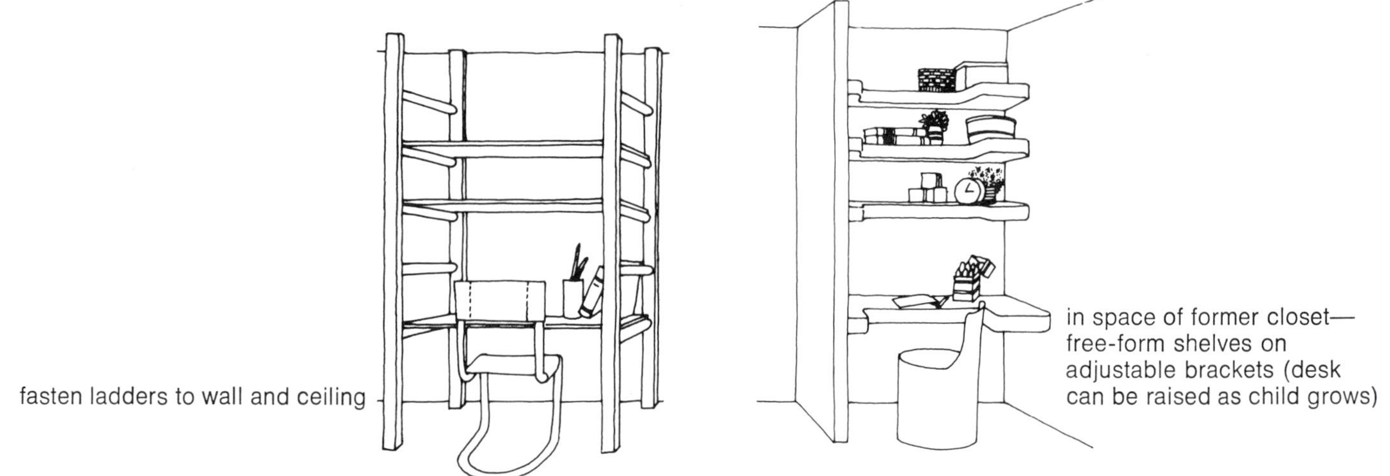

SHARING, PRIVACY, AND OTHER PROBLEMS

Although all the space-saving ideas in this book are applicable to children's rooms, this chapter focuses on some special situations:

1. *Privacy.* How to arrange furniture in a room that is shared by two, or more, children? How to divide it to give each child some privacy? Should there be a common sleeping area and a separate but common working area instead of the more routine division of space into two (or more) areas, each with a bed and desk? Children love to have their very own storage space, no matter how small. Is this possible?
2. *More floor space.* What kind of furniture is available that can be installed on the walls, thus clearing the floors? Wall-hung chests and cabinets? Foldaway beds, fold-down desks and tables? What kind of multipurpose furniture will help? A storage bed? A chest of drawers with a temporarily padded top that can be a changing table for baby?
3. *Flexible and disposable furnishings.* What styles will grow, literally, with the child? (There are tables, desks, and chairs that can be raised and lowered.) What styles might be adaptable to other uses? Can't a crib with one side removed and mattress as low as possible be a small love seat? What kind of furniture can be bought and then discarded without breaking the bank? Secondhand pieces fixed up? Boxes, bags, free for the taking?
4. *Expandable beds.* What kind of sleeping space should be reserved for young visitors or a new child in the family? Trundle, high-rise, or bunk beds provide extra beds in the space of one, making them wonderful space savers. Just be sure an upper bunk is not too difficult to climb in and out of and that it has a safety device such as a railing to keep a youngster from rolling off the bed.

STORING KIDS' CLOTHES AND POSSESSIONS

To begin with, clear out the clutter. Dispose of last year's clothes, toys with over two missing parts, the odd socks and gloves whose mates have not surfaced for over a month, and those hand-me-downs from a fat cousin that will never fit your string bean. Then decide what goes where.

- *Closets.* Try to plan the closet not only in terms of what it will hold but also for easy access. A rod placed within a child's reach—30″ for three-to-five-year-olds, 45″ for an older child—and drawers, boxes, or shelves that are low will make putting clothes away easy and be, it is to be hoped, an inducement to neatness. (A

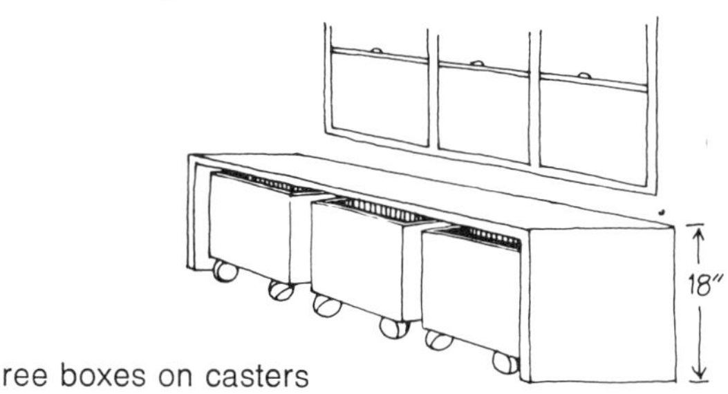

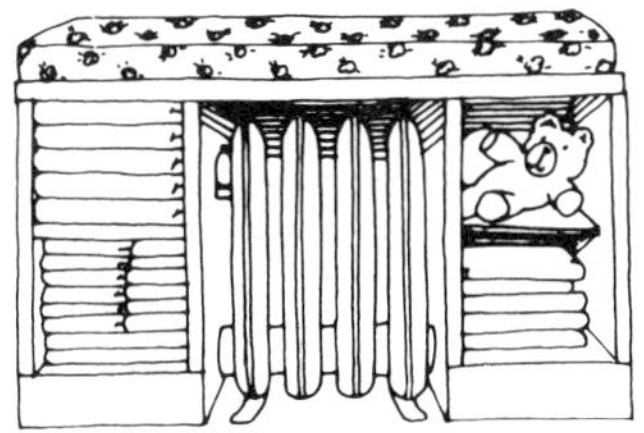

rod may be unnecessary in a boy's closet where little hanging space is needed.) Removing the closet door may serve as a reminder that the closet exists, make it more "available," and add to self-sufficiency (if not to chaos). In the same way, clear plastic boxes should, theoretically, be a boon to effective organization even by a child.

• *Chests of drawers.* To save floor space try to fit a small chest into the bottom of a closet or group two or more next to or on top of one another rather than in different corners of the room. Children often inherit cast-offs, their parents' old bureau or a relic from grandmother's attic. Sometimes these can be sturdier than a new piece, and generally they offer to the creative parent or child enormous decorating possibilities. They can be modernized with new moldings and hardware. An old chest can be completely covered with paint, paper, or fabric attached with white glue; or it can be just partially decorated with designs cut from fabric, wallpaper, magazines, or with stickers, small posters, colored tape, or decals. An unfinished chest can be colored with crayons and Magic Markers. Although a plastic "paper" or a glossy paint has built-in protection, a coat of polyurethane plastic should be sprayed or brushed on where necessary. A chest that is being decorated for a young child might have drawers of different colors, each standing for the category of clothing it contains, that is, white for underwear, pink for pants. Similarly, pictures could be pasted or painted on the drawers to indicate what is inside. Store-bought dividers or several shallow boxes help a child organize the many odds and ends in top drawers. Incidentally, heavy drawers are hard for children to pull in and out, so try to avoid overloading a large drawer or select a chest with shallow drawers that just hold less.

• *Shelves.* Shelves should be deep enough to hold games and toys and certain ones should be covered to conceal a mess. These can also be painted or papered.

• *Wall storage.* Cork, pegboard, Homosote, or wallboard are good surfaces upon which to hang things. They can be installed in one small area or over a large surface, such as wall-to-wall, floor-to-ceiling, and painted in bright colors to add pep to a room.

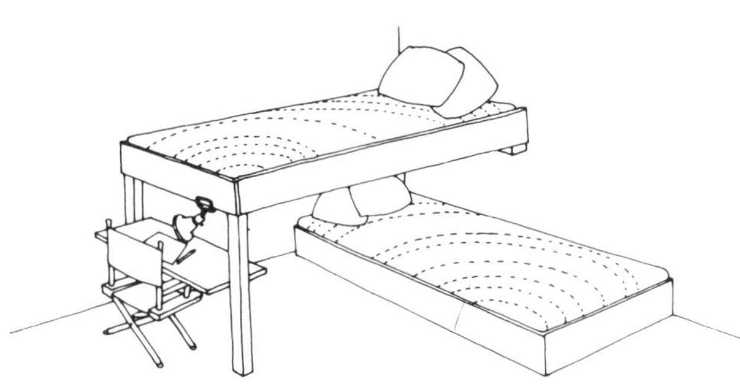

A room divider is often placed perpendicular to the long wall, but in this children's room it is parallel to it, free-standing, and long enough to include in it a bed, desk, and storage for each child.

triple trundle bed

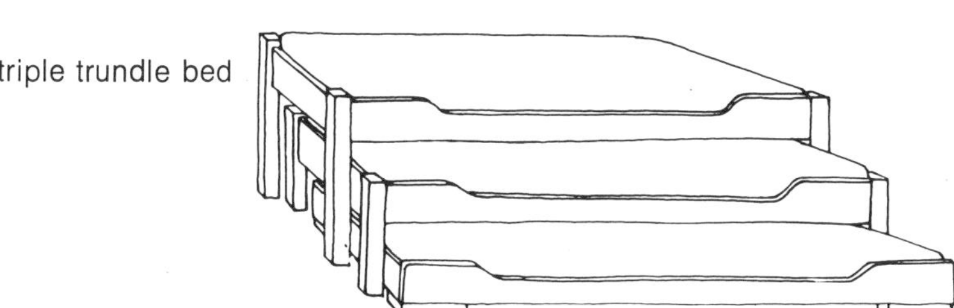

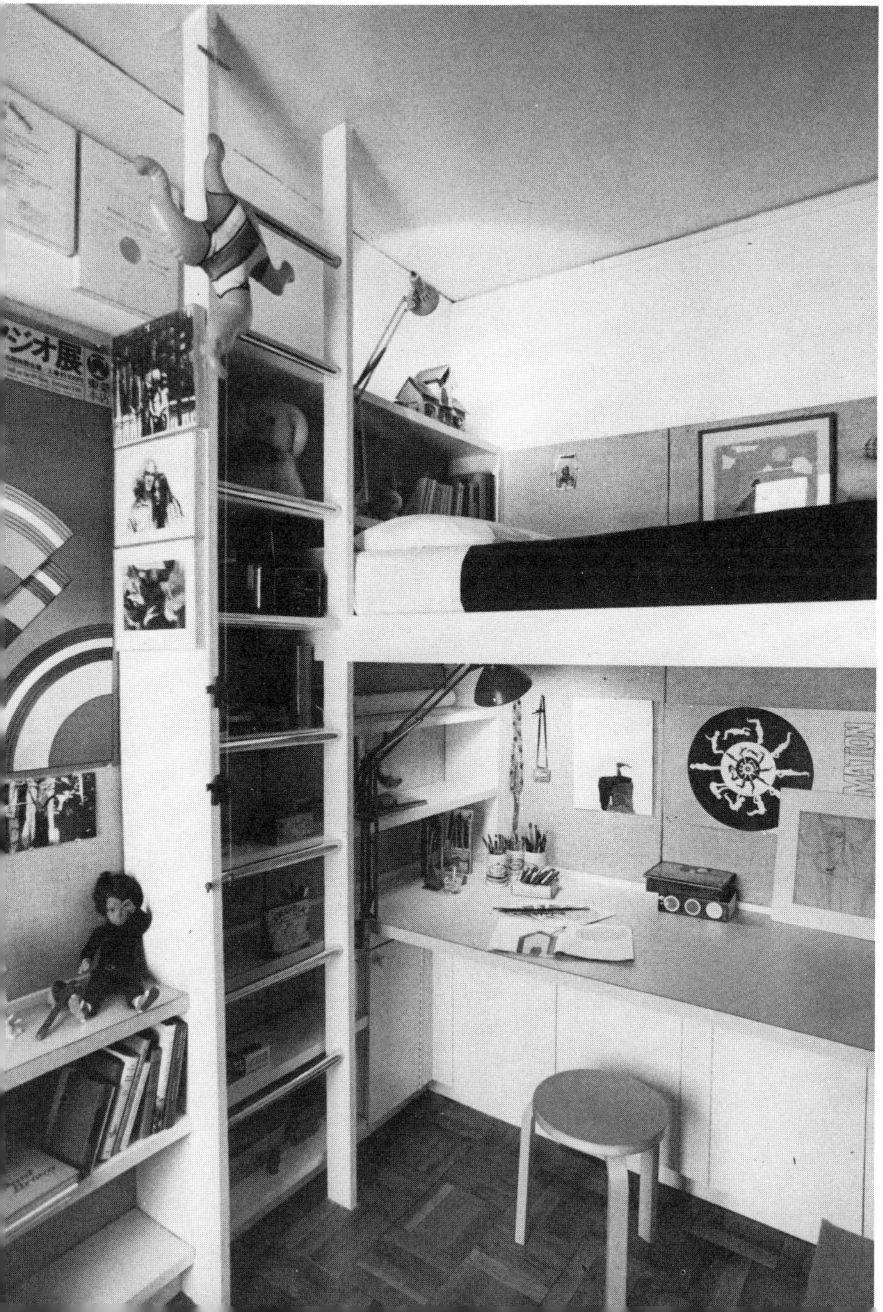

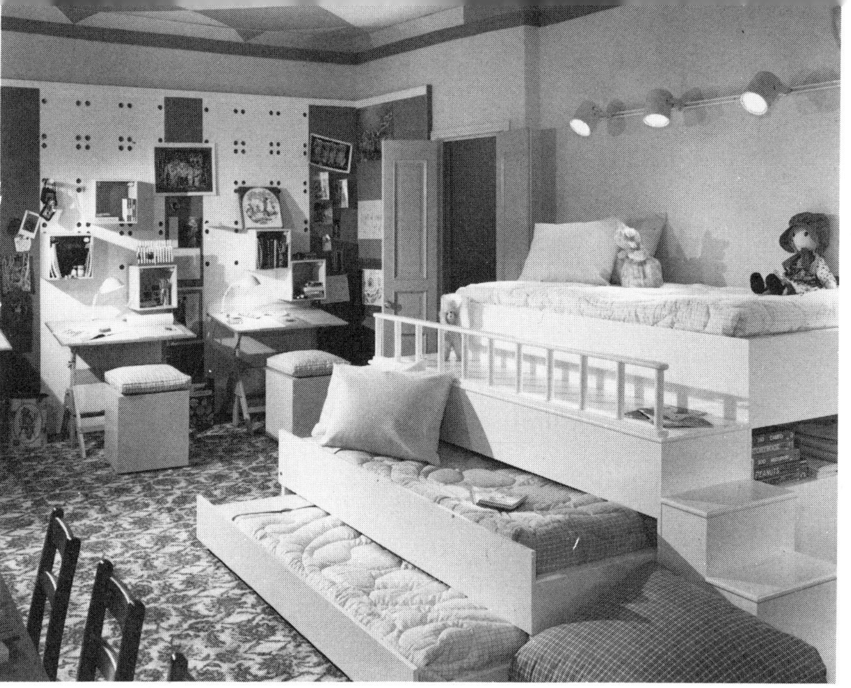

Above: A triple trundle is the ultimate expandable bed, providing sleeping space for three in the floor space of one bed. The designer has used drafting tables instead of bulky desks, with cubes beneath them for both sitting and storage. *Left:* In a small 7′ × 12′ room the architect has built a three-foot-wide loft 5′ 4″ above the floor and 3′ 8″ from the ceiling. The shelves and cabinets are covered with white semigloss paint; the desk counter and top shelf are covered with yellow plastic laminate; and the giant bulletin boards are ¾″ Homosote covered with burlap.

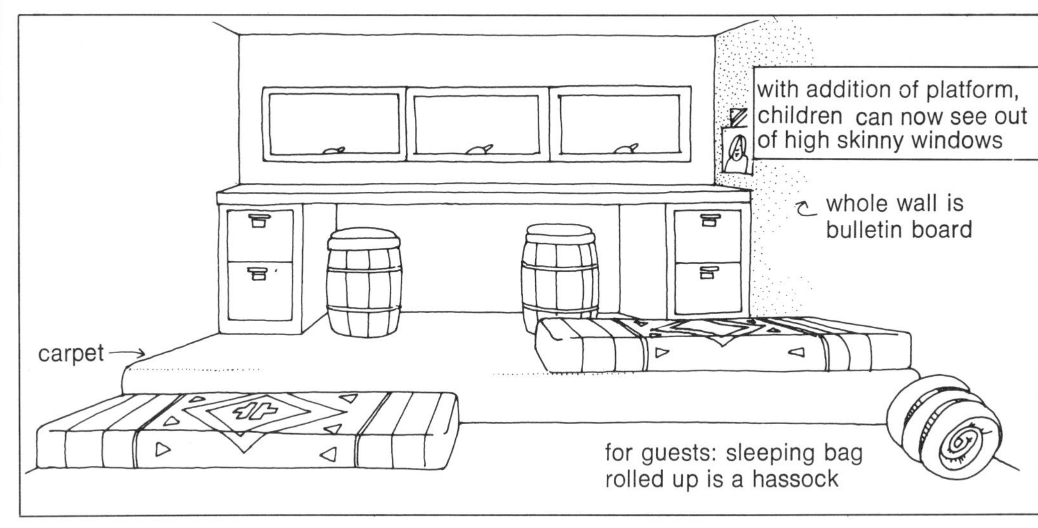

Fold-Down Furniture

closed

bulletin board with posters

open

mattress

shelf

①

work table or train / racing-car table

BLACK BOARD

②

Decorating Storage Units

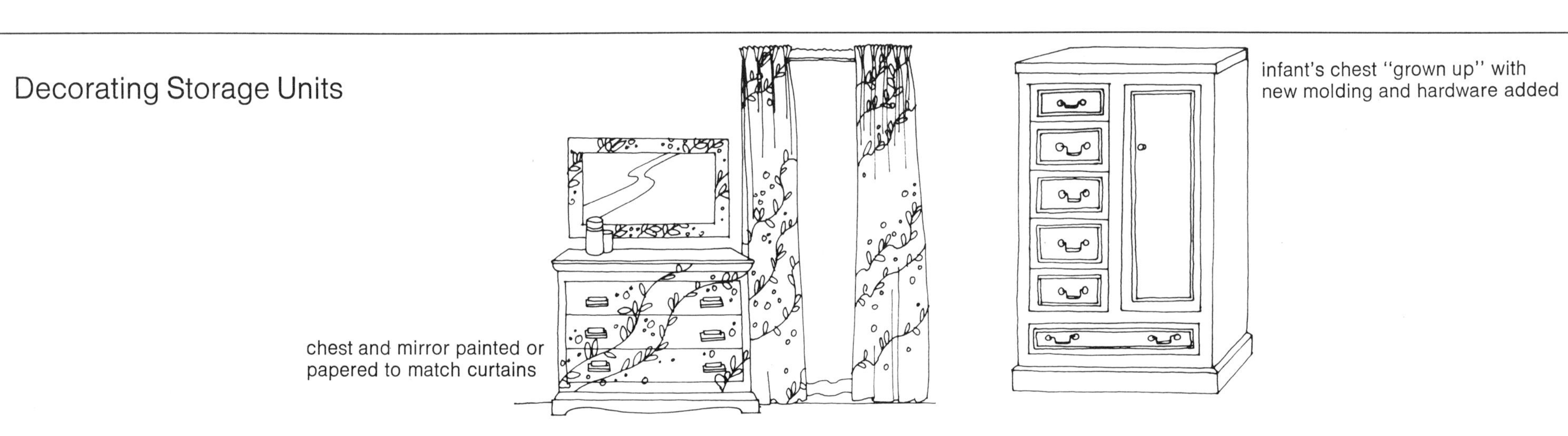

Disposable Storage

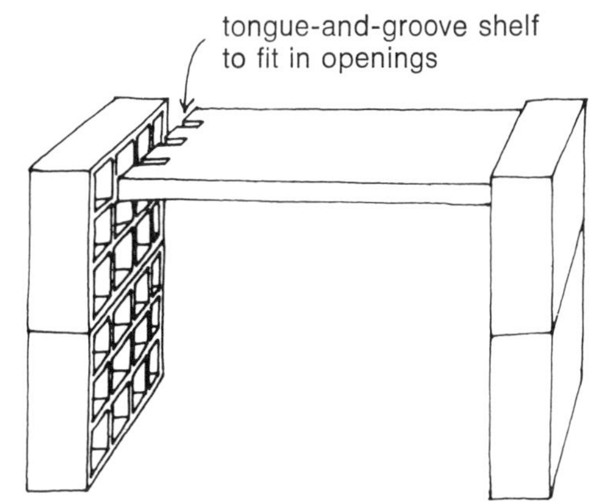

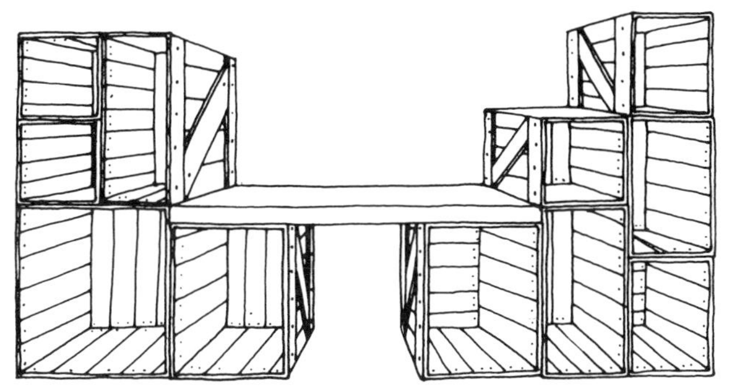

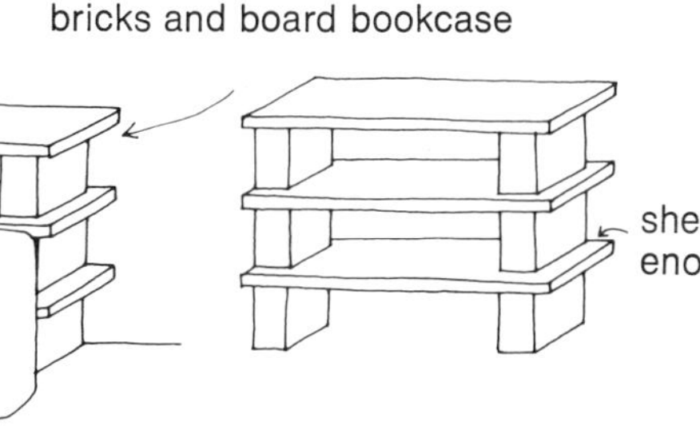

Wall-Hung Storage

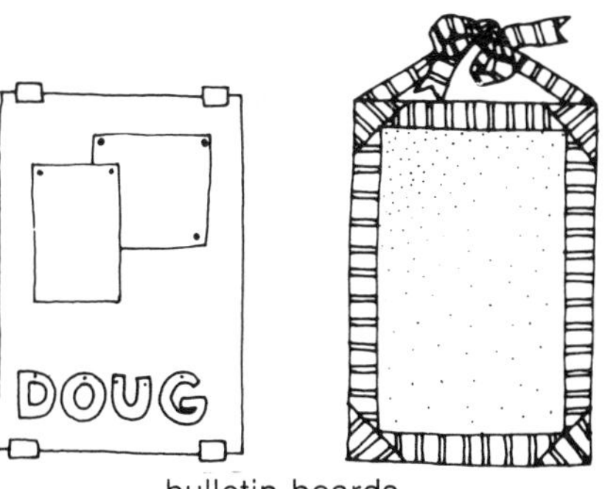

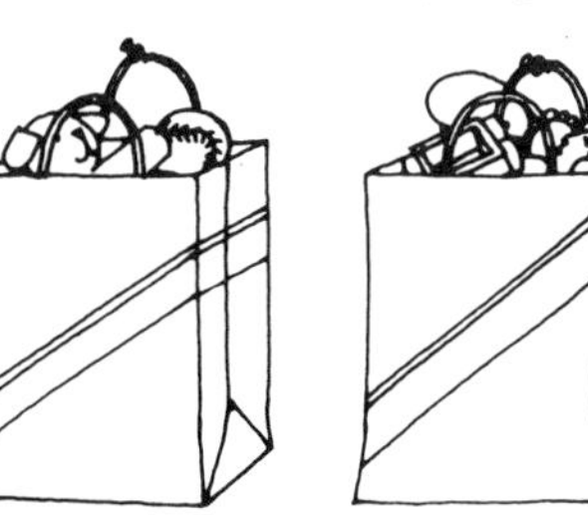

It is an unfortunate fact of life that although we have more leisure time today to pursue the pleasures of reading, having a drink, watching television, and listening to music, we have less space in which to do it. As TV sets get bigger, rooms get smaller; as book and record collections expand, shelves shrink. But, fortunately, with a little planning, many of our pastime possessions can be attractively displayed or handily stored.

BOOKS

Books are a beautiful wall treatment, and an attractive arrangement of them adds character, warmth, and interest to any area. The book-storage unit itself can be an important decorative focal point if its structural elements are emphasized. It can carry through the design theme with modern shelves in a contemporary room; period bookcases in a room with antiques; stained shelves to match wood beams in a provincial or country room.

This wall unit not only contains a bar, a desk, entertainment equipment, and bookshelves (on both sides), but is also a movable room divider separating the guest room–study from the living room when necessary. It is made of plywood with an oak finish and has sections (on casters) that fold back easily. The built-in television set rotates and is accessible to both rooms.

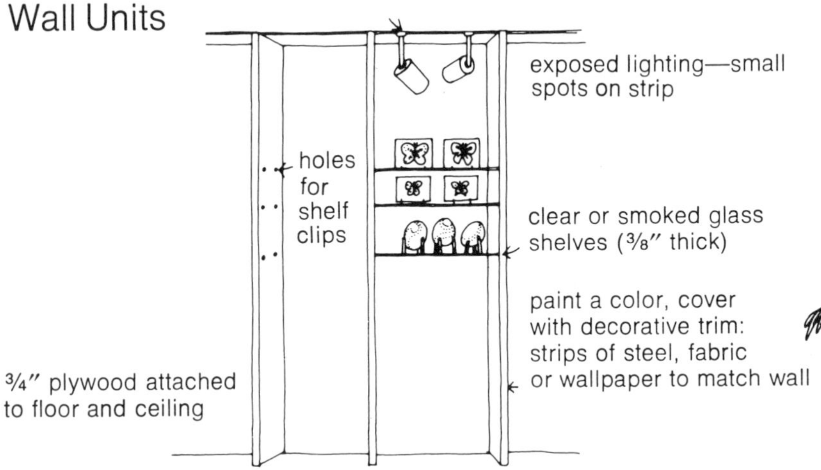

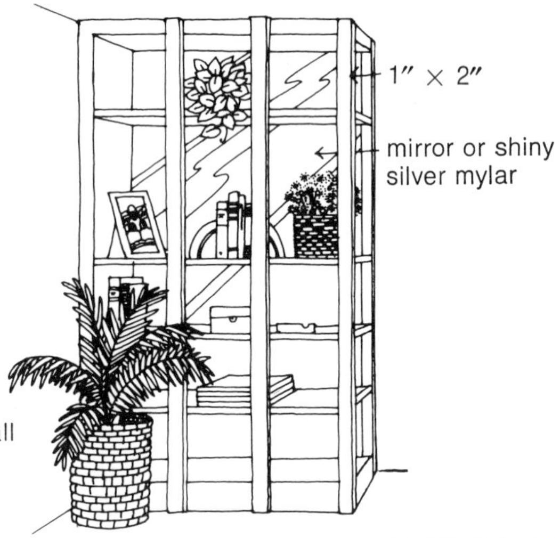

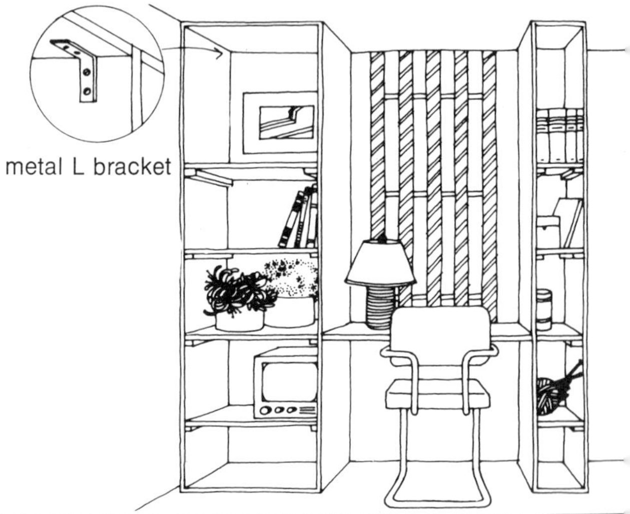

• *Decorative effects.* The wall behind an open-backed bookshelf, and the shelves or the case, can be covered in a coordinating fabric or paper or paint; for example, the same fabric on the wall as the drapery fabric. And often cloth-covered shelves are not only more striking but much less expensive than a good wooden shelf. Any material can be glued or tacked onto the shelf, with a piece of glass, cut to the size of the shelf, placed on top for protection if necessary. Colorful felt can also be used in this way. It is particularly effective on the wall behind a bookcase displaying art objects as well as books (ornamental accessories mixed in among books relieve the monotony). Attractive books can themselves be a decorating device. Those with tooled-leather bindings and colorful jackets can be displayed with spine out or with covers faced out.

• *Off-beat places for books.* Since an ever-expanding collection of books may quickly outgrow its quarters in the living-room area or den, search for book-storage space in one or more of the following places: bedroom, dining room, kitchen or pantry, foyer, guest room, or playroom. A wide hall covered on one or both sides with books can become a walk-through library (an added bonus is that wall-to-wall books will unify a hall that has too many doors). And those lucky enough to have a large spare closet can convert it to a mini-library by covering the walls and both sides of the door with bookshelves.

Within any room, books may be put in the following places: between or around windows or doors, behind draperies or sliding panels or doors, on mantels. Book-storage units can act as room dividers with access to the books from one or both sides. End tables can be bookcases, and books—large ones piled high—can be interesting end tables. Also, books can be put in drawers, spine up.

• *Store-bought book shelves vs. custom-made cases.* A unit bought from a store may be not only considerably less expensive than custom carpentry, but also more decorative and easy to disassemble and adapt to another home. Popular styles include spring-suspension poles with closed and open cabinets and drawers of different depth (the deepest one to be used as a desk); shelves installed on standards and brackets; a wide variety of metal, wood, and plastic units sold knocked down but very easily assembled; and wall-hung or stacked boxes. Commercial metal-shelf units are inexpensive and available in many size combinations. But they are made only in dull colors and often sold only in large quantities.

• *Designing book storage.* Any shelving system should be carefully planned—where it will go what it will hold: books, as well as the myriad of other things that manage to intrude, such as magazines, television, artwork, records, tapes, phonograph, cabinets, drawers, writing sur-

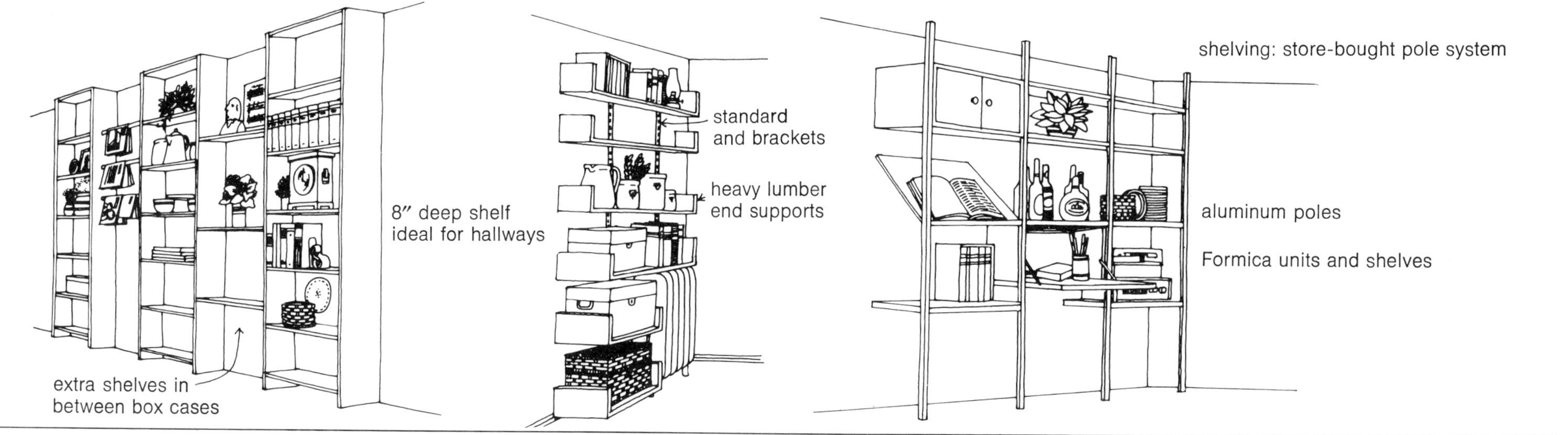

faces. The size and shape can be calculated and sketched on paper, and to test the design visually, strips of long paper or tape can actually be lightly attached to the wall. Determine also whether the visual emphasis will be horizontal or vertical, or a mixture. And take accessibility into account. Since it is hard to reach higher than 6½′ without a ladder, or lower than 30″, use these spaces for other storage, such as cabinets below and display above.

• *Something about shelves.* Shelves can be made of wood (¾″ plywood or pine are the most common kind used, unfinished, stained, painted, or covered with wallpaper, fabric, vinyl, leather, self-adhesive plastic, or Formica. Wood tape on the edges of a plywood shelf will make it look like solid wood. Transparent shelves may be glass or Plexiglas.

• *How to calculate the amount of space needed for books.* If you are designing your own shelf system, measure both the wall space necessary for the unit and the number and size of shelves that best suit the size (height and depth) of your books. Shelves are most commonly 8″ deep, but they may be as narrow as 4″ or as deep as 12″—even more. Shelves for the average book might be 8″ to 11″ apart with a larger interval between shelves to accommodate the height of bigger books. When calculating the height of a unit based on this, add on to your figures the thickness of the shelf. You will also have to estimate the number of running feet of shelving required. To do this, allow approximately one linear foot per seven average books standing upright. Allow also for future acquisitions. Adjustable shelves are always an asset, and even the most common standard bookshelf will look more interesting if the distance between shelves is varied. For visual balance, consider putting the largest books lower down and the smaller books higher up.

INSTALLATION ADVICE

1. There are several basic methods for attaching shelves based on the idea of resting the shelf on a protrusion in the case or in a side wall. The protrusions—which must be at exactly the same height to make a level shelf—can be brackets, a long metal piece with holes for screws; or shelving pins, small metal pieces that go into a hole drilled in the side of the case that can be removed and adjusted; or narrow strips of wood about 1″ × 2″ and as long as the depth of the case that are nailed in. Strong, well-secured nails can sometimes be used alone in a similar way.
2. Some experts say that a shelf made of ¾″ plywood and up to 30″ long does not need a center support. Anything longer requires some support to prevent sagging and to reinforce the unit. These supports also act as a divider between books.
3. Brackets or other hardware that holds shelves to a wall should coincide with and be screwed into studs in a wall. If this is not possible, molly or toggle bolts should be used.
4. For greatest security a large, high bookcase

Places to Put Shelves; Places to Put Books

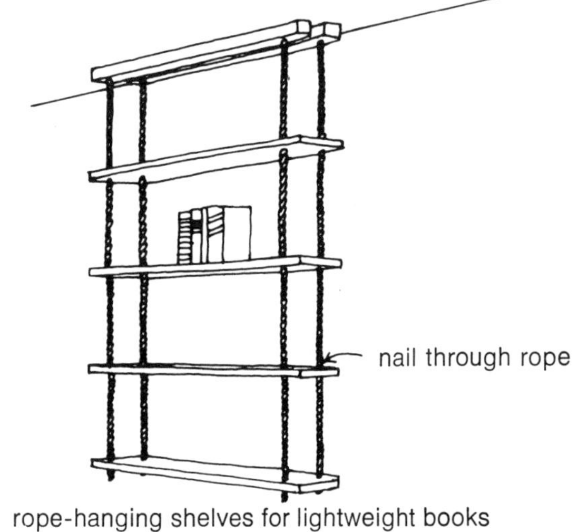

rope-hanging shelves for lightweight books

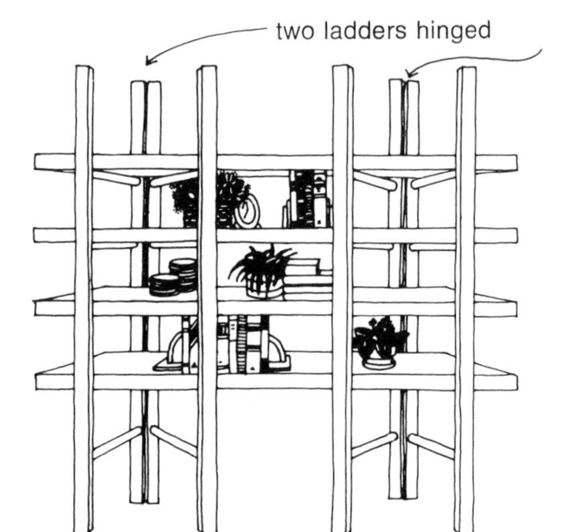

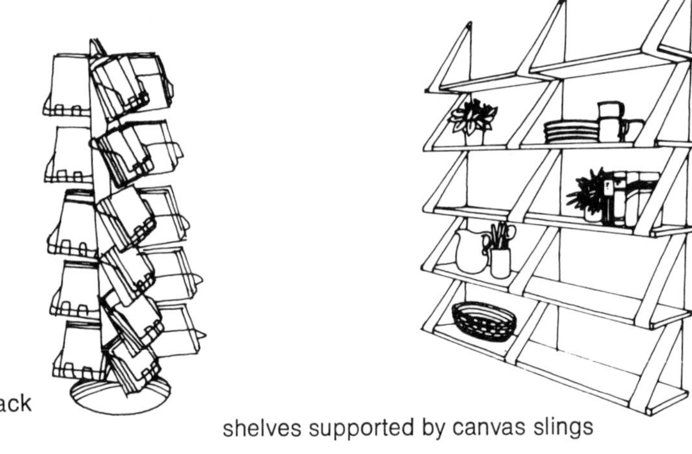
paperback display rack

shelves supported by canvas slings

fancy picture frame
nailed to plain-Jane surface

hung over back of door

unused door or window

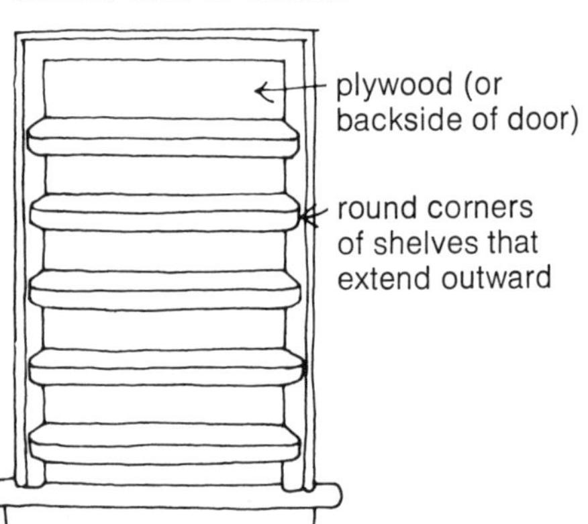

around doors or windows,
and down hallway

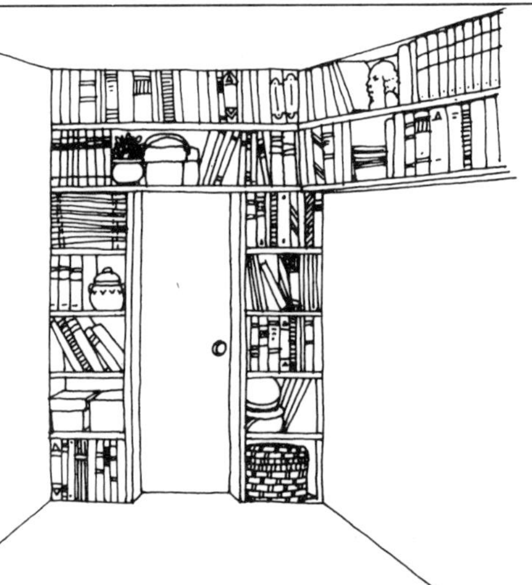

combination book storage / end table

circle of plywood, cloth covered

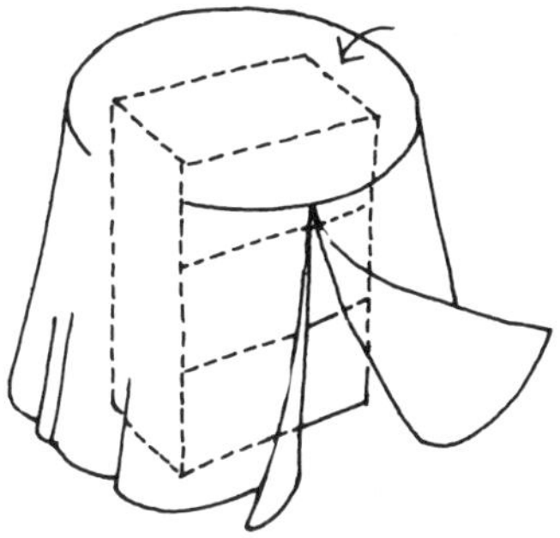

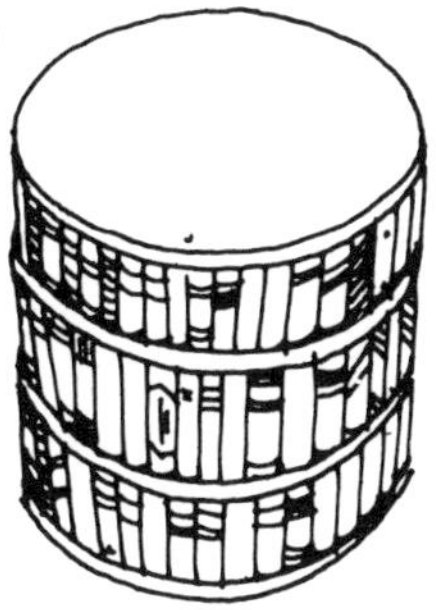

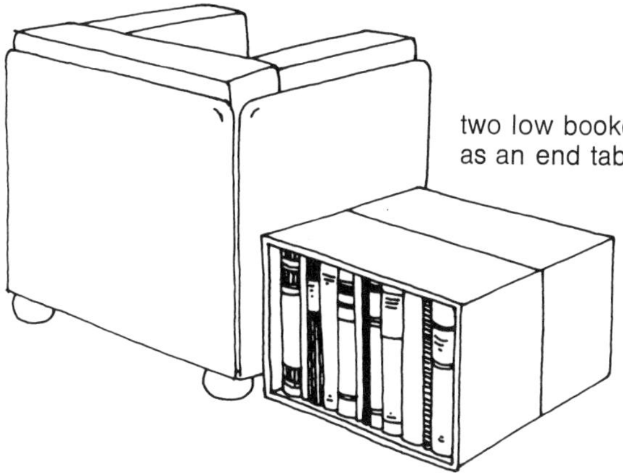

two low bookcases
as an end table

seat

shelf desk

book nook

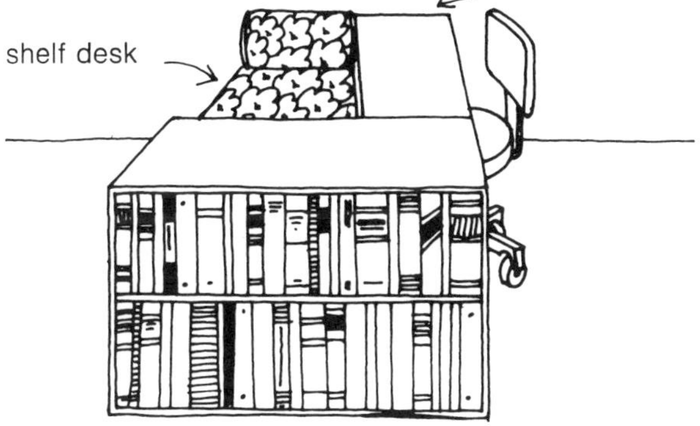

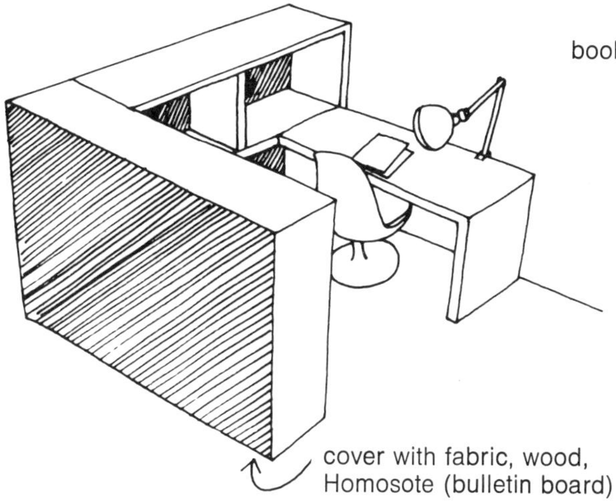

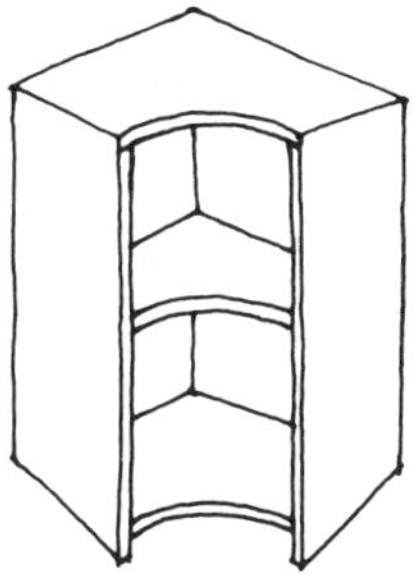

cover with fabric, wood,
Homosote (bulletin board)

in corners

alternative: use closed cabinets

bedroom bookcase
divider and headboard

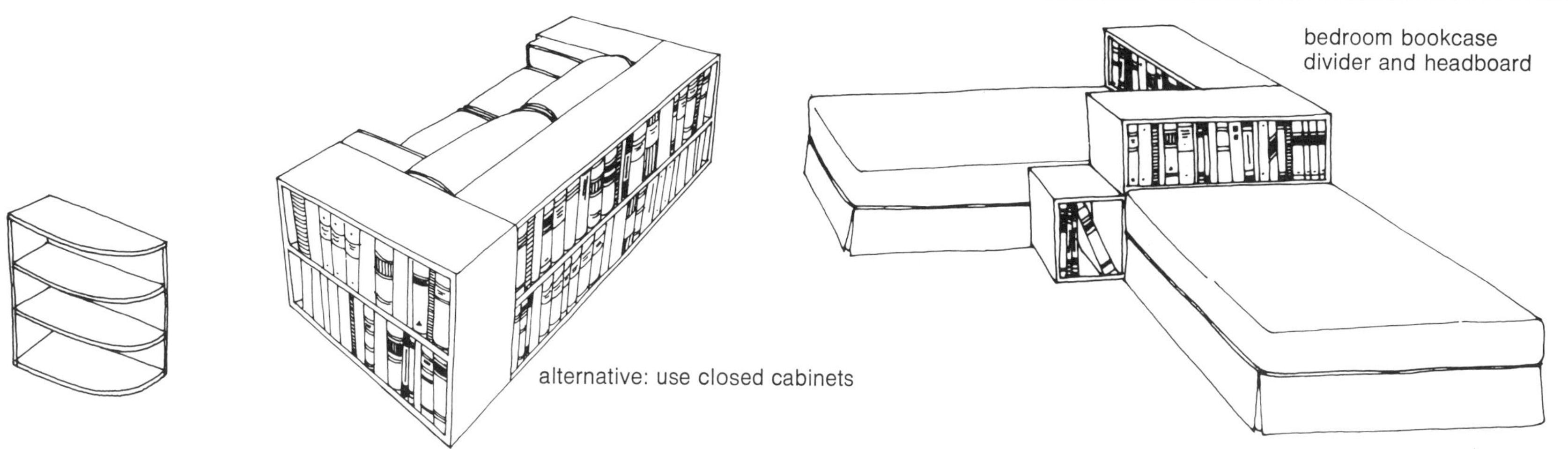

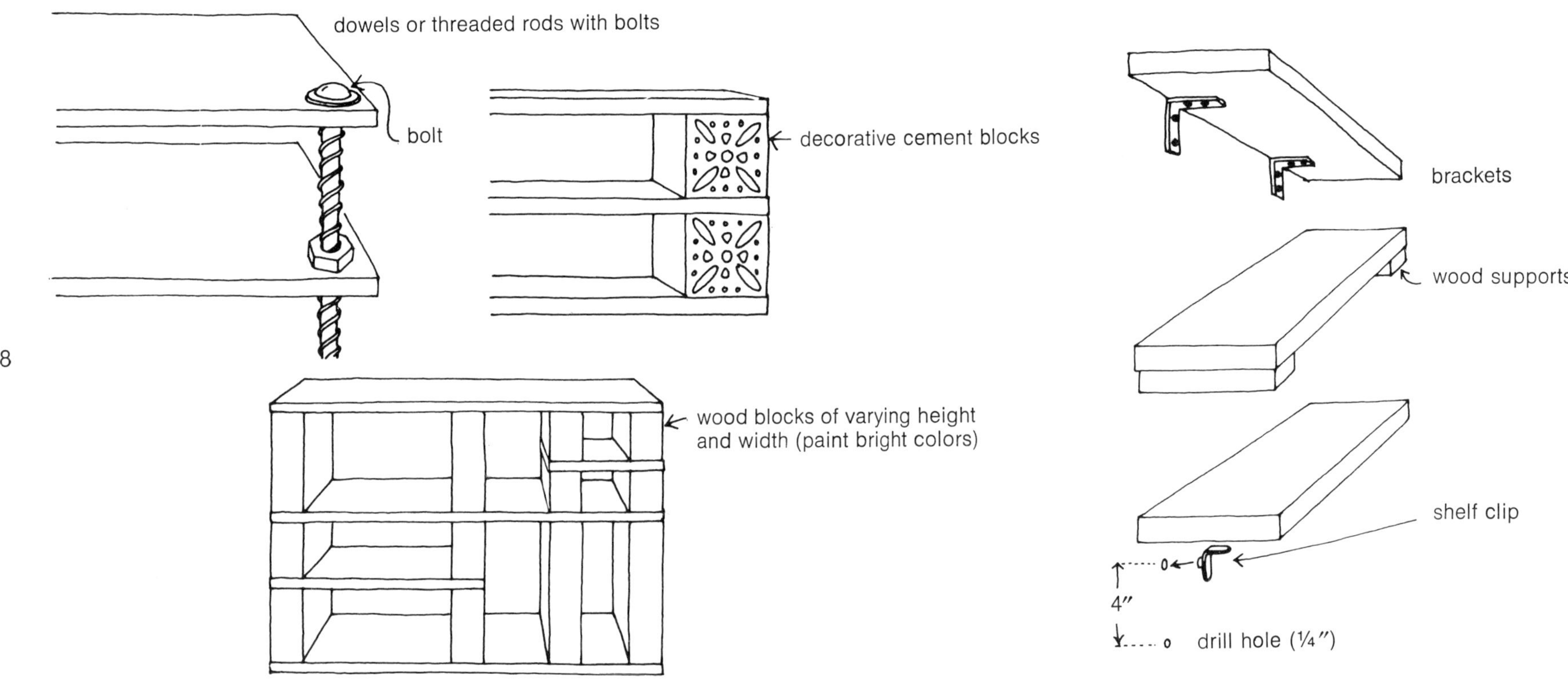

unit should incorporate the back or side of a wall. Bookcases can be secured to walls with L brackets with one arm screwed to shelf or case and the other to wall or ceiling (again through studs in wall). And if you do not trust the strength of the walls to hold shelves or bookcases, use poles floor-to-ceiling instead.

5. Many bookcase units can be built separately rather than attached to the wall, but a unit that is floor-to-ceiling may be too tall to be lifted up and should therefore be built directly onto the wall.

6. Put bookcases or shelves into existing recesses such as alcoves and niches, and try to plan bookshelves when new construction takes place so that they can be built into walls.

7. Separate bookcase units placed together will look built-in if molding is attached to cover their meeting point.

8. To gain extra storage and to add the appearance of height to an area, raise an existing bookcase up to the ceiling by adding more shelves to the top.

9. Book stops or book ends must be placed at the ends of open shelves to hold back books.

10. Paint or paper the wall behind open-backed units first before installing shelves, except if shelves are to be painted or papered also.

11. An easy way to steady a free-standing unit is to put very heavy books like an encyclopedia on the bottom shelf.

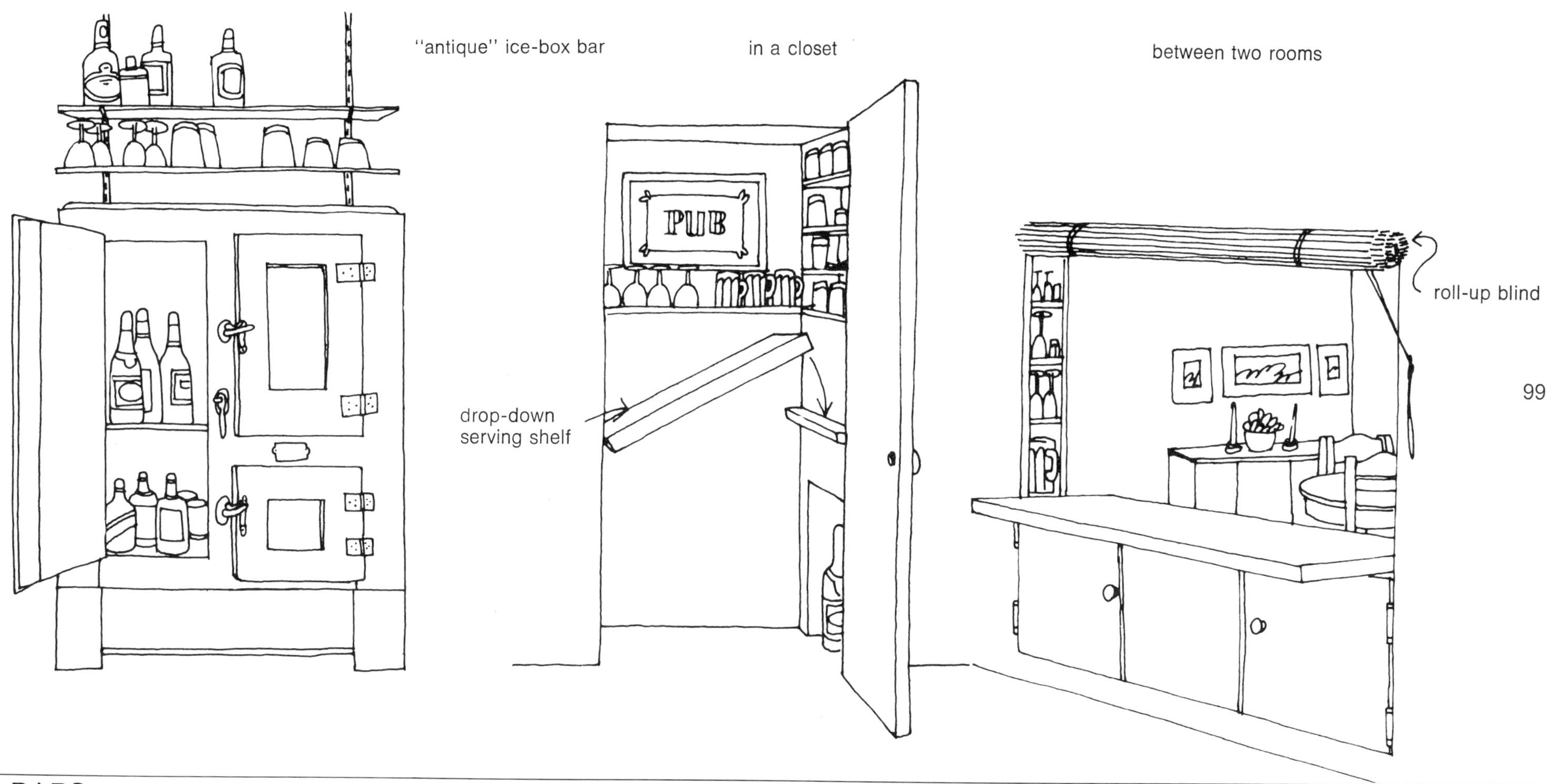

BARS

An elaborate arrangement for storing and serving drinks is not really necessary. Depending upon your life-style, a portable cart or tray can be wheeled or carried to the cocktail area, or drinks can be prepared and even served in the kitchen. A bar can be something as simple as several bottles on a bookshelf, or a group of beautiful decanters on a tray permanently placed on a side or coffee table. If you require a little more, then either buy a bar or convert a new or old piece of furniture, such as an armoire, a dry sink, an old wooden ice box, into one.

• *Closet bars.* Convert a closet into a bar by removing the clothes bar and other obstructing fittings and by adding a rolling cart, or a shelf at serving height, narrow shelves above for glasses, deeper shelves for bottles below. (The storage shelves can be concealed with doors or a curtain.) Decorate the bar closet with paint and paper, an interesting lighting fixture and accessories, a mirror, picture, and so on. Glamorous but expensive additions are mirrored walls, glass shelves, concealed spotlights, sinks, and small refigerators. Remove the closet door to display the bar or leave it on, and use the back side of a swing door for additional storage.

storage cube on wheels—swings around for viewing

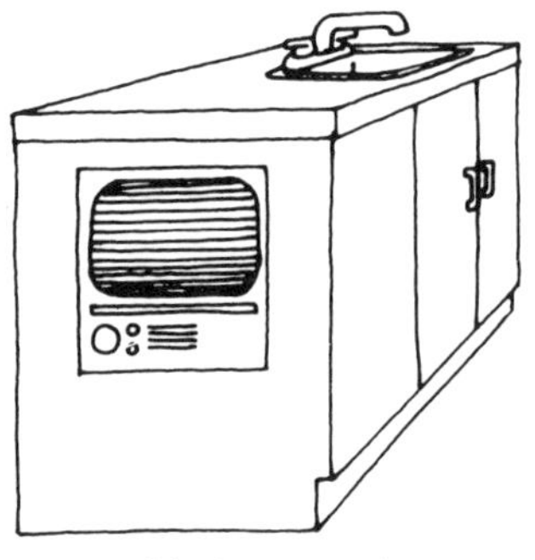
end of kitchen counter

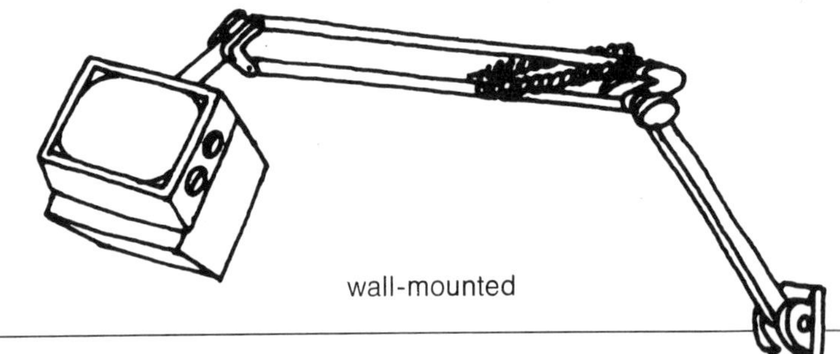
wall-mounted

shelves or closet covered with folding doors

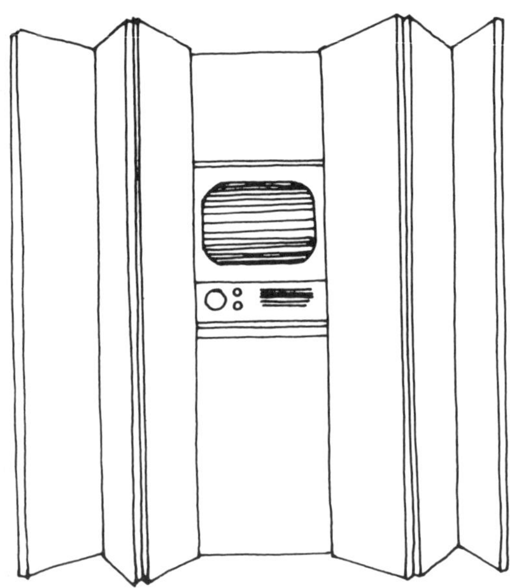

TELEVISION SETS

The manufacturers' instructions point out that television sets have ventilation openings in their cabinets to allow heat generated during play to be released. If these openings are blocked, heat builds up within the television set and can become a fire hazard. So keep this in mind when placing a set in a built-in enclosure or on a carpeted floor. (The manufacturers also caution against placing the set over or near a radiator or heat register.) And be sure that a wall- or shelf-mounted television is properly supported. Keeping this in mind, as well as the position for the best viewing, proximity to outlets, accessibility to controls, and whether or not to hide or show the set when not in use, here are some storage ideas for the television set:

1. On shelving systems, in built-in book-case/cabinets; or on a simple table of the same size, for example, a Parsons table. Since the backs of many television sets have something of a triangular shape, they fit quite neatly into a space-saving corner shelf.
2. On a table or small chest with wheels for ease of movement. Although I personally do not like the design of most commercially manufactured TV wagons, they are, I must concede, convenient for getting the set smoothly from place to place or from room to room or in and out of a closet.
3. Built into the wall, in a recess or between studs or where there is a closet on the other side. One excellent idea is to put the television on a swivel mechanism into a wall shared by two rooms, for example, the bedroom and the living room. Then the set can be swung around for viewing in both rooms. Some kind of covering such as a curtain or sliding door should conceal the ugly exposed back side of the set. If a set is placed on a shelf in a closet that has folding or sliding doors, these can be opened just far enough to expose the set but not the other contents of the closet. (Again, a curtain might cover the exposed closet storage that shows above and below the set.) A television built into the wall can be hidden behind a removable wall hanging or a picture that has hinges to one side and "opens" for viewing.
4. Suspended from the ceiling—an idea often used in hospitals and adaptable to home use with a special wall or ceiling-mounted unit.
5. On the floor under a skirted table.

MUSIC AND MOVIES AND GAMES

• *Movies.* Put the screen behind a valance or a beam and pull down for showing and put the projector in a closet with a hole cut out for the lens to peek through. The ideal distance from projector to screen is twenty feet.

• *Games.* Allow for storage of the actual game, as well as for a game table that folds away (the standard card table is 30″ square). The important thing to remember in active games, such as pool or Ping-Pong, is to allow enough room to move around. (See page 17.)

• *Music.* The music system—phonograph, tape deck, speakers, whatever—should be placed for greatest audio enjoyment and take the following into account:

1. accessibility to equipment and controls, and ventilation of the receiver;
2. a shelf for the turntable should be about 16″ deep (measure your equipment) and the turntable should be near the amplifier;
3. long-playing records are about 13″ square, 8-track tapes roughly 6″ × 4″, cassettes 4½″ × 3″. So plan storage space for them accordingly. This should be near equipment and never near the heat at windows or radiators.

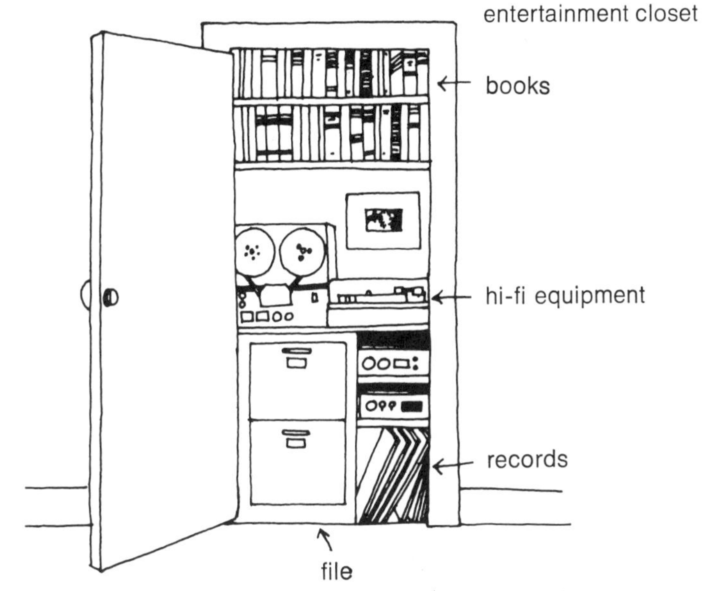

12. THE DISAPPEARING DINING ROOM

Many homes no longer have a dining "room," or if they do, it must fulfill other functions at non-mealtime hours. Since furniture can easily be adapted for dining, this is not a problem. An instant dining room can appear in a corner of the living room or bedroom, the front porch or foyer. Indeed, one enterprising apartment dweller used the elevator foyer: she set up and entertained there in the evening with complete privacy because the other apartments on the floor were doctors' offices.

The dining area can be defined with light—by lowering those in the rest of the room and by highlighting the table with candles, a chandelier, or a spotlight. Or an actual divider such as a curtain or screen can pull out and around the dining area, making an intimate dining ambiance.

Throughout a house there are many suitable eating and sitting surfaces. Those used should relate in size to one another. For example, if occasional chairs, which are usually lower than dining-room chairs, are used, the table should be proportionately lower. Pillows or other almost-on-the-floor seating would be suitable for use around a coffee table doubling as a dining table.

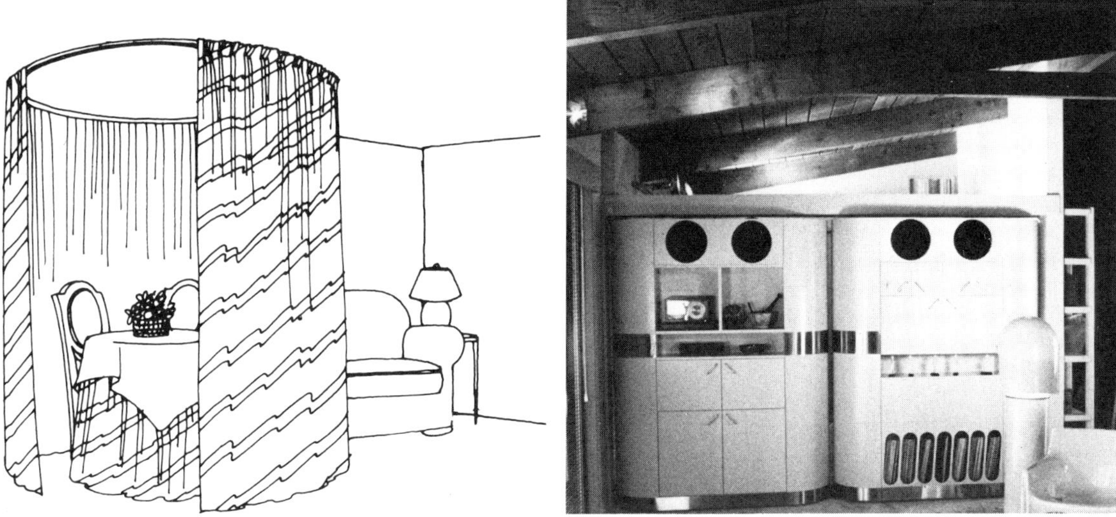

These Formica-covered plywood units rotate almost 360° to expose or close off the dining room. They hold a bar and eating equipment on the dining side, and records, speakers, hi-fi equipment, and a flip-down desk on the living-room side. *Drawing:* The dining area can be completely set apart from the rest of the room by hanging a curtain on a curved track attached to the ceiling.

Adjustable Dining Areas

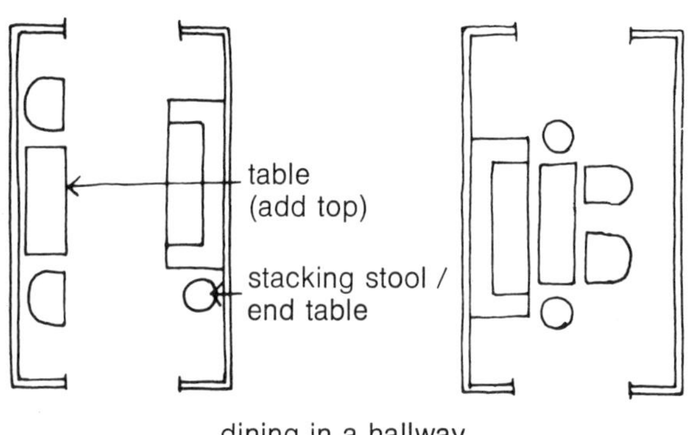

dining in a hallway

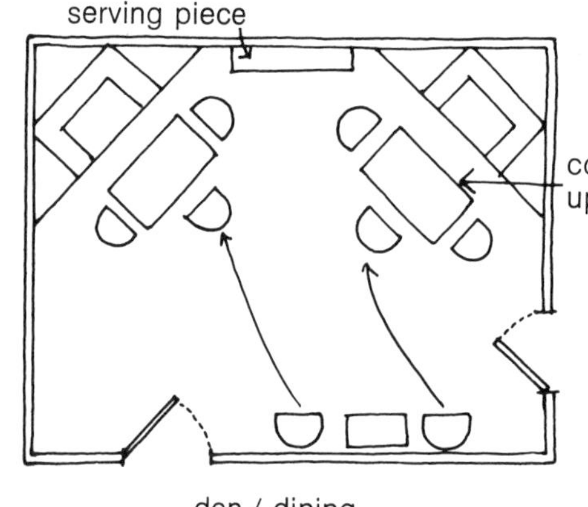

den / dining

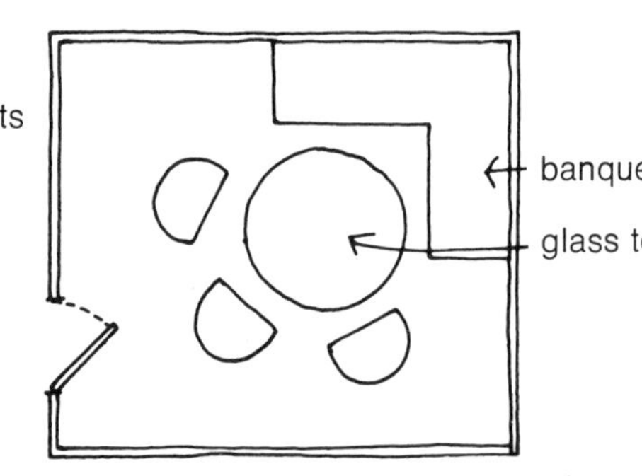

corner arrangement

TRICKS WITH TABLES

• Tables that metamorphose at mealtimes include:
1. A console table that opens up or expands with the addition of leaves, or two thin consoles put together to form one table.
2. A flip-top or drop-leaf table, or a drop-down shelf/table.
3. A desk, lamp, or work table; or game table for Ping-Pong, pool, backgammon. A folding tabletop, usually a round piece of plywood, can be added to make a larger and more solid eating surface, where necessary.
4. A stationary or folding card table (or two together).
5. A picnic table (good for a narrow area), individual snack tables (singly or in groups to form a table), or a coffee table (some adjust up to eating height) for more informal meals.

• If a table is a more or less permanent installation in a room, place it to one side or in a corner where it will take up less floor space.

• Placed in front of a mirror, table, chairs, and lighting fixtures will double in quantity and size, looking almost like a complete dining room.

• Round tables seat more and take up less space, and a glass-topped table (with glass at least ¾″ thick, please) belies its size.

• When additional eating surfaces are needed, a folding table or a table with an expanding top can be used alone or placed next to a smaller table or surface of the same height to make one big table.

• Two permanent surfaces—for example, a desk and a large end table—can each be set for big dinner parties. If the end table has a permanent cloth cover, a nice idea is to add a smaller top cloth for dining.

• If parts of the table or the table itself must be stored, make allowances for this. People have been known to use off-duty plywood tops as bed boards, or vice versa, but boards, tabletops, extra leaves, and folding tables are more often stowed under the bed rather than under the mattress. A screen with flat panels can also double as a tabletop, and colorful dining-table leaves or card tables with decorative covers can be hung on the wall as "art."

• Before buying, check out a folding table for sturdiness, as some can be quite shaky.

• Many space-saving table-and-chair combinations can be found in stores. One of the most ingenious has drop leaves and storage for folding chairs inside the table.

• A perfectly respectable table that is easy to store can be made from ½″ to ¾″ plywood or a flush-panel hollow-core door. Attach folding legs or wooden legs that can be unscrewed for storage or place the tabletop on two folding sawhorses.

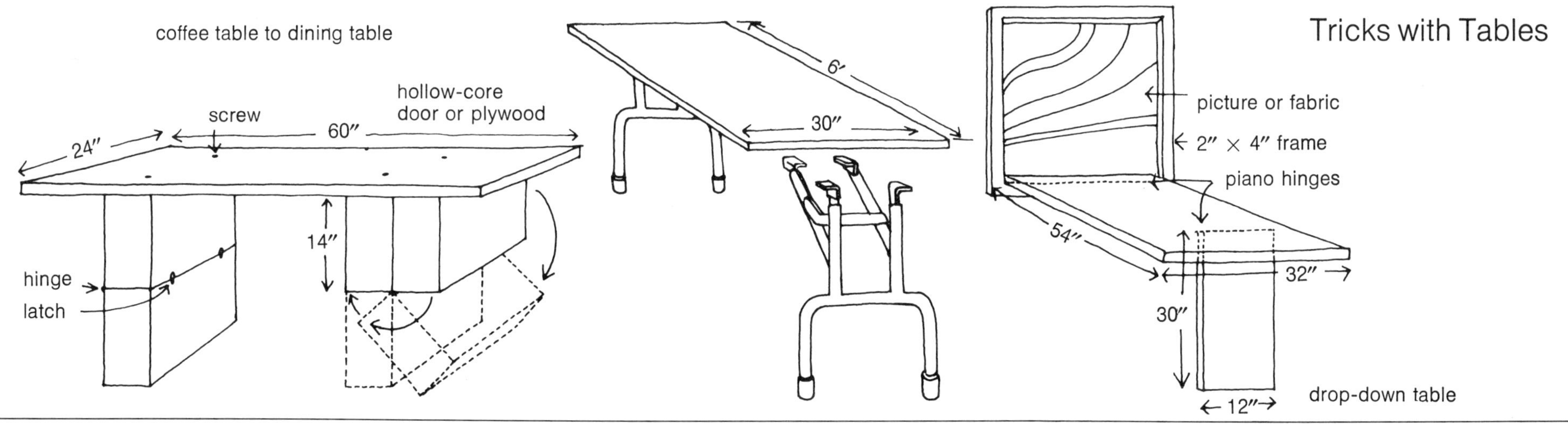

SEATS AND SERVERS

• *Seating* can be supplied by stools, benches, floor pillows, folding or stacking chairs, odd chairs gathered from around the house, and banquettes or couches already in the room.

Seats can be folded and stored when not in use or concealed beneath other furniture. Some may perform other functions, such as stools that are alternatively small cigarette or end tables.

• *Serving.* If it is covered with a lovely cloth, no one need ever know that the buffet is really the top of a radiator enclosure, a desk, a bookcase, chest of drawers, or fireplace mantel. (For dimensions of dining tables and chairs see Chapter 2.)

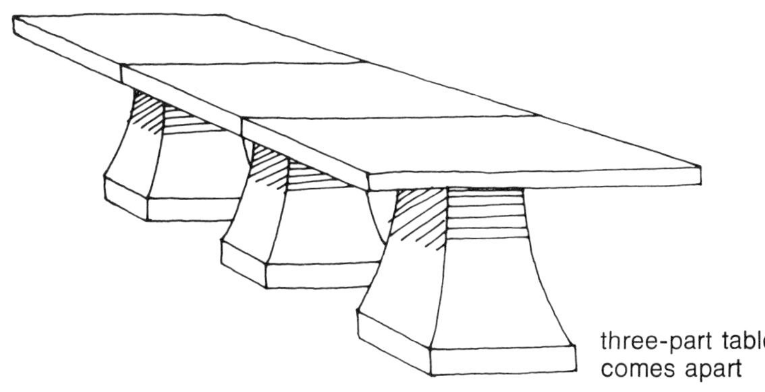
three-part table comes apart

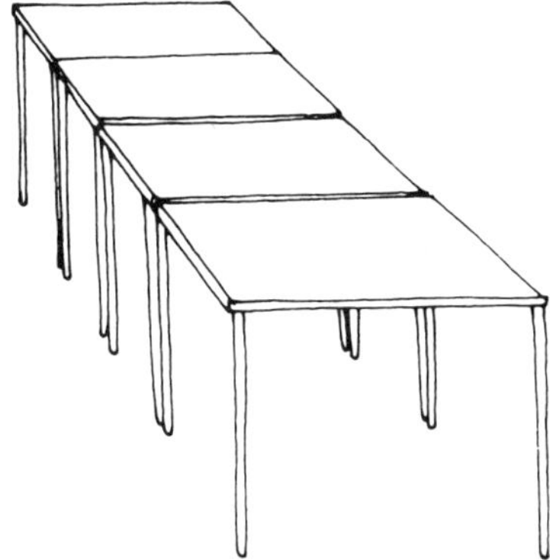
folding snack tables placed in groups

13. MORE EFFICIENT BATHROOMS & KITCHENS

Bathrooms and kitchens must house a variety of fixtures and appliances arranged in a way to permit efficient use. Space is therefore at its greatest premium in these places.

For a feeling of more spaciousness in kitchen or bathroom, duplicate the color and design scheme of the adjoining area. For example, the kitchen and dining room might have the same floor and wall covering; the bathroom and bedroom might have the same curtains and colors. Also, decorate to distraction! Plants, antique accessories, wonderful wall hangings add character to even the most medicinal rooms, so that a small size is barely noticed.

Sometimes a simple solution to the space crunch is to remove items normally stored in these rooms (but infrequently used) to a closet or cabinet outside, but nearby. Even a minor structural change can have a major effect—like blocking up or relocating a door. This may easily and inexpensively solve a problem such as inadequate space in the kitchen for eating. In the same way, a new door cut in the back side of a bedroom closet, giving access to clothing from the bathroom rather than from the bedroom, may serve two purposes: greater convenience when getting dressed and more wall space for the bedroom. Any new arrangement, however, should take into account that plumbing costs will be lower if new plumbing lines are near each other and if new equipment is installed where the old was.

Left: In this compact kitchen rounded windows, white walls with a brown graphic design undulating from the ceiling, and green plants create a striking environment. Note the economy of design achieved by connecting the eating surface to the wall and to the center island. *Top right:* A rack with pretty pots and pans is both practical and decorative; a center storage island provides both eating area and extra work space. *Bottom right:* Serving cart doubles as eating surface; narrow shelves surrounding window provide storage in a small space.

THE BATHROOM PLAN

Before planning a new bathroom or fixing up an old one, take the following into consideration:

• The sink should be near a source of direct light and preferably next to a window.

• A large mirror over the sink not only is practical but will also enlarge the room visually. A mirror can also be put behind the bathtub on one or more walls, or on the ceiling.

• The bathtub should not be under a window. It's drafty. In addition, you'll have to step into the bathtub to close and open the window.

• If the bathroom is big enough, include some form of divider, either a decorative screen at least 3′ high, shelves, towel holders, or even a narrow closet between the toilet and the rest of the bathroom.

• If the bathroom is too small for a regular door that takes up space as it opens into a room, substitute space-saving pocket or folding doors.

• If the space and the demand for a bathtub are limited, use a stall shower instead. Some models that are prefabricated of Fiberglas or metal take up less floor space (as little as 32″ × 32″) than the standard bathtub/shower combination (at least 30″ × 60″).

• Sinks are available in many sizes and shapes, with or without legs (these are wall hung and easy to clean beneath) or with a pedestal base. Some sinks are designed to fit into corners. If money and space allow, a double sink is a great convenience at the bathroom rush hour.

• Toilets, like sinks, can stand on the floor or hang on the wall, and here, too, some models fit into corners.

• In busy households the bathroom may be the only place to hide away—to escape to and relax in. So if space allows, furnish accordingly with comfortable chair, chaise longue, small writing table, books, telephone, and other conveniences and luxuries.

• By using a combination washer/dryer, or a front-loading washer that can go under a counter or the dryer, part of the bathroom can be a laundry, with supplies kept in the medicine cabinet or under the sink and a drying rack hung from the ceiling.

BATHROOM STORAGE

Plan for storage of linens, medicine, cosmetics, cleaning supplies, magazines, books, dirty and clean clothing. Shelves or cabinets can be put above the sink, toilet, or tub, and cabinets below a sink not only look neat but serve as extra storage.

In addition, install towel bars (they should be wide enough to hold towels easily) and plenty of hooks on doors and on the walls, especially near the bathtub. Medicine cabinets can often be re-

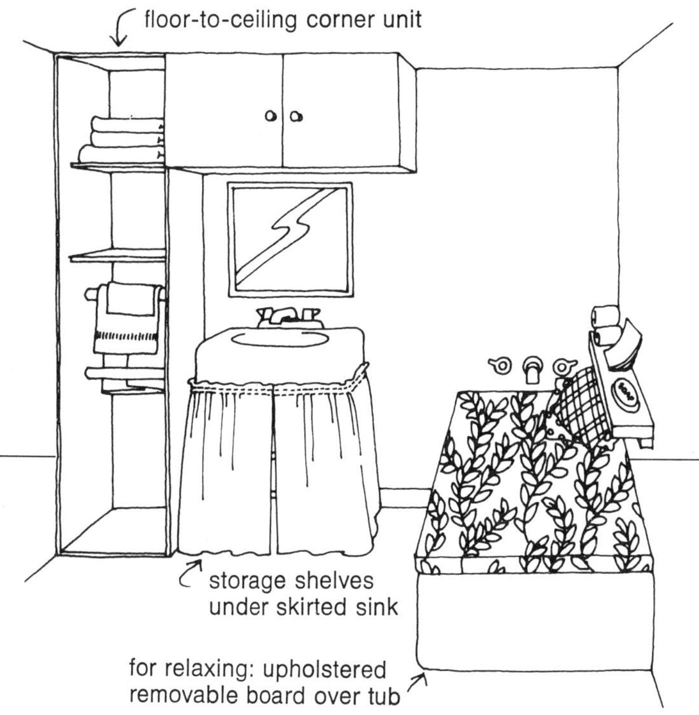

cessed into the wall between studs, small ones stacked one above the other. Medicine-cabinet shelves should be 4″ to 6″ apart with one spaced 9″ apart for tall bottles. There are also many wonderful gadgets for stretching bathroom storage space, such as shower caddies that hang from shower heads, magazine racks, compartmented tank-top trays, and many back-of-the-door organizers like drying racks for laundry, hanging cabinets, and towel holders.

Almost any furniture that will not be damaged by moisture can be moved to the bathroom, and these might include an attractive old chest or bookcase for toiletries, a hassock that opens up and can be used as a hamper, or, for towels, antique coat racks or folding hat racks.

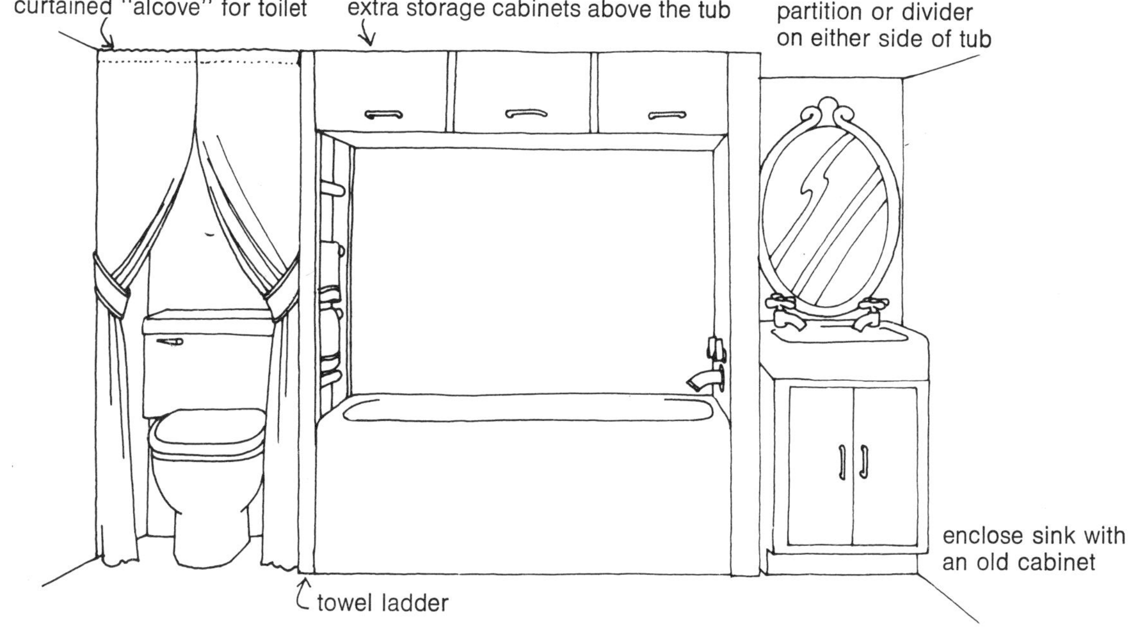

Dressing Unit

110

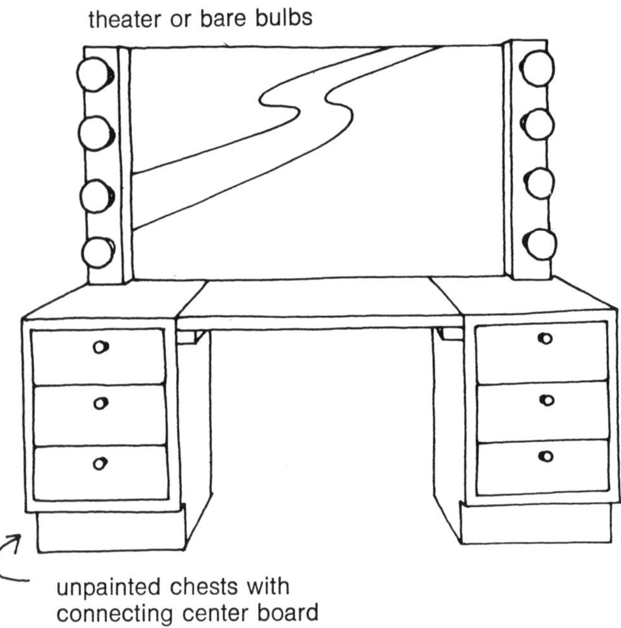

Over-the-Sink Storage

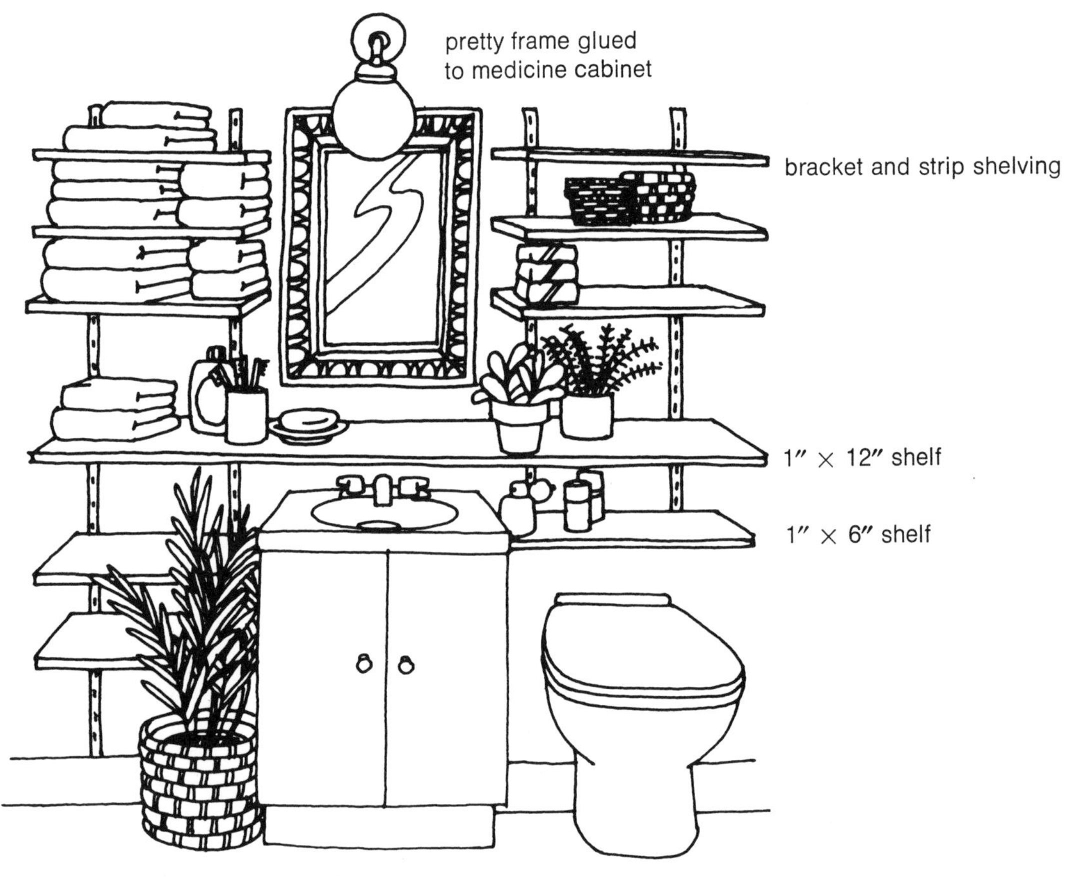

Under-the-Sink Storage

Towel Holders

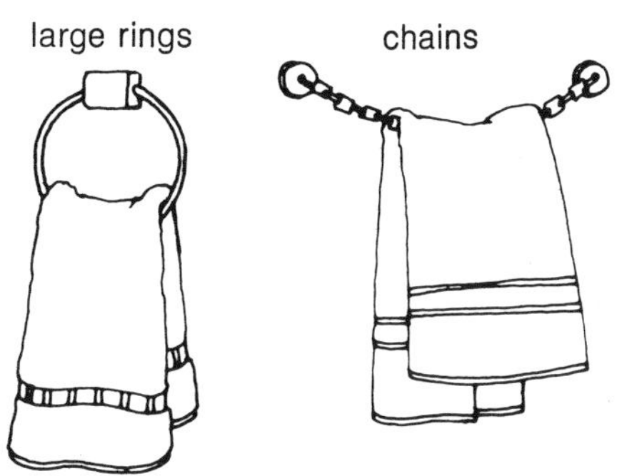

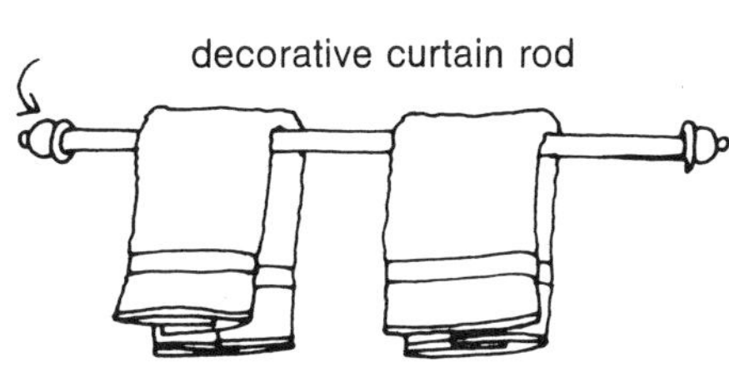

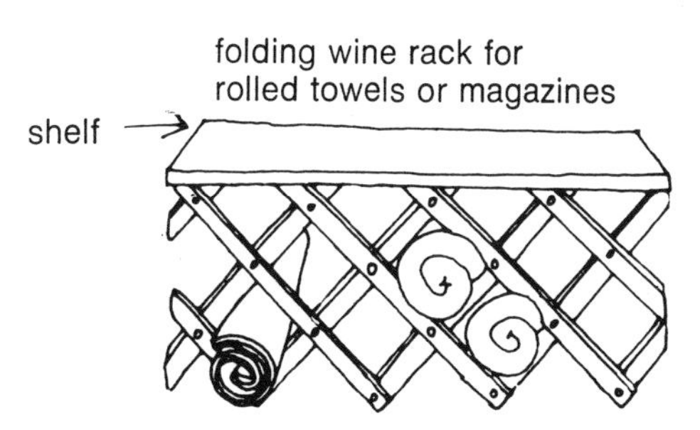

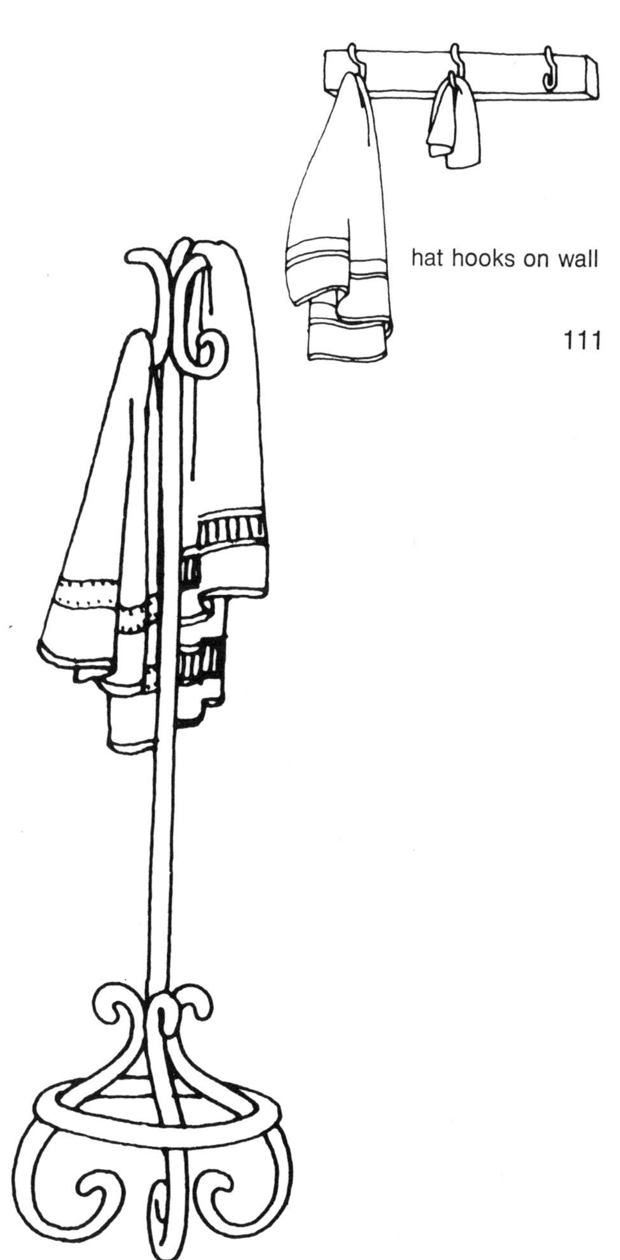

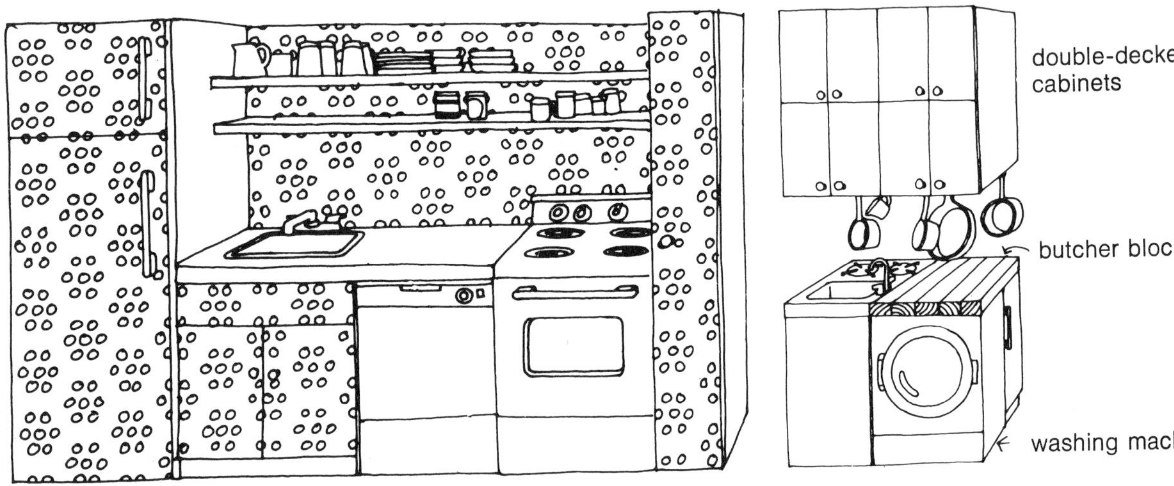

THE KITCHEN PLAN

Cabinets and appliances should be arranged whenever possible in a convenient order. It's easy to do this in a kitchen built from scratch; in an old kitchen, you have to plan around existing appliances, beams, radiators, windows, and plumbing that cannot be moved or that you cannot afford to move because of the cost.

• The four basic layouts are the U, L, double strip or row, and single strip. If possible, arrange appliances and cabinets so corner space is not wasted, and so the distances most frequently traveled, the so-called work triangle from refrigerator-to-stove-to-sink, are small enough to save steps but not too close to be cramped.

• For ventilation the stove should be on an outside wall, not under a window where it is a fire hazard (save this spot for the sink) and, if possible, not next to the sink or a door. There should be at least a little counter space on each side of the stove.

• It's preferable to put the refrigerator at one end of the counter and not in the center.

• The sink should be centrally located and the dishwasher should be near the sink and the cabinet that holds dishes.

• Most base cabinets and appliances are 34″ to 36″ high and 24″ to 26″ deep. Most wall cabinets, 12″ to 33″ high and 12″ to 15″ deep.

• Wall cabinets should be within an easy stretch. The lowest shelf is usually around 18″ from the counter. To make more space a cabinet could be hung lower, provided it was not too close to the stove or did not interfere with the use of the counter. Then, if there was room enough, another cabinet could be hung above the first.

• Allow enough clearance for opening dishwasher, refrigerator, cabinet, and stove doors. These should not collide with counters and other appliances.

• The kitchen plan might also include room for a telephone; a place for family paperwork—like a desk; a place to relax—a small couch or comfortable chair; and an eating surface—anything from a large dining table to a narrow shelf or drop-down table that takes up practically no room and disappears when not in use.

• To gain extra counter space consider a small table that can slide out from under a counter, a work center/island placed in the middle of a wide kitchen (a compact movable model on wheels is handy), a flip-top table that is either attached to the end of the counter or to a wall, or a removable cutting board made to fit over a top-opening washing machine or a sink.

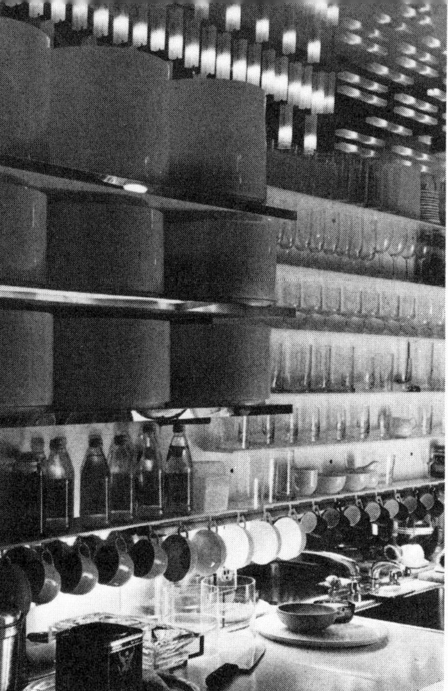

Plastic-covered lazy Susans protect china and require less space than swinging cabinet doors.

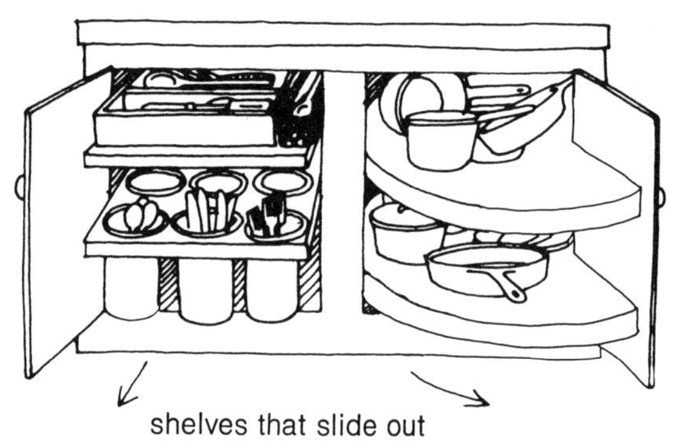

shelves that slide out

shelves between cabinet and counter

plywood rounds rotate on one-inch pipe

horseshoe-shaped narrow shelves built between existing shelves

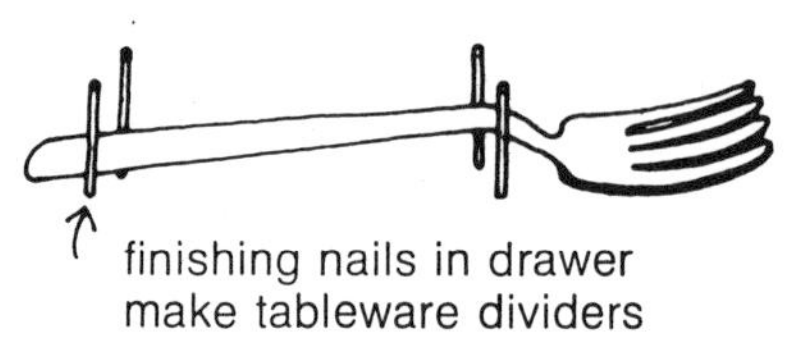

finishing nails in drawer make tableware dividers

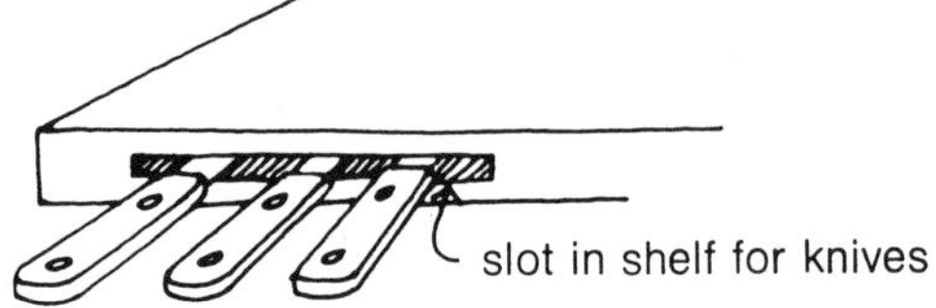

slot in shelf for knives

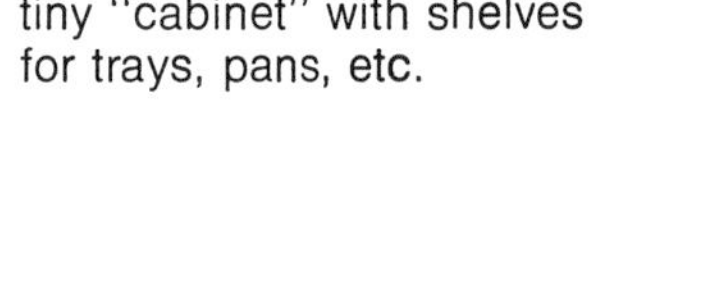

tiny "cabinet" with shelves for trays, pans, etc.

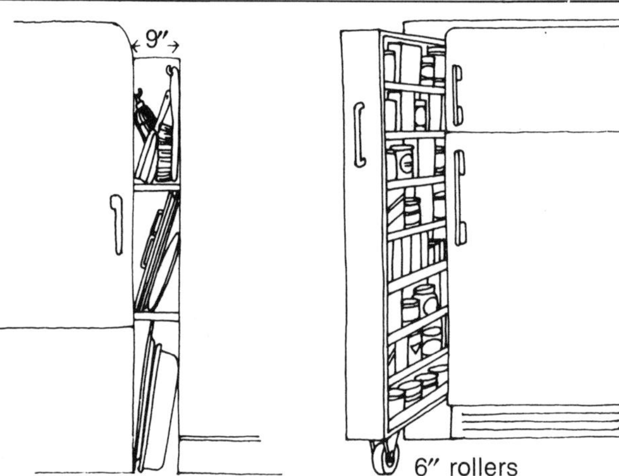

Islands

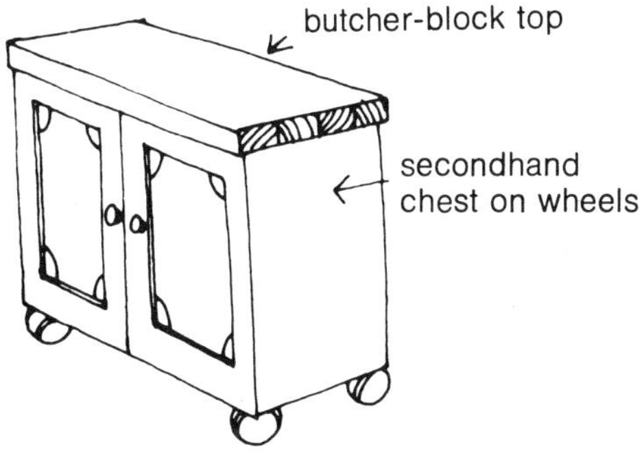
butcher-block top
secondhand chest on wheels

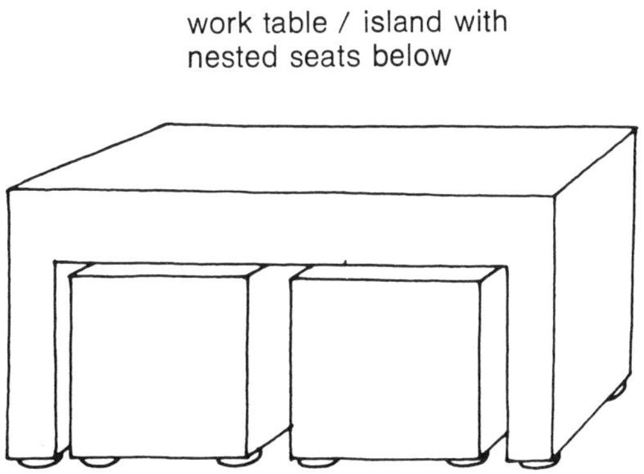
work table / island with nested seats below

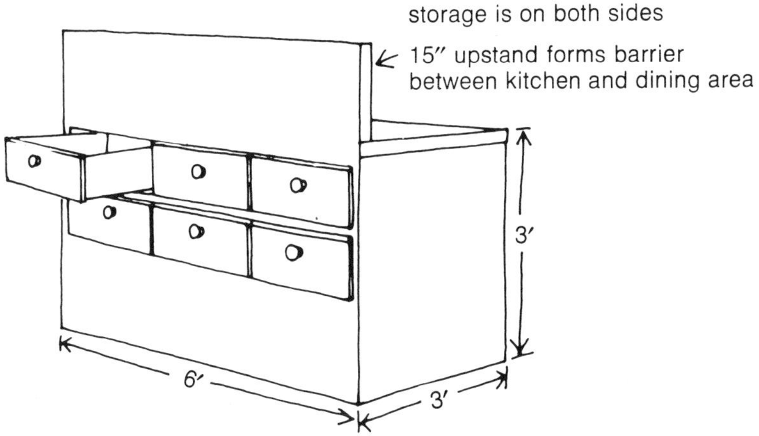
storage is on both sides
15″ upstand forms barrier between kitchen and dining area
3′
6′
3′

Ironing Boards

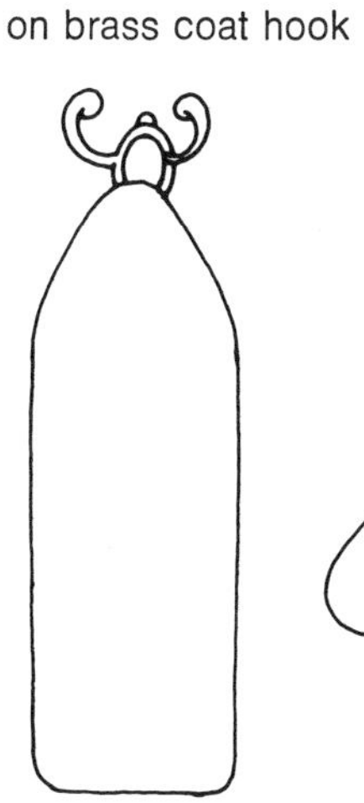
on brass coat hook

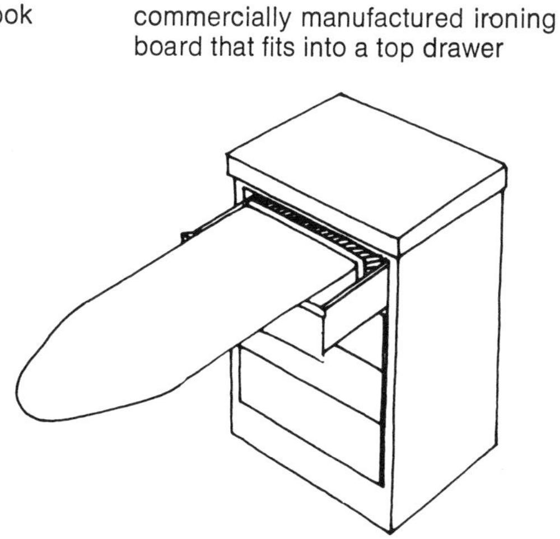
commercially manufactured ironing board that fits into a top drawer

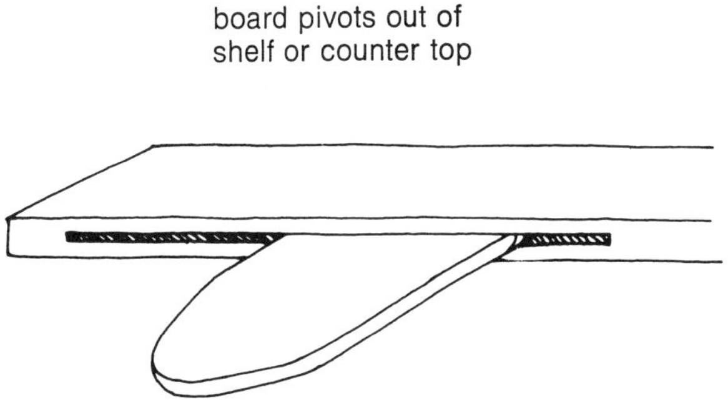
board pivots out of shelf or counter top

Eating Areas

15″

block with turn-button catch on wall
flip-down shelf in front of doorway
counter
hinges

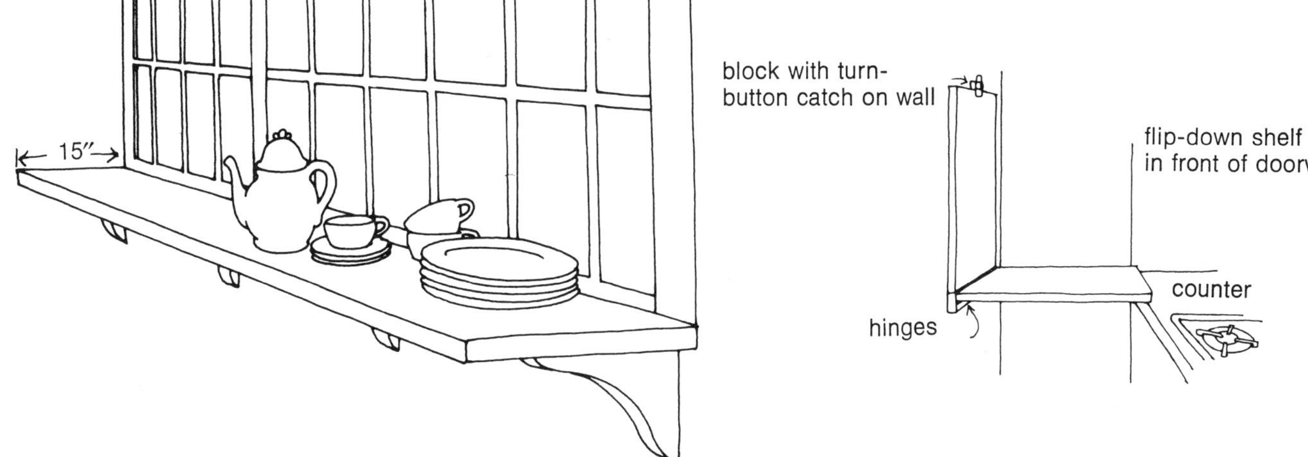

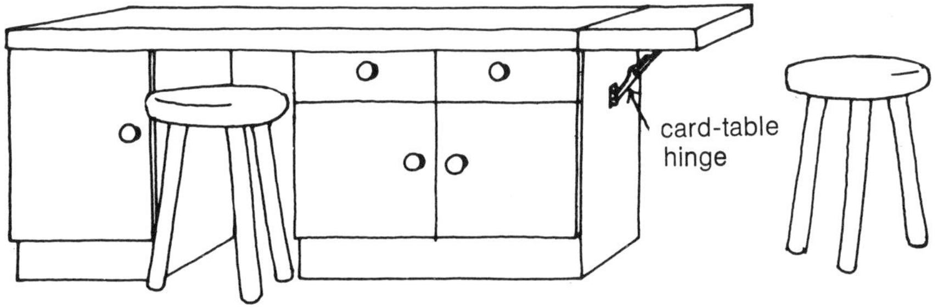

an opening in cabinet / counter unit
or extend counter one foot

card-table
hinge

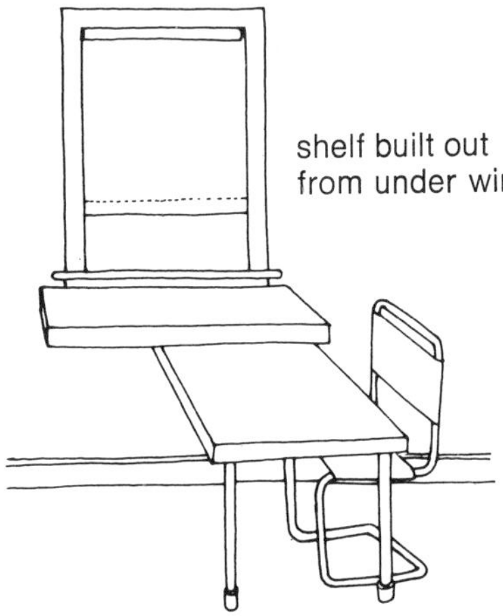

shelf built out
from under window

• Easy access from the kitchen to dining areas can be achieved by making an opening or pass-through between the two rooms. This can be closed off with folding doors, shades, or shutters for privacy.

TRICKS FOR TINY KITCHENS

With the availability of new appliances such as an all-in-one refrigerator-sink-stove combination, kitchens can be quite compact. It is now possible to have a kitchen-in-a-closet that is only about 18″ deep and 4′ wide or an even smaller one in an armoire, with storage on the armoire doors. Just be sure there is some ventilation—a window or exhaust fan nearby—and keep the following in mind:

• The direction of opening doors is especially crucial in cramped quarters, and sliding doors on cabinets may be space savers.

• Although appliances may have to be standard size, cabinets and shelves can be custom built around them, and walls and doors covered with pegboard to use all extra inches of space.

• Use as few different colors and materials as possible: try to paint cabinets and shelves and walls the same color (and use a matching floor covering). Paper everything in sight, including the refrigerator (which will look smaller and seem to "disappear" into the wall). Use the floor covering—tile, for example—on counter tops and on walls.

• Stoves and refrigerators can be quite small, but always try to use a standard-size sink.

• If there is a divider between kitchen and adjoining area, keep it low and the kitchen will be less claustrophobic.

• Hide a kitchenette (pullman kitchen) behind a curtain, shade or roller blind, a folding or sliding door, or simply behind a screen (put pegboard on the kitchen side of the screen).

KITCHEN STORAGE

Plan storage for food, cooking, utensils, dishes, flatware, cleaning supplies, and tools as close to where they will be used as possible—in cabinets (wall and base), in drawers, above the refrigerator and wall cabinets, below the sink and, sometimes, in the stove.

• *In cabinets:* Anything that has the misfortune to be a little way back in a base cabinet can be lost to view and almost forgotten. Various products help to make the contents of deep cabinets visible and more accessible: pull-out trays and bins; sliding shelves; a lazy Susan device, or turntable (excellent in corner cabinets); or stationary semicircular shelves

attached to the inside of a door.

- *Under cabinets:* Ready-made units that are easy to attach beneath a cabinet include towel and wrap dispensers, bread drawers, and utility drawers. Put hooks here and under shelves.
- *On shelves:* Add additional shallow shelves between existing shelves in a cabinet (use adjustable shelves and leave at least 2″ between shelves so items are easy to remove) or between counter and cabinet. A shelf 12″ deep will hold most dishes except larger platters and serving pieces, one 4–6″ deep will hold glasses, and one 6″ deep will hold cans one deep. Exposed shelves—as an alternative to cabinets—are nice for neat cooks, but can be terrible dust collectors.
- *Storage on wheels:* Cabinets that slide out from under a counter, wagons, and movable storage islands can house food and equipment, bringing them within easy reach of the cook.
- *Decorative storage:* For extra storage and extra decorating dividends, put interesting furniture in the kitchen—an old carved chest of drawers or wrought-iron butcher's rack. Be sure they are easy to clean and, if necessary, cover top surfaces with washable and heat-resistant materials such as glass, marble, or self-adhesive plastic.

LAST BUT NOT LEAST, THE LAUNDRY!

Washing machines can be front or top loading, are available along with dryers in space-saving combination and stacking units. Handy to have nearby: shelves and a counter for supplies and sorting of laundry, a hamper, an ironing board, a sewing machine, a large sink. The laundry may be in the kitchen or basement, in a bathroom or guestroom, in a corner of the dining room hidden behind a screen or in an alcove in the hall hidden behind a curtain. But keep in mind that this machinery makes a lot of noise and can be annoying if left to run where people are dining or relaxing.

AFTERWORD

The space-saving ideas described and depicted in this book are illustrative, not exhaustive. Each idea, I hope, will suggest another. Style and space economy are compatible and no space problem is too small to be solved. The only formula required is a sense of your real needs, an eye for unused space, boldness in imagination, and a willingness to experiment. These, more than driftwood, saved the day for the Swiss Family Robinson. They can help you conquer space as well.

With the addition of a small table and chairs, a wasted area beneath a staircase could be used for dining.

PICTURE CREDITS

The author and publishers wish to thank the following for their kind permission to reproduce the photographs on the pages noted: **7** Design: Joseph Paul Durso; Photo: Richard Champion. **9** Design: William Turner Associates, Inc.; Photo: Jaime Ardiles-Arce. **15** *top* Design: Milo Baughman for Thayer Coggin, Inc. **15** *bottom* Design: Robert Rhodes, architect. **21** *left* Design: Barbara Schwartz, A. S. I. D., and Barbara Ross for Dexter Studio Inc.; Photo: Norman McGrath. **21** *right* Design: Richard Abbott, architect; Photo: Norman McGrath. **29** Design: Gerda Clark for Abraham & Straus. **31** Photo: John Dominis, Time-Life Picture Agency, © Time Inc. **32** Design: Monsanto Textiles Company. **43** Design: Denning & Fourcade, Inc.; Photo: Edgar de Evia. **46** *top* Design: Robert Rhodes. **46** *bottom* Design: Paul Segal, A. I. A.; Photo: Darwin Davidson. **47** Design: Alan Buchsbaum and Howard Korenstein, architects, Design Coalition, New York City; Owens Corning Fiberglas Corporation. **49** Design: Paul Segal, A. I. A.; Photo: Darwin Davidson. **54** Design: Jeanna Carr. **57** Design: Mel Lerner; Photo: Darwin Davidson. **65** Design: Alan Buchsbaum and Howard Korenstein, architects, Design Coalition, New York City; Photo: Alan Buchsbaum. **67** *left* Design: Arthur Leaman, A. S. I. D., for Celanese House. **73** Design: Paul Rudolph, architect; Photo: Cervin Robinson. **85** Design: Charles Moore, architect; Photo: Bill Maris. Reprinted from the October 1970 issue of *American Home,* American Home Publishing Company, Inc. **88** Design: Robert A. M. Stern and John S. Hagmann; Photo: Norman McGrath. **89** *left* Design: Russell Childs of Armstrong/Childs Architects, New York; Photo: Robert Perron. **89** *right* Design: Carl Fuchs for Celanese House. **93** Design: Alan Buchsbaum and Howard Korenstein, architects, Design Coalition, New York City; Photo: Norman McGrath. **103** Design: Alan Buchsbaum and Howard Korenstein, architects, Design Coalition, New York City; Photo: Alan Buchsbaum. **107** *left* Design: Emily Malino for Window Shade Manufacturers. **107** *bottom right* Design: Richard and Barbara Rubens of Tomorrow Design Ltd.; Photo: Jaime Ardiles-Arce. **113** Design: Paul Rudolph, architect; Photo: Donald Luckenbill. **119** Design: Denning & Fourcade, Inc.; Photo: Edgar de Evia.

SPACE
SPACE